ADVANCE PRAISE FOR
GONE MISSING

"I did not put the book down for an entire day; read for eight or nine hours straight. Still thinking about the characters . . ."

—INGA S.

"Contains everything—love, mystery, intrigue; so perfect for a movie. . . . [It] stayed with me, and I thought about it during the time I wasn't reading it; it kept me company."

—DOROTHY R.

"I usually read for pleasure at night. . . . I caught myself during the day thinking about the book, and I was eager to get back to it and find out what happened next."

—JERRY A.

"Good page turner . . . Dean is a one-dimensional asshole! Great story with terrific plot twists."

—LEONARD R.

"Loved the courtroom scenes, exciting . . . [T]he twist with the [evidence]."

—DAYNA M.

"I read it in two days! Great read! You had me from the first chapter. . . . [F]elt like I was there: the car chase, the stakeout, the rescue, confronting the mother. Make a good movie."

—ROBERT A.

"The end? Wow, I never saw it coming."

—JIM A.

GONE MISSING

A MARIN COUNTY MYSTERY

GONE MISSING
A MARIN COUNTY MYSTERY

BY COLIN C. CLAXON

CAIRN STONE PUBLISHING

ISBN: 978-1-7325278-0-5
Ebook ISBN: 978-1-7325278-1-2

Manufactured in the United States of America.

Produced by Dean Burrell, San Francisco
Design by Maureen Forys, Happenstance Type-O-Rama
Cover photo © L. Vargas/Stars Artists

10 9 8 7 6 5 4 3 2 1

A portion of the proceeds from the sale of each book will be donated to
Trout Unlimited, CalTrout, and/or a foundation dedicated to preventing
child abductions, at the discretion of the author.

This book, including the names and descriptions of the characters,
is a work of fiction inspired by an actual case handled by the attorney author.
Any resemblance to actual events, places, or persons, either living or dead,
is purely and entirely coincidental.

Website: www.thenovelgonemissing.com
Email: contact@thenovelgonemissing.com

Cairn Stone Publishing
23 Grant Avenue, 4th Floor
San Francisco, CA 94108

*To my wife, who knows what it is to
be married to a sole practitioner trial attorney.
I did promise that it would never be dull.
It has not been. I love you.*

ACKNOWLEDGMENTS

TO ALL THOSE FAMILY AND FRIENDS, some of whom know Jason's story, who told me that I could do this: my thanks. To my father, who shared his love of books; to editor, Dean Burrell; to critic and editor, Tom Thompson of Marin Catholic High School; to all those who read, commented, and encouraged; to teacher, editor, and critic, Tom Jenks, for teaching me how to tell a story; and finally, to Susan Taylor Chehak and the University of Iowa Summer Writing Festival (2012), who helped me put it all together. Thank you, all.

And to the real Jason, wherever you are. Your disappearance will continue to haunt me forever.

PROLOGUE

"It is no great wonder if in long process of time, while fortune takes her course hither and thither, numerous coincidences should spontaneously occur."

—PLUTARCH, *Plutarch's Lives,* Vol. II.

"I do not believe in meaningless coincidences. I believe every coincidence is a message.... When you live your life with an appreciation of coincidences ... This is when the magic begins."

—DEEPAK CHOPRA, *The Spontaneous Fulfillment of Desire: Harnessing the Infinite Power of Coincidence.*

"What connexion can there have been between many people ... who, from opposite sides of great gulfs, have, nevertheless, been very curiously brought together!"

—CHARLES DICKENS, *Bleak House.*

Part 1

1973

CHAPTER 1

FROM HIS LEDGE ACROSS THE RIVER, he watched them on their small beach, the men often naked, the women usually topless. Always with the boy. Sipping wine from his bota bag, smoking his weed, John sunbathed and shared the deep river pool that separated them, looking for an opening. His idea had been to hang out with them at their favorite swimming hole, try to make friends, get invited to party with them, somehow get into their house—anything to get to the boy. A casual, "Hey man, how ya' doin'?" A nod. Smiles exchanged with one of the women. That was it. So far it had not worked. John was beginning to doubt his plan, and he was running out of time. Until she screamed.

~

Four days earlier, gathered around the small conference room table, Burt, his uncle's partner in their investigation firm had challenged him: "How? How, John, do you plan to get in?"

"I'll find a way," John replied. "They're hippies. It won't be that hard. They hang out, they party. I have some ideas."

"Right!" Burt swiveled in his chair, fanning a dismissive pudgy hand. "You're just going to walk in, say, 'Hi, I'm here to snatch your kid!'" His hand dropped. "Fat chance!"

"Relax, Burt," John's uncle, Fred, smiled, as he leaned forward considering his nephew. "There's a right way to do this. John looks the part . . . long hair. He certainly has a better chance than we do," he nodded at the noticeable paunch of his older partner. "If John can get in, if they let him in, we have an opportunity to get the evidence we need, and he might be able to recover the boy. I think we should let him try."

Lean, tall, and tan, his hair to his shoulders, John Meagor had jumped at the offer of a summer job with his uncle's firm, EKI Investigations, hoping to gain real-world experience that might lend some relevance to the grueling first-year law studies he had just concluded.

"I think I can get in with them," John continued. "We know where they live . . . that they hang out at the river almost every day."

"The river! You may just have to get naked, John-boy. To fit in!"

"Well," John replied, recalling the details of their investigation report and, smiling, ran a hand through his long hair. "There is that."

"Yeah," Burt continued, "*that*, and the dope, the drinking, the partying, the 'free' love. Some place for a three-year-old boy! Christ, we ought to just break down the goddamn door!"

Fred interrupted, "We are only going to get one crack at this, you know. And we don't want to let her get away or screw up the custody case for our client. If John can pull it off, we have a winner all around." He paused and looked at his nephew.

"We'll give it a week, John. You've got one week." Standing, Fred extended his hand to his nephew. "One week. Then we send in the cavalry."

"Cavalry!" Burt snorted. "Better the sheriff and Child Protective Services!

~

Today, fingers laced behind his head on a pillow of his clothes, basking naked in the afternoon sun, John watched them through the vee formed by his feet until he had dozed off. Then she screamed. He awoke, looking right at the blonde woman standing at the water's edge on the opposite bank, her outstretched arm pointing at the boy in the river. The water had risen dramatically from the day before, and their beach had all but disappeared. John stood. He could see the boy's dark curls barely above water; one small upraised arm reaching as the current began to carry him downstream, toward John. Faster. Soon the boy would be beyond his reach.

John Meagor leapt—out and down. The slap shock of the water cleared his head, and when he surfaced, the child was swept into his arms. He clutched the boy close to his chest. *Perfect*, he thought, *now if we both don't drown, this might work.*

Unlike the placid pool near their beach, the river here narrowed among the boulders as it gathered strength and speed. He held the boy tightly with one taut encircling arm. The boy's eyes were closed, but John could feel the heart pumping against his forearm. He had to get to the shore before they were swept away. In late summer the water was not yet cold, but he could feel the little body start to shiver, and John knew that his own efforts would soon sap his strength.

Fighting the current with his free arm, he struggled them into a sitting position—his feet now ahead, the limp boy cradled in his lap, as they surged and bounced downstream through the whirling foam. Struggling to keep their heads up, John wiped his long hair back. He felt slippery rocks, and they tumbled headlong over and through the froth of a roaring chute. For a moment they were both submerged, and it took all John's strength to hang on to the boy and claw his way back to the surface. He gasped, his lungs ached and his arm was stretched and numb. He spit; the boy gagged and coughed.

They continued to drift. The water was deep now, its grip stronger. John was tiring. He strained to see ahead. He tilted to his left and kicked furiously to gain the passing bank. He stretched as he felt for a rock, the bottom, any footing, that might slow their drift. *I have to get out of here!* He let the current carry them as he caught his breath. *That was lucky, really lucky*, he thought. *If I hadn't almost landed on top of him, I would have never got him.*

Ahead, the river bent to the left around a small sand spit formed by the sloping bank. He knew they needed to reach that spit, or they were in for big trouble in the cataracts below. He rolled, turning at a right angle to the current, and he kicked fiercely toward the sandbar, struggling to keep the boy's head above water. One foot felt a smooth stone, then another, and then nothing. He strained against the strong current, thrusting toward shore. He feared they would round the point, and then? He didn't want to think about it.

He lunged desperately toward the approaching bank, kicking powerfully, pumping his legs, grunting in time to his efforts. "Shit . . . shit . . . shit . . . !" He could feel the current tightening its hold, reluctant to give them up.

What had been a distant roar from the waters below was now becoming a crescendo. One foot touched a boulder, slipped off. Then he felt some stones, but still the current held them. For the first time, John had a sense of panic. *What if we don't make it?* Kicking, lunging, pulling with his free arm, he fought for the riverbank. He held the boy tightly. Then he sensed the current relax, and he was onto some smaller rocks and then gravel. With a final thrust, he had bottom under both feet. The pull of the river slackened. He pushed on farther up the sand and slumped in the shallows, in water to his waist, exhausted. It was over. His lungs heaved; he could hear his heartbeat. He sat there exhausted. The boy lay still in his lap, his head resting on John's chest. John watched the river slide by.

Finally, he struggled to stand and he cradled the small, limp body in his arms, turned, and walked slowly away from the river.

The fatigue of his efforts hit him. His legs folded, and he sank down onto the wet sand, on his back, the boy still on his chest. John fought to get his breath. The boy moved up and down with the rhythm of John's breathing, his heart pounding. They lay there. He watched the clouds thread the trees, a hawk circling high overhead. It took all of his strength to control his own breathing.

He felt the boy stir. *Thank God,* he thought, *he's O.K., because I don't know what I would have done next.* John stood up, steadier now, and, carrying the boy, he walked up the sand. Seated again, he rested his back against a log, the boy nestled in his lap. He looked down examining him: the boy's wet curls covered his forehead. *His hair is almost as long as mine,* John thought. *A love child. Almost one dead, drowned, love child. Close call.* John smiled. *This was a whole lot more than I signed up for, but it just might get me in.*

The boy stirred, eyes opening as he realized that he didn't know this stranger who held him. Fright showed in the boy's eyes, but there was no strength in his brief struggle. John held him tightly, warming him.

"It's O.K., little guy," he rocked gently. "You just took a little dip. Your mom's on the way," he hoped.

The boy shuddered, chilled from the cold water and the excitement. They sat there rocking, and John was glad for the quiet, and the now soothing, pulse of the river.

Soon he heard them coming, crashing through the branches, bushes, and leaves on the riverbank behind. Shouting: "J-A-S-O-N, J-A-A-S-S-O-N-N!" A woman's voice.

The boy's mother reached them first. She stumbled onto the small beach. She had not seen them on the sand against the log and might have run past.

"Here," John said, surprised at the weakness of his voice. He was not sure if she had heard him. She stopped in her tracks, a few yards away.

"Over here. We're . . . he's . . . the boy . . . He's O.K." *What had happened to his voice?* "Just a little wet and scared."

In one frantic movement, she cleared the space between them. She grabbed the boy from John's arms.

"Jason. Oh, my God, Jason!" she cried as she examined him, oblivious to the man seated in front of her. He had watched her from across the river, but never got close. From the pictures in the investigation file he knew it was she. John leaned back against the log, suddenly bone tired. As he watched her with the boy, he glanced down and realized that he was completely naked.

"Oh-h-h . . . shit!" He wondered if he had said it aloud.

"Man, that was out of sight! Where did you come from?" a male voice called. A young man, followed closely by a short, plump woman, had stepped down onto the sand spit. Tall, gaunt, clad in a tank top that came almost to his knees, the man walked toward them. His eyes widened as he saw that John, still seated, was naked.

"Shit, dude, you ain't got no clothes on," he said. "How is he, Mara? Is he O.K.?" he turned to the woman. "Man, that was awesome . . . freaked me out! Totally!" he said. "When he went under, I thought, 'shit, that's all she wrote.'"

"Shut the fuck up, Phil." A second man stepped out of the bushes, down onto the riverbank. *Well, that's all of them,* John noted.

"Whoa, Dean, did you see that?" the skinny one inquired "It was awesome. He—"

"I said 'Shut up,'" Dean snarled. Dean had dirty-brown, disheveled hair to his shoulders. His shirtless body was too lean to be healthy; his look and disposition reeked of hostility and suspicion. Dean had an angular face, hollow cheekbones, and darting dark eyes that gave him a distant, detached look as he eyed the rescuer. Phil, cowed by Dean's rebuff, cringed.

"If you had kept your eyes on him, you dumb fuck, this would never have happened," Dean glowered at Phil. They were now all standing in front of John, looking down at him.

"Leave him alone, Dean," the shorter woman spoke for the first time. "It wasn't your fault, Phil," she said, resting a hand on Phil's shoulder. "We all should have been paying more attention. Shu'dda watched him closer. Surprised he hadn't gone in before. I kept telling—"

"Stop it! All of you!" the boy's mother interrupted. "It happened, O.K.? He's O.K., that's all that counts!" She turned toward the woman. "Stay out of it, Penny," she continued. "He's my son and my responsibility. I can take care of him. I don't need help from any of you."

"Well, then maybe you ought'a start," Penny muttered. The shorter of the two women at barely five feet, Penny was wearing a faded, flower-patterned sarong tied at her hips, beneath a dirty, tie-dyed T-shirt, the sleeves cut off. Tufts of hair protruded from her armpits. Her breasts, large for a small woman, pushed the hem of the T-shirt away from her body and revealed a tanned abdomen with a noticeable belly.

The boy was beginning to fuss in his mother's arms. The excitement of the rescue and the confrontation produced an awkward moment until she stepped forward and set Jason on the ground. She offered her hand to John who was still seated. The boy hid behind her, clutching her legs and staring out at John.

"Look . . . Thanks for, well, saving him, I guess. You saved him, that's what you did," Mara said.

"What's his name?" John asked.

"Jason. His name is Jason," she replied. She withdrew her hand, realizing that since John was covering himself with both his hands he was not going to take hers. "He's only three."

"It's O.K.," John replied, "I was just lucky to see him. I was almost asleep when you screamed. I looked up and saw his head in the water. All those curls. When I jumped, I practically landed on top of him. The rest was . . . Well, we were lucky, I guess," he said, smiling at the boy. "He was pretty scared. Can he swim?"

"Christ, he's only three, and we don't have a pool at the club," Dean snapped. "I'm Dean and she's Mara," he said pointing to the blonde woman.

"Pleased to meet you, Mara," John replied, ignoring Dean and staring at Mara. "And you are welcome. Just glad I could help. He is a great-looking kid."

Mara smiled at the corner of her eyes, reading his disdain for Dean. She showed no emotion. *Cleaned up she would almost be beautiful*, John thought. Slightly taller than Dean, her blonde hair fell long, down her back. Tanned, lithe, John knew from having seen her on the beach that she was long-legged and shapely. But there was something about her eyes. Green, with a startled, wary look, as if her eyes, ever alert, were planning an escape route for the rest of her body.

"I'm, John," he said to Mara. No one had asked. "And I don't have any clothes, uh, with me. My stuff is back up, across, the river."

Dean had continued to stare at John. "What were you doin' here, or up there?" He gestured back upstream. "We seen you a couple of days ago."

"I heard about this spot, the river and all, from some people I met in Frisco. I wanted to check it out," John said, "and I—"

"My God, Dean, get a grip! He saved Jace's life! He's sitting here wet, no clothes, and you're giving him the third degree! What kind of shit is this?" Penny interrupted. "We should be thanking him!"

"You're right," Dean responded. He turned. "Look, Phil, give him your shirt. That ought to work. And I have an extra pair of 'stocks' in my pack. You can wear those for now, until we get your stuff back."

Mara and Jason had not moved. Phil stripped off his shirt, revealing a chest that seemed to shrink, undefined, into his waist, which somehow held up his cutoff jeans. *One deep breath, his shorts will fall off,* John thought. Phil tossed his shirt to John, who caught it in his lap. John looked at them as they watched him. He started to stand. No one turned away. Mentally shrugging, he stood and pulled the shirt over his head. *At least I can't see them. What the hell,* he thought. *Burt should see me now.* The shirt fell to mid-thigh. Dean handed him a set of Birkenstocks, and John stooped, balancing on one foot and then the other. He looked up. Penny had not taken her eyes off him, a trace of a smile. Mara was now looking away, one arm draped over the shoulder of Jason. John winked at the boy.

"Tell you what," Dean started, "Phil can handle it, hustle back up to get your stuff. There's a footbridge downstream. We can all go back to the house. You can come with us if you want. If you got no place to go, you can chill with us, man. He can catch up with us there. O.K., Phil? O.K., with you, man?" he asked John.

"Sure, if that's O.K. with Phil," John replied, looking at Phil.

"Whatever . . . sure . . . O.K.," Phil replied.

"My threads are up on the ledge," John said, and he took Phil by the arm and pointed back up the river, where he had jumped. "See the bush? On the right?" he indicated to Phil. "Near it is my backpack, my shoes, and other stuff. Be careful when you pick it up 'cause I think my wallet is on top, not inside," John explained.

"Cool. O.K. I can handle it," Phil responded.

"We need to get our stuff, back up at the beach," Mara reminded Dean.

"Right, I know," Dean said. "C'mon." He turned and started toward the bank. Phil, loping ahead, turned downriver and disappeared into the brush.

~

They followed the fire trail along the river down to the paved county road. While they walked, John asked Penny, who had fallen behind the others, where they were staying, and she explained that they had all come from the Haight, in San Francisco, about six months ago. Except for Mara, who came along later. Dean found the house sort of by "accident," and the door was unlocked, well, broken, and the electricity and the water were still turned on. Nobody was around, so they spent one night and then just sort of stayed. Most of the houses were boarded up, and the few people using the road kept to themselves. They "liberated" some furniture and "stuff" from one of the abandoned houses. The sheriff drove by once and stopped Dean who said that the house belonged to an uncle of one of the girls.

Following the shoulder of the pavement, they came to a small cluster of buildings set at a bend in the roadway. A weary church, too many of its faded red shingles fallen away, advertised "Mass, 10:00 A.M., every other Sunday" on a crooked sign set in a pile of stone, part of a crumbling wall, on the edge of its small parking lot. Across the broken pavement of an intersecting lane that ran uphill and disappeared in the trees were a store and its former service station. A cracked glass pump, brand markings peeled away and its hose missing, separated the store from the county roadway. When they arrived, Phil was lounging on a wooden bench, in front of the store, John's pack between his feet.

"What took you guys so long?" he grinned. His third tooth on the right side was gone. "I been here for hours."

"Bullshit!" Dean snorted.

John picked up his pack and tossed one strap over his shoulder.

"I stuffed your shorts and shit in the top," Phil explained. He reached into his pocket. "And here's your wallet."

John removed his khaki shorts from the pack, and slipped them on under the T-shirt.

The store was taller than wide, its false front at least three stories, the worn wood and shredded stucco stark in the late afternoon sun. The door was open. Mara and the boy had gone inside.

"We need some stuff," Penny said to no one. "Milk, bread, some cereal. And there's not much for dinner."

Dean settled next to Phil on the bench, watching John. "Don't have my wallet," he said.

"Well, I don't want to walk back down here again," Penny said, "I'm tired."

"Hey, man?" Dean asked still looking at John, "You got any money we can 'borrow'? There's some stuff we need, and you're staying for dinner, right?" His grin was a challenge.

"And TP. Get some shit paper," Phil added, "those magazines—"

"Shut up!" Dean dug an elbow into Phil.

"Sure," John smiled, "I can help, I have a few bucks on me."

"C'mon," Penny motioned, taking his arm as she led him into the store. He could feel her warmth through her thin top. Phil and Dean remained seated on the bench. "I know what we need," she smiled at John.

The store was cool, and the old building's small windows, some at the second-story level, provided little light. The owner was seated on a stool behind a chipped, stained counter, which was topped with cracked and warped linoleum. He looked up warily.

"Hi, Mr. Mattuzig," Penny said cheerfully. "We just need a few things, and guess what, we've got money," she smiled at the elderly, unshaven man, whose frown seemed to erode at the news. "For a change," she added.

"Hope so," he replied, "'Cuz you ain't got no credit left," his eyes fastened on Penny's breasts, peering over his filthy, crooked half-glasses, one ear-piece held by a bent paper clip. Mattuzig wore a torn, sleeveless undershirt, pelted with remnants of forgotten meals. His face was puffy, *ex-boxer or a serious drinker,* John thought. A purple mole projected just below the crease of his mouth, a long, stained hair curling outward.

"C'mon," Penny tugged John as she led him down the center of the three dimly lit aisles to a cold case at the rear. She removed one half-gallon of milk and some butter.

"How about some beer?" John offered, as he opened the other door.

"Sure, that would be great," Penny replied. "Lucky Lager—do you have enough for a six-pack?"

"One won't go far with that bunch, I bet, I'll get two."

"They'll like that. 'specially Dean," she said. "He loves his beer, but then so does Phil," she laughed. She moved over to another aisle and stopped at the paper goods. John looked at her. "He was kidding about the magazines, right?"

"Not really. But newspaper works sometimes." He wasn't sure if *she* was kidding.

"Let's get another roll," he said, nodding.

"Sure," she grinned. She turned, shifted one of the packs under her arm, and grabbed a large box of Kellogg's Flakes from an adjoining shelf. Penny headed back up the aisle toward the front of the store, and John followed. He set the beer on the counter. The store owner licked his lips, watching Penny.

"I thought Dean said something about dinner," John inquired.

"So did I," Penny said turning toward him. "We really are low on stuff and—"

Price is the object, John knew, and turning to the man behind the counter, who had not moved, he asked, "You got any meat? Steaks, maybe?"

"All he has are frozen, in the back. But we don't usually get steaks. Some-times hamburger," Penny replied.

"Well, we're celebrating about Jason, aren't we," John said meeting her gaze.

"What's with the little guy?" Mattuzig interjected. Penny's vacant stare provided no explanation. Mattuzig rested on an elbow, a thumb under his jaw, one index finger wore a constant path under his nostrils—back and forth; back and forth. A sheen had formed on the finger.

"No," John replied. "He had his first swimming lesson today. He did O.K.," he said, smiling at the man and then at Penny. "Where's the meat?" The grocer stared at him, at the items on the counter, and then the woman, and John realized that the he did not trust them. "Here," John said and put down a twenty-dollar bill.

"We got some fresh meat today, not just frozen. She knows where the meat is," he replied as he picked up the money, "Don't ya, sweetie?" he grunted.

"Back by the beer?" John asked.

"Second door over," she replied. "On the left."

"You wait here, I'll find it," John turned away and walked to the rear of the store. He found the meat and mentally totaled the items: six dollars, maybe. As he shut the cold case, a side door opened, and Mara and the boy reentered the store. She looked up, startled to see John.

"Hi," he nodded. When they walked past, he ruffled the boy's hair.

She paused, her hand holding the boy. "I see you got your clothes."

"Yeah. It felt very weird hiking down here in that shirt," he smiled, reaching out to run his hand through Jace's hair. "You O.K., little guy?"

"He's fine," she answered. As she started past, Mara paused and looked back at John: "I really appreciate what you did. I'm sorry if we ruined your plans or whatever."

"I didn't have any plans, so hanging with you guys is cool," he said. "I like it out here, and maybe I can stay a few days. If that's O.K. with you and Dean and the others."

He could feel the chill creep back into her voice when she replied, "I don't care. It's up to the others, I guess. It's O.K. with me, but I'm just one." Her eyes took on that wary look again. He followed her to the front of the store. Mara walked past Penny without a word.

"See ya, little man," the grocer smiled at the boy as he walked outside.

"Bye, Mr. Ma-too-sick," the boy said shyly, glancing over his shoulder.

John set the steaks on the counter. "That should do it."

Mattuzig rang up their purchases, each entry a hand crank on the old register.

"That it?" he asked. "All comes to $13.30." John nodded and the grocer made change from John's bill. Penny had already bagged the other purchases. Mattuzig reached over and shoved the meat down, crushing the cereal.

John's look challenged the older man as he said, "Saving on the overhead?" John rearranged the contents.

"Right," Mattuzig snarled as he slammed the cash drawer and slouched back on his stool.

"Let's go, John," Penny said quickly.

"Like that little guy. I like him," Mattuzig said softly. "Damn shame that he's with you hippies," he hissed. "Needs a real home, is what he needs. Not that shit hole some people are squatting in!"

"Thanks, Mr. Mattuzig," Penny replied. She took John by the arm and nodded for him to pick up the beer.

Outside, Penny spat, "He's an asshole! A miserable, grade-A asshole!" The sun was lower, almost hidden behind the forested hill to the west. But the late summer afternoon was still warm. The others were gone. Penny stepped off the store porch, onto the road, gesturing with her head, "This way," she turned to her right and started up the hill. John followed. What had once been a paved roadway was now fissured and broken. Ahead of them he could see Mara and the boy.

"You O.K. with those bags?" he asked Penny.

"Yeah, sure," she replied looking up the road, "They could have waited."

"How far is it?" John asked, as he saw Mara and Jason pass by several houses, until the overhanging trees obscured them.

"Not far. Couple of minutes. The house is in those trees, on the left," she nodded up the road.

~

Ahead, near the turn to the house, Dean asked Phil, "Did you get a look at his stuff?"

"Yeah, sure, like you said. Hope he didn't notice."

"He won't. He didn't say anything when you gave him his pack and got his shit out." He paused, waiting. "Well, what—?"

"Like he said. His name is John. John Meagor, that's his last name. Meagor, I think. Something like that."

"I don't give a flying fuck about his last name. What else?"

"He had a California driver's license, with a Berkeley address, and a student body card this year, 1973 . . . from Berkeley. Cal. It had a bear on it. I didn't go through it all, just the stuff on top."

"A fuckin' bear! College boy! What else?"

"He's got some weed. Matter of fact, a pretty good stash. I didn't take any. It's wrapped in a plastic baggie. Bet it's good stuff."

"Money?" Dean pressed.

"Oh, yeah. He's got a roll. Looks like it might be a couple hundred. A twenty was on top."

"Really? Wonder what's up with him?" Dean pondered aloud as they turned down the path to the house.

~

In answer to his questions, while they walked, Penny explained that she was one of six kids, from Minnesota, a city so far out of it that she split at the first chance with her then-boyfriend from high school, who freaked and fled Frisco after his first acid trip (*which I don't do… ever*), but she stayed. She made cool macrame and fern plant hangers that she sometimes sold at the weekly street fair in Fairfax. She didn't miss her family or they did not give a shit about her, and did he have someone or what?

"What's with Dean? He is sort of in charge?" John asked.

"You could say that. At least he thinks so." She gestured. "Here, down this path." She nudged him to turn left, careful that her breast made meaningful contact with his arm.

The single-story house was set back from the road, at the end of what once was a driveway. Overgrown in the front and surrounded by trees, it was almost invisible. Built in the 1930s as a summer home when the area was popular with weekenders from San Francisco, it was little used or maybe abandoned until they discovered it. A porch ran across the entire front, beneath a sagging overhanging roof. Smoke coiled from a slanting metal stack to the rear. The front door was open, a screen door hung to one side. John recognized the house from the surveillance pictures in the investigation file.

The front room was bare except for broken wooden and cardboard boxes lining one wall, a fireplace on another wall. To the right was a dining room with a long wooden table and an assortment of metal and wooden chairs. A broken chandelier, bare bulbs, dangled over the table. Peeling paint and dirty, dented walls throughout. The floors were bare, worn, tracked, and dirty.

Penny led him past what looked like bedrooms, one on each side of the hall, to the kitchen at the rear. The windows were dirty, a few missing panes, and torn screens hung like shrouds. It was dingy, dark, depressing, and smelled worse: damp and neglected and old. He did not see Dean or Phil when they entered

"Elaine!" Penny called out, "We're here." As they entered the kitchen, a tall, gaunt woman standing over the sink, turned to face them and wiped her hands on a stained apron. The sink behind her was cracked, mottled dark brown on the sides, and it tilted forward. Counters on either side were peeling, warped, the tiles chipped and missing. There were the makings of a salad or maybe soup spread out on the countertop.

Open shelves held several pots and pans, a coffee pot, and jars, mostly empty. The windows behind her looked out onto redwood trees, the outside indistinguishable in the settling darkness. Paper bags, take-out food cartons, and bottles were piled to the side. Under the sink, vegetable greens hung out of a bucket garbage pail.

"This is Elaine," Penny said. "We got some stuff, Elaine. Wait 'til you see what's for dinner. Steak!" She smiled at the other woman, as she set her bags down on a card table set in the center of the room.

Elaine was the tallest of the three women, probably the oldest. Stern looking, suspicious, she wore her hair down, in long, kinky curls. She was dressed in a long, cotton, tie-dyed shift in shades of orange and blue. Barefoot, the edges of her feet were black. She was standing on a pink faded towel, a floor mat. She looked slightly better than the pictures John had seen of her.

"Put it in the fridge. The beer, too," Elaine nodded at John and leaned back against her counter. He placed the beer in the box. The refrigerator was cold inside, but the door was wired on, one hinge missing.

"We met at the swim—" Penny started.

"I heard," Elaine interrupted. "Sounds like you were at the right place, at the right time," continuing to wipe her hands. "And Mara was very lucky you were," she studied John.

"Just lucky, I guess," he said. "I'm John."

Elaine's eyes narrowed, and he realized that she was looking behind him. He turned when Penny said, "We got the stuff, Dean, and guess what, Phil? Steak tonight! Cool huh!?" Penny announced.

"You got steak? You got that kind of dough?" Dean asked.

John turned to meet Dean. "Yeah, I had some left over, and as long as you were kind enough to invite me in, and it's been a weird day. I thought, what the hell? Is that O.K.? Or what?"

"Cool, man. It's cool. We ain't poor, but it also ain't prime rib every day. Or every week, for that matter," Dean's eyes softened and for the first time, his mouth widened in a slight grin.

"Well, man, it's cool with me," Phil stuttered. "Steak! Shit, that's bitchin!"

"Well, let's not have it too *cool*, Phil. Better hot, like cooked," John joked. They all laughed, and he felt them relax, except Elaine, whose frown suggested unasked questions.

CHAPTER 2

THE SLIPPING LIGHT PAINTED THE REDWOODS DARK. The slumped remains of a barbecue were set behind the house, close to the creek: a raised pit, the original cooking area, and a pile of recently stacked loose bricks that served as a counter. Three aluminum lawn chairs, some wooden armrests missing, faced the pit, their plastic seats and backs stretched, frayed, fragile. Phil tended the glowing coals with a poker made of a wire hanger. He knocked the ash off a pyramid of briquettes and spread them evenly.

"Hey," John said approaching, "Looks good." He handed Phil an open beer.

"Almost ready. Give me a hand with this," Phil said pointing to a grease-encrusted grate. "Old, real old. They don't make 'em like that anymore. Last forever," he smiled as they eased the grill over the coals, sliding it onto two metal rails.

"This may be 'forever,'" John replied, brushing off his hands.

"Yeah, but that shit will burn off. We haven't done this for a while. And this helps," he held up a rusted tire iron and slowly ran the grooved end over the metal grate, knocking off leaves, dirt, rust, and congealed grease. The coals flared and sputtered. "That'll clean it up."

"I guess you're right," John said. "And let them get really hot."

"Right on," Phil responded, continuing his efforts.

Sparks rose and wisps of smoke puffed from the dripping grease. Satisfied, Phil carefully added new briquettes. He had wrapped a rag around one end of the coat hanger, it was getting hot. He smiled to himself.

"Cool, very cool," Phil said backing away from the grill. He took a chair and reached down for his beer. He took a long pull from the chilled bottle.

"Hot. More like very hot," John grinned.

"Cool fire, I mean," Phil said. "I used to be a grill cook, assistant really, one time in a steakhouse. In, well—" he stopped.

"Right," John leaned back, testing his chair. He enjoyed the stillness, the glowing fire, and the cold beer. "So you're the man for this job, right?

"Yeah, that's me," Phil nodded.

Neither man spoke as they watched the glow, and John tracked the smoke as it rose through the leafy blackness.

"So, Phil? That's what I should call you, right?"

"Sure. You know, Dean makes fun of me sometimes and stuff. Yeah, 'Phil's' good. Shit . . .," laughing, ". . . it's my name." They laughed together.

"You can call me John, 'cuz that's *my* name."

"I know, I saw it on your license," Phil replied.

"How's that, Phil?" He leaned forward, resting his elbows on his knees. Phil avoided his gaze. John could feel that his question had sucked the air out of Phil.

After a moment he looked away and said, "Oh, I get it. You checked my wallet to be sure you got the right stuff, that it was mine. When you picked it up on the rocks. Right?"

"Ah, yeah. Sure," Phi stammered, "I sure as shit didn't want to get some-one else's shit. I checked it, right. Saw your name and you lived in Berkeley. That was O.K.? Right?"

"Sure. No sweat. Skoal!" John lifted his beer to Phil, smiling, and they clinked bottles. Phil's hand shook slightly.

"Skoal!" Phil responded.

John felt him relax and sat back. "I understand you guys have been here for a while. This is a really great pad."

"Yeah it works, and the river is . . . well, you saw it."

"I guess I did, I sure did. And so did Jason," John added.

"Right, he sure did."

"Interesting place for a kid . . . a little kid . . . here, I mean."

"Well," his eyes downcast. "He came with Mara, so . . . I don't know."

John leaned forward, until Phil looked up and met his gaze. "How did that happen, Phil?"

~

"Getting pretty chummy, aren't they?" Elaine observed to Penny, both standing at the sink. Outside, the two men were silhouetted against the glow of the fire.

"He seems O.K.," Penny answered, "Kind of nice. I mean he bought the food, and he seemed nice when we walked up the hill." She shook the water from the lettuce leaves as Elaine handed them to her.

"We don't know anything about him, Penny. Where he comes from."

"He seems O.K. Cute, too," Penny mused, "and he is really—"

"My God, Penny! Is that all you can think of?"

"I just meant . . ."

"I know what you meant. Whatever, he sure saved our asses. If little Jace had got hurt, or drowned, we would all have been in big trouble." Elaine dried her hands on a paper towel. "It's Mara's fault. I told you sooner or later he was going to get in trouble unless she kept an eye on him. He's only three. People like her shouldn't have kids. Shouldn't keep them if they do, and he doesn't belong here. No way, not here!" she said.

"Elaine!" Penny whispered, leaning toward her, "they're in the other room," Penny warned.

"I don't care. It's not right," she replied. "Why did he come back with you? I don't like it."

~

Outside, tending the fire, Phil explained that Elaine and Penny were hitch-hiking back from Fairfax one day, and Mara, driving her VW bus, picked them up. By the time they got to Toca (*there was a battered broken sign on the gas pump that had once read "Tocaloma," some Indian word . . .*) they had invited her to stay, or she had invited herself, whatever, since she had a car. They thought the kid was cute but might be a problem with Dean. Dean and she hit it off, sort of, and she's been here ever since, couple of months, maybe more. The kid was cool, and we all look out for him, especially Elaine. As long as someone else looked out for the kid, Mara could care less; it freed her up. Elaine thought it was wrong for her to stay here with him; like she's a bad mother, but she would not face down Mara or Dean.

"Where is she—Mara—from, do you know?" John had asked.

Phil continued that she doesn't like questions, so we, at least not me, never asked. She never says anything about where they came from, the kid's father, nothing. I think it is the Midwest or maybe back East, but the car had

California plates. One time Elaine brought it up, and Mara got pissed. Told Elaine and Dean the kid and her were none of their business, and that if they had any questions or didn't like it they, or her, whatever, they could get the fuck out—split. Told them to make up their minds. (*It was tense, man*). Dean told her to chill out. He told Elaine to back off, and that was it—never came up again. She had the car and a few bucks, so it all worked out. Phil liked the kid at first, but he never got close to him because of Mara. Elaine was very protective of the kid, which Mara resented, and Penny stayed out of it. The kid sort of took care of himself. (*He is a cool little dude—for a kid.*) But he guessed that some of the stuff they were doing may not be the best thing for a kid, but no one ever said. Lately, Dean and Mara really got into the weed, she was fucking Dean, sometimes on the beach, swimming naked. We scrounge for our food and shit, whatever. (*He took a long, thoughtful pull on his beer and stared into the blackness*) Elaine was afraid that the store guy, that asshole Mattuzig, might report us, because the kid spends a lot of time with him at the store.

"How's that?" John asked.

"Oh, you know, the weed's O.K., but not all the time," he hesitated, stood up, and raked the coals. It was obvious he had finished the story. John drained his beer, and, tilting back, he tossed the bottle into the blackness. He did not hear it land.

"What about those coals? Look pretty good to me," John said, breaking the silence.

"Should be about right."

"O.K. I'll get the meat?" John stood up.

"Yeah, O.K. Now's good," Phil replied.

John stretched as he walked back to the house. The screen door banged behind him when he entered, and the women stopped talking, he guessed about him from their look. He smiled at both.

"Coals about ready," he said. "S'cuse me, ladies," he grinned at Penny as he removed the plate of steaks from the fridge.

"How you want yours?" he asked, stepping back.

"Medium rare," Penny blushed. .

"Me, too," Elaine said absently.

"Well done," a voice behind him replied. John kicked the refrigerator door closed and turned. Dean was standing in the doorway.

"No blood in mine. Well!" Dean ordered.

"And you, Mara?" John asked. She was standing next to Dean.

"Medium is fine," her voice was soft in marked contrast to the others.

"O.K. Two MR. One medium. And one well, no blood. Got it!" John recited. He pushed the screen door open with his back and stepped outside, smiling to himself.

"Here we go, Phil," he called out as descended the few steps. "Work your magic!"

~

The five of them and boy ate seated around the large table in the dining room, which had a long crack running diagonally across it and was held together by metal, wavy brads pounded into each side of the crack—Phil's work. There were three chairs that might have matched the table, but on two the split fabric seats had been replaced with plywood. Dean took a taller chair at the head of the table; Mara sat to his right, next to Phil. John found himself across from them, next to Penny. The steaks were heaped on a chipped platter. Notwithstanding his specific cooking instructions, Dean quickly grabbed the largest of the steaks. A cracked wooden bowl held lettuce, tomatoes, and cheese-encrusted taco chips (*nachos in an earlier life*, John guessed). Ketchup, a jar of mayo, and a bottle of Thousand Island dressing completed the menu. As she sat down, Elaine set a loaf of French bread in the middle of the table with the butter John had bought. An assortment of cutlery was scattered in the center of the table, some plastic, some metal. Elaine produced a jug of Mountain Red, and Phil did the honors twisting off the top with a flourish and a comment, "Da-daah!" They all laughed. John took one of the jars used as a wine glass; the others were plastic. Phil cradled the jug in his arm and presented John with a test pour, pausing. John swirled the wine, sniffed, tasted, and pronounced it "bitchin'."

They all laughed. Phil was delighted.

"Give me a break, you dork," Dean moaned.

Later, John could not remember if he had eaten anything. By the time they got into the second jug, they had replayed the drama of the day, with Phil taking the lead, through a reenactment of the rescue. They got into the dope over the steaks, using John's stash; Dean and Mara were smoking heavily. The mood eventually turned critical, Elaine blaming Mara for "the almost tragedy," she called it. Penny came to her defense to no effect. As the euphoria of the marijuana erased the tension of the afternoon's events, they recalled their meeting with John, dripping and naked on the beach, and a drug-fueled hilarity took over. John had no recollection of how or when the evening came to an end, but at some point he knew that he was "in," at least for now.

~

"He's in!"

"Who's in?" Burt replied, looking up from a file and across his desk at the smiling Fred Meagor, his partner, who rested against the door jamb.

"John is. He got in and spent last night in the house, with them. We just got the call," Fred replied.

Burt shook his head and rocked back in his chair. "No kidding. That's great," he said. "Well, you guessed right, then. Did John call or what?"

"No, not John. Our contact left a message. John doesn't know that we have a set of eyes on him, and the contact doesn't know that John is working for us. We set it up that way."

"Right, I remember. Well, now what?"

"We wait until he makes his move," Fred replied. "I need to call the client and alert him that things may happen fast now, so that he's prepared." He straightened and started to turn away, but then paused and looked back at his partner, "... with or without the cavalry!"

~

For the next three days John hung out. They slept until late morning. By midday they were either at the river or stayed at the house. Once when Mara drove into town, she left Jason behind, and Jason quickly attached himself to John, who played with him. If Elaine did not run the kitchen, John doubted that they would eat. Phil did the odd jobs without prompting: wood for the fireplace, repairs to the house, garbage dumped in the creek behind the house. John had seen the rats during the day and heard the raccoons at night. He kept Jace away from the dump and warned him not to touch anything the rats might have been into. They all bathed in the river.

By default, Penny appeared to be in charge of the inside of the house, picking up after everyone. Dean, the self-appointed leader, did nothing except bitch at the others. He was either hungover or stoned, on edge during the day, wasted at night.

Mara, while seemingly accepted as part of the group, did not fit in. She ignored the others with an air of aloofness that he heard Elaine more than once deride as "stuck up." Yet, she was sleeping with Dean, and she was the only one with whom Dean did not argue or kid. He rode Phil mercilessly, and Phil took it.

They sent John down the road to the store twice at Elaine's suggestion. He had wondered how they would treat him when his money ran out. They had helped themselves to his stash of marijuana, and it was almost gone. Jason had gone with him to the store, but he was unable to coax any information out of him. The boy seemed to have no memory of where he had come from, or of his family. *He is only three,* John told himself, *what do I expect?*

Once at the river, John had worked with the boy in the water. Getting him to go in beyond his feet had taken all afternoon. But now he was running in, and he even jumped off a log into John's arms as he gained confidence.

This morning John woke to find the small boy sleeping on the floor against him.

After breakfast of dry cereal and coffee, Dean mentioned to no one in particular, "Well, we are low on food and stuff. Might be time for a grocery run tonight."

"I'll take the car," Mara replied, "I'll drive this time. But who's going?" she asked.

"Take John with you," Dean teased. "About time he did somethin'."

"Christ, Dean, what's wrong with you? He's bought stuff all week!" Elaine protested.

"Hey, I'll go," John interceded, "But I'm running low on cash you ought to know."

"You won't need any money, where you're going," Dean laughed, joined by Elaine.

Mara smiled. "We'll go tonight," she said, her eyes bright, challenging.

~

During the one-hour drive Mara said very little. It was dark, and the city streets mostly deserted. By the time they reached the empty shopping center, they had already made two restaurant "stops," one Italian where they had "scored," Mara called it, pasta, sauce, and leftovers from the back door. The other was Mexican: stale chips, tacos, some mixed-up orders headed to the garbage, including, tonight, some burritos and runny quesadillas. Now, on the other side of town, Mara edged the VW bus slowly along an alley, an estuary on one side, the rear of the buildings on the other. Dumpsters, packing crates, piles of cardboard boxes lined the narrow lane. Bug-filled security lights and the glow from an adjacent marina across the narrow canal cast eerie shadows on the pavement at the rear of the stores. Her headlights off, Jason was standing on the passenger seat, his arm out of the window of the slowly moving car, trying to touch the dumpsters and boxes.

"Stop that!' Mara warned. "Keep your arms inside, Jacey. How many times have I told you? You'll get hurt."

Jace smiled back at her from under the dark bangs that covered his eyebrows. "It's O.K., Mommy. I like it," he answered.

"Jason, do what your mom says," John interjected from his perch on a plastic crate set between the two seats.

"Awww," the boy whined, squatting on his knees, his small arms no longer protruding from the van window.

"There. That dumpster, the one next to the blue door. That's the bakery." Mara pointed. "We'll check it out," and she eased the van in-between a parked truck and the large container. She turned off the motor. "You wait here and look out. We'll be right back. It will only take a second," she said turning to John.

"Leave Jason. I'll watch him," he replied.

"No way, he goes with me. You just watch the truck and keep your eye out for the security guards," she replied as she slid out of the front seat. "C'mon, Jacey," lifting the boy out of the car. Mara left the driver's side door ajar. John slid over into the passenger seat and watched them walk in front of the vehicle. She held Jason's hand. The dim glow backlit her long hair, with a golden effect. *Beautiful,* he thought, *if she washed it regularly.* Mara opened one side of the dumpster and leaned in to prop up the lid. Then she hoisted the boy up and lowered him down into the box. Almost immediately loaves of French bread and baguettes began appearing in her arms, and he could hear the giggles of the boy. Her arms full, she stepped back toward the van, and handed the bread quickly to John.

"Here, toss these in the back," she ordered. He took the loaves and placed them on the floor behind him, as she turned back to the dumpster.

After two trips, she told the boy, "C'mon, honey, that's all. Let's get you out."

"Mommy, help me," John heard the unseen voice reply, and the edge of a large pink box appeared over the side of the container.

"Oh, my God. Jacey! It's a cake. A birthday or wedding cake. Let me help you," Mara replied.

Suddenly the box disappeared back into the container, and almost immediately he heard the boy cry, "Mommy, I all icky. It fell on me!"

Fascinated, John watched as Mara leaned into the box, her feet off the ground as she stretched down to reach. She hauled him out, still clutching the pink box. John glanced up, distracted by a moving light, far down the alley, coming slowly toward them. *One light, not headlights,* he thought, but his focus was the woman, struggling with the boy who was still hanging onto the cake box.

"Let's go," he shouted at her. "Someone's coming!"

Looking ahead, John could now make out a man: uniform cap, a flashlight in his hand. *Oh shit,* he thought, *now we've had it.*

He slid over into the driver's seat, pulled the door shut and felt for the keys, as he heard her open the side door and throw the boy in. She slammed the door and dropped onto the passenger seat as John started the motor. The engine caught on the first try, and he saw the guard, closer now, pause at the sound.

"Go! We're in!" Mara yelled, and John let the clutch out, bucking the car, cursing his nervousness. The car headlights were still off. As they eased forward, the guard was now clearly visible in the center of the alley, and his bright flashlight was blinding John. Afraid of running him down, John eased off the accelerator. The guard was now directly in front of the van, and there was no way to go around him in the narrow alley without hitting him.

"Damn," John muttered, and he heard Mara sigh. The guard was now at her window, shining his long flashlight around the car.

"This is private property, you know. Don't like you hippies stealing stuff out of the garbage," he growled.

Inches from his face, she replied: "It is only garbage, who cares? It's not like it's *your* stuff."

"Don't give me any of your shit, hippie chick," he said shifting the flashlight to his other hand as he reached for the door handle. "Get out of there!" he ordered.

As John watched Mara and the man next to the window, almost in slow motion, she snarled "Fuck you, pig!" She spat directly into his face, only inches away. John saw the spittle hit his forehead and the visor of his cap, and trickle onto his glasses.

He heard her yell "Go!" as she hit John's arm and the van shot forward down the alley.

Hanging out of the window, she screamed back at the guard: "Dickhead! You private dickhead!" She laughed as the van bounced into the street and John turned on the headlights, as they veered right onto the parkway that would take them out of town.

"Do'n hang out of the window, Mommy, you'll hurt," he heard Jason warn from the rear.

They both laughed as they made all the green lights on the deserted streets. When they finally had to stop for a red light, the alley far behind, for the first time John took his eyes off the road and looked over at Mara. Her head was back against the seat, her eyes were closed. She looked tense and tired, her bravado gone.

"You O.K.?" he asked.

"Yeah, fine, just fine. I love going out to dinner, and getting screamed at by some pig night watchman with nothing better to do." And then she started to laugh softly. Jason had moved up between their seats.

"Look at Jacey, John. Look at his hair. Oh, shit, he has cake all over him!" They began to laugh as Jason licked at his frosting-covered fingers. John glanced down. The boy had cake packed into his hair, red and white striped frosting ran down his face and neck where the cake had landed on him when he tried to push it out of the dumpster.

"If there's any left in the box, it ought to go good with the Mexican," John offered.

"Oh, right," she answered laughing. "God, he is such a mess. But he is so cute," she said. It was the first time John had heard her refer to the boy with affection.

~

The fruits of their scavenging, highlighted by the cake, were cause for a celebration. After Mara related the encounter with the security guard, the group now accepted John, and he felt comfortable with them.

"I've seen him there before, the dickhead," Mara laughed. "But he is usually hanging out in front. So, we cruise around until he is at the opposite end, but that's the first time he has ever approached us."

John told the story of their confrontation with the guard, making much of Mara's bravado, and they toasted her retaliation.

"Fuck the pigs, private and public!" Dean said. "What do they care if we raid the garbage, for Christ's sake! It's garbage! It's not like stealing. Cheap fuckers!" He was drunk and a little stoned. The room was clouded with their smoke.

"You should have seen Jacey in that dumpster," John said. "I couldn't figure out what he was doing, Mara kept telling him to come out. He wouldn't let go of that cake. No way. And then he came up. All covered with the frosting in his hair. Man, it was everywhere. It was too much. And the cop coming at us. . . ."

"He's a tough little shit, that one," Dean said.

"Nice, Dean. He's all of three years old," Elaine inserted. "You shouldn't have taken him in the first place. My God, he is just a kid. He doesn't belong here, and—"

"He's my kid, Elaine, and I'll take him where and when I want, and it's . . . he's . . . none of your business, remember that. And don't you tell me what to do, ever!" Mara snarled.

"Chill out," Dean interrupted. "You too, Elaine."

Elaine glowered at him and avoided contact with Mara.

Elaine's displeasure with Mara as a mother was obvious to all, and she stared at her with complete disdain. *She should just leave us out of it . . . ought to get gone and take the boy,* Elaine thought. She was deathly afraid of somehow being held responsible for what might happen to him, and she was sure it would only be a question of time.

They were well into the wine and the weed since John and Mara's return, and all of them were buzzed from the combination of the food, dope, and sugar shock. Penny, sitting next to John, had paid particular attention to him while he told their story, but she remained quiet. She had offered him hits on her joints—she was now on number three—and both were high. Penny's hand rested high on his bare thigh, and occasionally her fingers clenched and curled under the hem of his shorts as she gazed at him. Watching her made Elaine sick—*she is such a pig!*

"Well, fuck it. Too much excitement for me," Dean interrupted. "'Private dickhead!' That's a classic, Mara. Shit, I wished I'd seen that," he continued. "I'm smashed and ready to crash," he said, one arm around Mara. She flinched. "C'mon, woman. Let's get it out of here," Dean said, standing. He held out a hand to Mara, which she ignored, but when she stood, she stumbled and knocked over her chair. Dean steadied her. "'Private dick. Dickhead!' That's famous," Dean repeated. Mara followed him out of the room into the adjacent bedroom. The door kicked shut.

"Wonderful. Just wonderful, the two of them," Elaine muttered, her wine glass empty. As she stood, she looked at the boy sitting on the floor, behind John and Penny, playing with a pile of the taco chips. She reached down and grabbed most of them. "Give me those Jason, they're dirty!" The boy cowered under her voice. On her way out of the room, she glanced at the others. "It *is* garbage. You're feeding the kid garbage, for God's sake!"

"I'm history, Penny," John said running his hand over her head. She leaned over to him, her lips on his cheek, then his ear; the smell of pot and the wine on her breath, mixed with patchouli oil she always wore. "And, I've got to piss." Gently, he moved her away and headed for the door to the outside.

"I'll wait," he heard her say.

~

He came back inside, the coolness of the night settling his head only a little. The house was dark now. He went into the parlor where he had been sleeping on the floor. No furniture. Penny was nowhere to be seen, he noted with a mixture of regret and relief. He slipped off his T-shirt and dropped his shorts, clad now only in his boxers. He lay down on top of the sleeping bag he had used as a mattress. The zipper was long gone—it was more blanket than bag. Hands behind his head, he wondered if they had been caught at the shopping center, what would the cops have done with the little boy? Taken him away? Foster home? Maybe. This was no place for a kid. His eyes were heavy.

~

The scent of the patchouli oil woke him. That and her hair on his face. Fogged by the sleep, the wine, and dope, he was uncertain where he was, and then, as if coming out of a dream, he couldn't figure out where *she* was.

But he knew it was Penny. She was behind him, her hair in his eyes, her lips on his face and on his mouth, nibbling on his ears, first one and then the other. He felt her breath in his ear and then her tongue. She was humming softly, and then he felt her hands massaging his bare chest. Her lips found one and then his other nipple, which hardened under her wet touch. He did not move.

Her lips were on his face, his lips, his ears; her fingertips tracing his ears. He felt his head start to buzz in response. Her face was now on his chest, her breath warm on his skin, her wet tongue traced the way for her hand. She raised her head, looked back at him, and smiled. Her fingers walked down his abdomen. He sucked in his gut when her hand found his enlarging member, paused, and was then joined by her other hand. She massaged him with both hands, through his boxer shorts, and he felt himself involuntarily straining to meet her, his pelvis lifting to her touch. Except for this motion, he continued to remain perfectly still; the breathing he could hear was his own.

She leaned over him now, sliding down his body. Her bare breasts smothered his face, her lips and tongue working now on his navel. He felt her reach inside his shorts and slide them lower. Her weight kept him pinned. He was now fully exposed to her, but her body blocked his view. Then he felt her take him, fully erect, in both hands, and slide her hands up and down his shaft, again and again, pulling and releasing. And as she adjusted her body, she took him into her mouth, long straight and hard, her lips sliding down into his pubic hair and then out, and again.

The entirety of his universe shrank, reduced to the length of his penis, focused only on it and the rush of feelings, which his body discharged with each of her movements. Time was suspended in her hands and mouth. He rolled his head back slightly, arching his back to meet her. And all he could think of as he gave himself up to her was, *"Shit, if she only knew I am getting paid for this!"* He rolled his head to one side, so he could breathe and there in the doorway to the living room, a silhouette only, the little boy stood, his blanket to his face, watching them.

~

John awoke confused, he had no idea of time. It was quiet. He arose and slipped on his shorts. In the kitchen, Elaine was at the sink. His mouth tasted sour, and he knew his breath must be worse. He leaned over Elaine and asked, "Any coffee in this joint?"

"Ugh. Oh, God, you smell like garbage! Get out of here," she pushed back.

Laughing, "C'mon, Elaine where's the coffee?"

"This isn't a restaurant, and I'm not your waitress. God, you stink!" She cringed.

He opened a cupboard, took out a jar of dehydrated coffee. *The guy on the label has half a face, that's the way I feel.* He opened the jar, and the stale smell caused him to gag.

"You'd have to be pretty desperate to drink that shit," Elaine said. "It has been here since we got here. But you go right ahead and try it."

The coffee was a crystalline mass, stuck to the bottom of the jar. "No way. I'm not that hard up," John tossed the jar into the garbage can. He went out the side door to the porch and saw the boy in the yard below.

"Hey, little guy," John called, as he went down the steps. "What'ch you doin'?"

"I got a stick, see?" offering it for John to inspect.

"That's a good one, Jace. Let's see if we can find me one."

"I have to pee, John," the boy replied, scrunching his hand into his crotch, "You help me?"

"Sure. Here," he said moving to him. "Lem'me show how to use a tree. Guys don't have to go inside. It's easy." John took the boy by the hand, and they moved over to a large redwood tree. The ground was level. He helped the boy pull his shorts down. No underwear. John watched as the boy directed his stream onto the tree trunk, making a trail on the bark. "Watch out for your feet," John laughed.

The boy backed up a step and giggled.

"That was fun," Jace laughed.

John helped him with his shorts, checking the zipper. The boy smelled faintly of urine, and John wondered if he ever bathed, except in the river.

"From now on, if you have to go, and you are outside, just find a tree," he ran a hand through Jace's hair.

"That's *my* tree. I'll use *it* from now on," he replied proudly, looking up.

"O.K. buddy, that's O.K.," he smiled back. "Where's your Mom?" John asked as they moved away under the trees.

"She took the car and told me to wait."

"Oh. Tell you what. Let's you and me take a walk. O.K.?"

"Sure," the boy replied, raising both arms up to him.

"Oh, so I have to carry you?" John bent down and, turning him, hoisted him over his head, onto his shoulders. His little feet dangled by John's face.

"Hang on. But not my hair. My shoulders. That's it. Here we go!" he shouted, and he loped up the slight rise, stepping onto the road. The boy bounced on his shoulders, laughing.

They zigzagged down the road, bobbing and weaving, John lifting Jace up to touch the overhanging branches. The boy giggled aloud as John swooped up and down, as if to drop him. At the bottom of the hill, John stepped up onto the concrete platform fronting the store and gently swung Jace off his shoulder and down. The boy skipped into the store.

"Hi, Mr. Ma-too-sick!" he dragged the name out as he had heard others do.

"Hey, little guy. How you doing?" the older man replied, leaning over the counter to muss his hair. Mattuzig was unshaven, his undershirt spotted and wrinkled, probably slept in. He reached back to close the magazine he had been reading. His glance dared John to remark.

"We're on a hike. John and me," Jace replied, looking over at John, who was standing in the doorway.

"Mr. Mattuzig," John nodded.

"Well, at least someone is watching him," the grocer replied. "Lots of times he just shows up here, all alone. By his'self. Someone could grab him. A car goin' by, and you would never know."

"Is that right? He's been at the house the whole time I've been there. I haven't seen him take off."

"Oh, he takes off all right. At least when he comes to visit me," Mattuzig answered.

"Well, now, we're hanging out together, Jace and me," John said.

"Hanging out! Somebody ought to 'hang.' The way they live up there and do nothing all day. Couple of times I almost called those county people to tell them about the boy. No place for a kid," he straightened.

"Well, that's something."

"You look, well, seem different from them," Mattuzig frowned.

"Look. It's cool. They are all right," John answered, "And I bet it's not forever. With winter coming on, I think they might go back to the City," he said. "Do you have a phone I can use?" John asked, looking around. "There's someone I need to call."

"Yeah, I got a phone, but I never let *them* use it. Never know where they might call and stick me with the bill," he said. "Where you *need* to call?"

"Berkeley. Here's a buck to cover the call. I need to let someone know where I am," John said.

"You do seem different. And you look out for that boy. Berkeley ain't so far. Go ahead," Mattuzig said. He stuck the dollar in his shirt pocket.

"Where's the phone?"

"On the wall just inside the back door. By the cold case," he nodded.

"Thanks," John said. "Come on, Jace, give me a hand." He turned and started toward the rear. "He can stay here with me," Mattuzig said, coming from behind the counter and hoisting the boy up.

"Can I touch these keys and make it ring?" Jace said, as he reached for the cash register, "Mr. Ma-too-sick?"

"Sure, little guy. You can maybe even ring up a sale, if your friend here buys something when he comes back," John heard behind him. The grocer looked down at the register and seeing the business card, EKI Investigations, picked it up and put it in his pocket.

~

John bought them both some juice, and they sat on the crumbling rock wall of the church parking lot, across from the store. They watched the occasional passing cars, taking turns guessing the color of the next one. Jace played with some of the larger stones that had fallen from the edge of the wall, trying to put them back. Many were too large for him. John watched him struggle, and then stepped down and began to help pick up rocks that might fit back into place. There was a pile of stones at the end of the wall that drew the boy's attention.

"Let's build a tower, John," he said.

"Well, there's not enough rocks for a tower, Jace. Not enough to do much with," he said. "But we could build a cairn."

What's a 'karn'?" Jace asked.

"'Cairn,'" John repeated. "It's a pile of rocks, large ones on the bottom, small ones on the top. Sort of like this," he said, and he began to make a base.

"Yeah! Let's build a karn!" The boy began handing him rocks. They selected rocks that would fit on top of each other, working at the corner of the parking lot. John explained that Indians, frontiersmen, trappers, and explorers would build and leave cairns to mark certain spots or trails, to show others who came after, or even for themselves when they returned, marking the direction they were to take, or that this was a spring with good water, or a ford to cross a river, often to mark the way home. Sometimes they were used as a warning or even as a signal, he explained as their cairn grew. Soon they were finished.

"See?" he said standing and hauling the boy up onto his shoulders. "From now on anyone driving by can see our cairn and know that this was the right place, or that it was time for something to happen."

"Why, John? Place for what?" he asked.

John laughed and mussed the boy's hair. "To go to church, I guess, Jace. Or to park here. Or some kind of a signal."

"A signal for what?"

"Oh, I don't know. Maybe for a meeting or a party."

"I don't like parties," he pouted.

"O.K., then a meeting." John reached up and grabbed both of the boy's hands as he stepped off the wall, and they headed back toward the house. He felt Jace turn and look back.

"I can see our karn, John," the boy said. "Think someone will see it?" he said.

John smiled down at the boy. "They can't miss it, Jace. No way," he said. He felt the little hands tighten in his grip. *No way, not after my phone call.*

~

Dean was sitting on the front porch, trying to roll a joint, hands shaking. He dropped the small package of Zig-Zags and cursed. As he bent over, Elaine stepped out onto the porch, the screen door slammed behind her. Dean jumped.

"Fuck, Elaine! Don't sneak up on me like that."

"I am not sneaking up on you, Dean. You dropped that before I came out. I was watching you."

He picked up the pack and settled back into his chair. "Spying on me?" he said.

Elaine sat on the top step, facing him, her back against a post.

"Look, Dean, this is not working, at least not anymore."

"Not working for who? You, Elaine?" he snorted.

"Not working. Period," she replied. "Look at you, you're a mess, Dean. You are stoned all the time. Angry most of the time. You weren't like this when I came here with you. And Mara—"

Dean leaned forward, the Zig-Zag package between two fingers, and pointed at her. "Leave Mara the fuck out of it, Elaine. Not your business!"

"Well, it is my business. Our business. She has her kid here. You let her stay, and this is no place for him. She could care less about him, he almost drowned for God's sake. This is going to lead to trouble. The authorities. We still don't know anything about her. Now you invite this college boy to camp out because he has a few bucks and some of your precious weed."

"Stuff it, Elaine! No one promised you, or anyone, anything when we moved in here. Right? You wanted to party with me, and we had some good times, didn't we?" he leered. "Now you're just jealous. Maybe you should check out the college kid, try something new," he scoffed.

Elaine reddened, her eyes narrowed and met his for several moments. She stood and turned to walk back into the house.

"Elaine!"

She looked back at him.

"He is just some college boy having a summer fling, don't sweat it."

"I am not so sure, Dean. There is something different about him. He seems more interested in the boy than in us."

Dean shook his head and laughed. "Right. The boy—and Penny!"

CHAPTER 3

THE LATE-MODEL FOUR-DOOR SEDAN, Stone Realty tastefully lettered on the passenger door, pulled up in front of the house and stopped behind the rental car. The driver leaned over and, seeing the man, smiled, straightened, and got out of her car. Short, fortyish, stylishly dressed in skirt, jacket, and high heels, she stepped onto the sidewalk. Hand extended, in a pronounced English accent, she said, "Hello! I'm Angela."

"Rob Williams," he replied, returning her firm handshake. "We spoke on the phone."

"Cute, isn't it," she nodded to the house.

"I like it." he replied. "I got here a little early and took a look around."

She considered the young man who was neatly dressed, collegiate-looking—open polo shirt, khakis, Top-Siders. "Well, let's have a look inside. You will love it, all redone, actually. She removed a key from her pocket and opened the lockbox hanging from the brass door hardware. Unlocking the door, she said, "Deadbolts, double locked. One can't be too safe these days, can one?"

Williams followed, and together they walked through the home and out into the fenced backyard, a steep drop-off behind. "No one will be coming up there," she pointed. "It is very secure."

"I like it. Is it still three hundred dollars a month?"

"Of course, it is, if you commit today. Is that possible? The owner wants at least a one-year lease."

"I can go six months with an option to extend. My option," he countered.

"I think perhaps we might do that. The owner is overseas. Saudi Arabia? Some desolate place, I believe," she shuddered. "He does not expect to return for at least six months to a year, so that will do nicely, I should think. Yes, I can do that."

"I can give you a check now for six hundred, and you can send me the lease or rental agreement. Would that be enough of a commitment?"

"My goodness, yes. You *are* certain, aren't you?" she smiled. "That would be super."

"What is this area called?" Williams gestured behind and to the side. "This neighborhood? I forgot what you said on the phone."

"Why, it's Sun Valley. Isn't that a charming name?" she smiled as they moved back inside.

"Incidentally, Angela," he said, "could you recommend a good lawyer? Not for this. I have some legal business once I get situated and would appreciate a referral. Someone who handles child custody cases, trial work. Somebody good," he inquired as they paused in the living room.

"Absolutely! I know a young local chap who might be just perfect. Very nice, respected, though quite young. I believe that he does trials, that sort of thing. I may have his card in my car. Yes, I know, Grant, Will Grant is his name. Helped me with a sticky mess once," she paused, pensive, and then she smiled. "Now, when would you be moving in?"

~

The boy woke John with an urgent nudge. "John! Wake up! Pee-pee tree, John!" The boy was kneeling next to him, shaking his arm. "I wanna go pee tree," he repeated.

"You sure, Jacey?" He rested on one elbow and looked at his watch. It was just after 2:00 A.M. "It's the middle of the night, little guy," John said.

"You said to use my tree," his tone left no doubt.

"Ok. Let's go, but use your soft voice, O.K.? He slipped on his shorts, checked for his wallet, and stepped into his sandals. In the living room, he spotted the boy's shoes, picked them up, and slipped them on Jace's feet as they walked quietly out of the darkened house through the kitchen. "Careful," he lifted him up and carried him on his hip, down the stairs and across the forest floor. The large tree was barely visible.

He set the boy down, "Not my tree," Jason said.

"Sure, it is," John answered

"No. *That's* my tree," the boy pointed and stepped away, "See? There."

"You're right," John shrugged and moved the few steps to the other tree. "Need help?" he asked.

"No," the boy responded, and he didn't, John could hear.

"I told you this was *my* tree, John. See?" the boy said looking back at John.

"Careful," John warned.

"I know-w-w."

John studied the darkened house. Not a sound. He felt a tug at his shorts. "I'm done," the boy said.

"Tell you what," John said, "Let's you and I take a walk, or a ride. How 'bout a ride?" He hoisted the boy onto his shoulders.

"Yea! A ride!" Jason said, excited. "Let's go!"

"But no noise, O.K.?"

"O.K.," the boy whispered in his ear.

John threaded the stand of trees, the boy's knees clutching his head as he bent to clear the low branches, and then stepped up onto the road. His vision had adjusted to the darkness, a splotchy sky was partly visible through the canopy of overhanging trees. He turned and started slowly down the road. He looked over at the house as they passed the entrance path. All dark, quiet. He moved carefully over the uneven pavement and dirt. Once he slipped but quickly recovered his footing. The small hands tightened in his hair.

"Hey. My shoulders, not my hair, remember?" He felt the boy's hands move.

"Are we going to Mr. Ma-too-sick's?" Jason whispered.

"No way. It's the middle of the night, kiddo. Mr. Mattuzig is sound asleep."

"We could wake 'em."

"Not tonight," John smiled.

He walked carefully down the crumbling roadway, pausing once to look back. He knew if they were missed, that he would have seen the house lights come on. Satisfied, he continued down the road, cautiously picking his way. At the end, opposite the store and in the open now, he could see the empty roadway. The light of a faint moon reflected off the stones of their cairn.

"See this?" John pointed. "See? Now we know where we are, even at night."

"My tower! That's my tower, John, right?"

"Right."

Reaching up to steady the boy, John stepped up onto the wall and walked quickly across the parking lot. He paused and lifted the boy up and off his shoulders and settled him onto one hip as they crossed the lot.

"Oh! Oh!" Jason cried softly. "My shoe, John. It fall down."

"Its O.K., little guy, we won't need it." In one smooth motion he reached down and opened the driver's side rear door of the waiting car and eased the boy across the seat, sliding in after him. He reached back and pulled the door shut.

He nodded to the face in the rearview mirror. "Go!" he ordered.

The sound and tension of his voice startled him. He heard the engine catch, the brake release, and the car shot forward across the lot. Bouncing once, the tires spit gravel, and they were on the paved roadway before the driver turned on the headlights.

The dome light came on, and Jason looked up in the half-light at the other man seated next to him. He stood on the seat and reached out his hand to touch the man's head. He leaned into his encircling arms and said: "Daddy! Did you see my cairn?"

"Yes, we did, Jason," the man replied, his voice broken. "We have been watching it for the past two nights."

"John and I build'ed it," he announced proudly.

"I hoped it was going to be tonight," the driver's voice strained. "After we got your call, we set up for each night. I saw the rocks, and we waited all night, last night."

"Sorry," John replied. "I was hoping to avoid a confrontation, for his sake," he nodded at the boy. "The timing had to be right, and tonight we just got lucky."

"Daddy?" The boy repeated softly, "Where have you been?"

"Yes, Jason. It's me, buddy. I'm here. Daddy's come to take you home."

John nodded at the driver in the rearview mirror, and the dome light went off. John watched through the windshield as the white center line dashes flew beneath. The trees, fences, and few buildings raced past the speeding car and behind into the blackness.

~

For its seventy-five years, the courthouse dominated the center of town. Fronting on the main street, an expansive concrete plaza led from the sidewalk to entrance steps that ran the width of the three-story building. The steps were flanked by tiered side walls and topped by four towering Corinthian columns. The building and a parking lot covered an entire city block. There was a rear entrance on the street behind. The Honorable Homer J. Halsey had his courtroom and chambers in a new section of the building, which had been added to second floor of the original three-story structure. The ground floor housed the jail.

"How ya' doin', Mr. Grant?" the uniformed bailiff inquired, looking up as attorney Will Grant entered Department Three.

"Fine, Frank. Is he in?" he asked.

"Sure, go on in and just knock. We don't have anything until after lunch," the bailiff smiled.

Located behind the courtroom, the judge's chambers consisted of an outer office, staffed by a court reporter who doubled as his secretary, empty now, and an inner, larger office. The door was open.

Grant hesitated, "Judge?" he called. "Will Grant."

"C'mon in, Will." A large partner's desk dwarfed the remainder of the furniture, three side chairs and credenza behind the desk. Shelves with the requisite law books, interspersed with pictures and memorabilia, lined the walls.

"Good morning, Will," the jurist said, and rising, he extended his hand to Grant. "How are you, the family?" the jurist asked cordially.

"Fine, thank you, Your Honor," Grant replied. "I just need this order signed, from the hearing we had the other day, and I thought I might walk it over. The Collins case." Grant explained.

"Happy to oblige, Will. Let me take a look at it." Well over six feet tall, the judge was a formidable presence, with a huge head and a thick neck, which disappeared into his shoulder pads in one of the photographs behind him. In the picture, he had a cut on his forehead and he held a dirt-smeared helmet under one arm, the other arm around a player whom he seemed to dwarf. *Lineman? Linebacker?*

"Linebacker," the judge offered, reading his look.

"Honorable mention, All-America," Grant added softly.

The judge smiled. He read Grant's order, signed it, and handed it to the attorney. "Well, that settlement avoided a nasty bit, didn't it, Will?" he said. "Bet you're happy not to have to try that case."

"You know me,Your Honor. Trying cases is what I do, and we might have done better," Grant grinned.

"Right. Give it to June on the way out, and she can process it for you," the judge said. "See you next time, Will. There is always a *next* time, isn't there, in this law business?"

Grant smiled at the jurist, "You never know, do you, Your Honor?"

As he passed through the outer office, he handed the order to the clerk. "Settled, June," Grant said.

"*He* has a way of doing that, doesn't he," she replied smiling. "Oh, and by the way, Mr. Grant, your secretary called. I was to be sure to tell you. You have a client, 'An urgent matter,' those were her words, waiting for you at the office. Do you want to use my phone?"

"No. Thanks, anyway. I'm headed right back," Grant replied.

Outside, as Grant waited for the light, he wondered about that "urgent matter" awaiting him. With the law, he thought as he stepped off the curb, everything is urgent and everyone is in a hurry.

~

Dean was seated at the head of a long, oval table. His chair was slightly higher than the other dozen or so that ringed the table. Men, each in a dark suit, white shirt, dark tie, shoes highly polished, sat in the chairs, facing him; one resembled his father. Someone muttered "useless . . . a waste . . .?" He knew he was supposed to speak. He looked down into his lap, gathering his thoughts. He was wearing cutoffs, a sleeveless T-shirt whose upside down message he could not read. His feet were bare, and they appeared incredibly big as they rested on the cold, empty metal of the table base. He looked up. The chair at the end of the table, opposite him, was empty. Was it occupied before? The men stared at him, waiting. One of them brandished a gavel-like hammer, poised to smash him. As he opened his mouth to speak, he heard his name, far off. "Dean!" Again. Nearer. Louder. Now it came from behind him, touching his ear. Inside his ear? He turned slightly to see. Nothing. He turned back. The chairs were empty. An infant sat in one of the chairs. The table was tilted in a large field, surrounded by dirt and dead grass. He was alone. "Dean!" He saw her now at the foot of his bed. Penny's voice was anxious. "You better get up. They're gone! Get up, Dean!" He wanted to roll away from the sound. Who the fuck put that bitch in my dream? His swollen tongue was pasted to the roof of his mouth.

"Dean, get the hell out of that bed. They're gone! Mara is freaking out!"

Dean groaned, raised up on one elbow. His head was throbbing, "Who's gone? What the fuck are you yelling about?"

"John and Jace. We can't find them. Mara is freaking out. You have to talk to her. We're all in the kitchen. Get up, now." Penny turned and left the room.

Dean sank back. He covered his face with his hands. His rubbed his eyebrows, then his thumbs searched his cheekbones. His fingers mined his closed eyes, forcing tears from them, as they dug for the sand that held them shut. He yawned and sighed heavily into his closed hands. He recoiled from his own breath. He glanced at his watch as he rolled off the bed—almost 11:00 A.M. Early, he thought. When his bare feet touched the floor, he paused scratching his head, *"What was that shit? Some meeting? Some kind of table? In a field. Fuck!"*

~

"No, I haven't seen him *or* John," Elaine said to Mara as they stood at the sink. "Don't *you* know where *they* are, at least where your son is?"

Mara, sensing the other's hostility, left the kitchen. She had already checked inside the house; they were not out front. She had noticed that John's sandals were gone, but some of his clothes and his sleeping bag were still on the floor. She half expected that she would hear them coming in— the bang of the screen door. She went down the stairs to the backyard and walked over to the BBQ. She called out half-heartedly, "Jason? Jason, where are you?" No answer.

Mara sat down on the pile of bricks and looked back at the house. She knew Elaine despised her as a poor mother. Damn it, she had never wanted a child, but she was not going to have someone, anyone, tell her how to run her life.

That was why she had left Boston. She felt as if she was missing out on life—the adventure, the excitement. The free things anyway, she was not enjoying any of them. She wanted the freedom to do what she wanted, when she wanted, whatever it was. But then she got pregnant. God, what a huge mistake that was. How could she have been so stupid, so drunk? And then the boy's father, wanting more of Jason—to see him, spend time with him and his goddamn grandmother... she could feel them closing in on her. Christ, he would probably have married her if she had given him a hint! No way. He was threatening her *options,* one of her friends had said.

So she split. She did not need him, anyway. She thought of leaving Jason, but right or wrong, he was *hers,* no one else's, and she would figure it out. What did Elaine want her to do? Leave him? Adopt him out? Well, fuck her! She had him—he was hers—and she would make it work. She had gotten here, made her way in that beat up VW bus, the two of them, across the entire damn country to San Francisco, but she could never fit in—not with the baby, not with her East Coast "attitude," they had called it. Well, fuck them! She thought she would like what they were doing here. This was more like it, but she did not like *them,* any of them, the assholes. Including Dean, but he was the only *guy* and he wanted her, and that was part of the scene, wasn't it?

She stumbled on Dean and the others, and everything was supposed to get better. The first time she stripped and dove in that river, lolled on the beach under the redwoods, smoking a joint, getting high whenever she wanted, for as long as she wanted, having sex, getting drunk on the wine, the beer, whatever, all of it, she felt that she finally had arrived, that *this was it! Don't confuse me with someone who gives a shit,* she thought! That was it, and she didn't give a shit. And for a while, it was it.

She lit a cigarette, took a long drag, and watched the smoke curl into the fractured light of the late-morning sun. It smelled so good here, she thought. Now, that fucking Dean. Demanding, nasty, grabbing at her. What *he* wanted, not what or when *she* wanted. They were all the same. Except that John. What was with him? Why was he here? He seemed different from the guys she had hung with in the City—nice, almost too nice. A frat boy slumming? Or was he something else? She stood and stretched. *Get a grip,* she told herself. Penny (*my God that slut!*) was doing him, and he was taking Jacey off her hands.

Elaine and Phil, all of them, losers. Losers. It might be time to think about moving on, anyway. The summer was almost done, and it would be cold and wet here once the rains started. But where? She stomped out her cigarette. *They will be back,* she thought. *Stop worrying.* But it's time to think of a new plan, because no one was going to make decisions for her. No one but she. The same for Jacey.

She should not have let John get so close to the boy. None of this was planned, it just sort of happened, meeting them and staying here, John . . . Maybe it was time to move on before things . . . Well, whatever, when Jace gets back she would sort it out so that she—not stuff that just happens, not other people, but some kind of plan, her plan—controls what she does. Looking around, she thought, this was not long-term. It was just something to do, what she wanted to do. Then. And maybe it was over. Well, she would fix that as soon as they got back.

Mara started back to the house, cutting through the trees and up the slight hill, so that she could check out the front and the road one more time.

Nothing. The road was clear as far down as she could see. She turned and walked down the path to the front porch. As she mounted the few steps, she saw Dean come out, the torn screen door banging behind him.

"They're not in back and not coming up the road," she said. "I can't figure it out, Dean. They aren't around. Where can they be?"

Dean sensed the stress in her voice. "Shit, Mara, that kid, and that John. They probably went to the store, or maybe to the creek across the road. They'll be back. Don't sweat it." He lowered himself into a wicker rocker and lit a cigarette.

"Big help you are," she replied, "You wouldn't give a shit if Jason disappeared. Probably would have been O.K. with you if he *had* drowned, except for the cops and the inconvenience."

"Christ, Mara, that's a crock and you know it. I know how important he is to you," Dean said leaning forward, the cigarette dangling from his mouth. Leaning back he rocked gently, "I'm telling you, John likes that kid and they are probably on one of their hikes is all." He exhaled through his mouth and nose, the smoke drifting to her.

"I'm not sure about that John," she replied moving away from the advancing smoke cloud. "There's something about him. Why is he here, staying, do you think?"

Dean laughed heartily, "Go ask Penny, why don't you?"

"You're sick, you know that?" Mara said. "When they get back, I'm going to talk to him. He worries me, kind of."

"Whatever. That's cool. But since he got here at least Jason has had someone to play with. May not want to rock that boat. Been easy for you, huh?"

She opened the door, pausing as she entered. She leaned down, inches from Dean's face. "Fuck you! You asshole!" she snarled. The screen door slammed behind her.

"Gotta fix that damn door," Dean muttered, rocking backward. "Bitch," he said to himself, checking to be sure she has not heard him.

~

The law offices of Will Grant were two blocks from the courthouse. He exited the elevator on the top, fifth, floor at an office suite that he shared with two other attorneys. The reception area clock read 11:15 A.M. As he picked up his message slips, Rene, his receptionist, nodded, "Got another one?" Grant assumed that June had called from the court.

"Hey, five figures are better than four, and both are better than a defense verdict. I'll take it," he kidded. He noticed that the young man who had been sitting when he entered was now standing. He turned.

Rene said, "Mr. Grant, this is Mr. Williams. He has been waiting for you. We called the court," she explained.

Grant extended his hand. "June gave me the message. I'm Will Grant."

They shook hands. "Rob Williams, Mr. Grant. Pleased to meet you. I hope you can help me," he said.

"Well, let's see. Come on in, Mr. Williams," Grant led the way.

Grant's office was spacious and bright with a view of the tree-covered hills and the downtown. A large desk, two client chairs, and adjacent credenza were complemented by a table with two matching chairs and a small couch, which permitted conferences to be held in his office. On the wall, framed certificates verified Grant's admission to the Bar, to various appellate courts, and the Supreme Court of the State of California.

"Sit here," he said indicating the couch, "and call me Will." Grant took one of the conference table chairs and sat. The man settled on the couch at first and then immediately stood up, nervous. "No, sit down, it's more comfortable," Grant gestured, and Williams sagged back onto the couch.

"How did you get my name?" Grant opened.

"Oh," the man answered, "a real estate woman. I rented a house from her. She suggested that you might be able to help. She wasn't sure, but I don't know any lawyers here. Angela Stone, she gave me your card."

"Sure, I know Angela," Grant replied. "We've worked on some probate, real estate matters. You were lucky to find her." Grant noticed that the man had calmed, and he continued, "Does this involve real estate then?"

Williams leaned toward the attorney, "No, not real estate. I'm not sure what you would call it. But it might involve kidnapping and . . . custody . . . of a child." He ran his hand nervously through his hair.

Grant studied him; he was serious. This was no joke.

"Well, let's see if we can get a handle on this. One *is* criminal: kidnapping. The other: civil, actually family law. They are sort of mutually exclusive. I mean, generally, you can't kidnap your own child. Have you been arrested?"

"No. At least, not yet. But I did kidnap my son. I mean, I took him from his mother without her knowing it, and without her permission," he halted.

Grant rose and moved over to his desk. He leaned over and pressed his phone, "Rene? Can we have some coffee, please?" He looked at Williams. "Coffee or soft drink? Coffee? Black?"

Williams nodded. "Two blacks. Thanks, Rene. When it's convenient for you." He turned back and sat on the edge of his desk measuring the young man. Early twenties, six feet at least. Fit. Button-down white shirt, pressed khakis, and loafers. The coffee arrived and was served. Grant waited a minute, sipping his drink.

"O.K.," he took a pen and legal tablet from his desk, moved to one of the chairs, and set his coffee cup on the table as he faced Williams. "Let's start at the beginning. Remember, you have lived whatever it is you are going to share with me, and I am hearing it for the first time. I will, I promise you, interrupt with questions. And, two rules. One. For this purpose, I am representing you. I am your attorney. Even if I do not take your case. So, everything you tell me is protected by the attorney-client privilege. It is confidential. No one can make me reveal it, and I would not. Second. If you want my help with whatever this is, no B.S. Excuse me, but there is no clearer way to make this point. I expect—demand—the absolute truth. If you are not sure about something, say so. First time you lie to me, we are done. Got it?" He concluded.

"Yes," he sighed, "Yes, I understand."

"O.K. Good. Let's see if we can find a beginning."

For the next two hours, the young man explained that he was the father of a three-year-old boy. Until recently the boy had lived in the East, in the Boston area, with his mother whose name was Tamara Evans. He had fathered the child—his name was on the boy's birth certificate, and the mother acknowledged him as the father. The boy looked like him. They were never married, but he had been supporting the boy: he had paid all the birth expenses and regular support ever since. They were sharing custody through an informal verbal agreement.

"Nothing in writing? No court order? No custody proceeding?" Grant asked.

"No, nothing like that. We worked it out, and I was living nearby. Maybe a mile or so across town. I lived, live, with my grandmother, and she helped out, babysat. She loves him," he sighed. "It was all working for the past three years. We had no plans of getting married. He was sort of an accident," he paused.

"O.K., we can get into that later. Continue," Grant said.

"I was having Jason, that's his name, at least once a week, and she began calling and asking me to take him more . . . overnight. I was never sure why. It wasn't because of her job. She was into something. She never explained. I didn't care because it meant I got to spend more time with Jason. So . . ."

He went on to explain that once he had gone to pick up some of the boy's clothes and found the place was a mess and reeked of pot. This was new. Usually, it wasn't too bad. Not good, just messy—dishes, cigarette butts. When he asked her about the pot smell, she became enraged; she swore that he could not tell her how to live, that *everything*, he assumed meaning Jason, was his fault.

He let it go, but he was determined to keep a closer eye on her. There were a few times when she was late—or did not show at all—to pick him up after a weekend; once not until late on a Monday and another only after he had called her, on a Wednesday. She was secretive about her activities, and he was afraid to ask. More and more she was affecting what he referred to as a hippie style—in her clothes, her attitude, the pot odor. Although he did not know it until later, his grandmother had gotten into an argument with her, suggesting that maybe she should not have the boy at all if the child was interfering with her lifestyle. He had caught only the tail end of that encounter when he arrived home as she was picking up the boy.

Once he had consulted an attorney about his options if things got worse, and he had been told that he would have to prove that she was unfit, neglectful, leading a lifestyle that was bad for the boy. He started to keep notes, to gather the evidence. Then she disappeared.

"What do you mean 'disappeared'?" Grant asked.

"Disappeared. Left. Moved out. She took off." He stood and moved to the center of the office, pacing. Grant turned in his chair to follow him.

"I called her in a few days, to check on her schedule. That's what we used to do. I waited to let her cool off," he said. "No answer. I tried that several times. So now it's the weekend, and I had him most weekends. I drove over there, when she would usually be home. No car, a couple days' mail in the mailbox. No answer at the door. I got the key from the owner. It was like a triplex, and he knew me from my coming over. He told me that she hadn't been home for days; that he hadn't seen her car. I went inside. Gone. Cleaned out. Everything. Furniture, dishes, toys. The whole works, gone."

"Empty?" Grant asked. "No one saw her moving out?"

"Gone!" he stared at the attorney, his eyes narrowed, pained.

He had scoured the neighborhood, reported her absence to the police, missing persons, social services, motor vehicle department. He had reported her car, a VW bus, as stolen. Nothing. She was just another runaway, with a child yet. No one did anything. The FBI would not even take a report. "No crime committed," they had told him.

After six months he was worn out. It almost killed his grandmother. She had never been involved in anything like this. It was affecting her health. So he quit looking. He was working in an office, nothing permanent, just something to keep him busy, his mind off it. But he never stopped worrying about the boy. He had been an only child, both parents dead while he was small, and he kept thinking how *he* had felt, imagining the parents he could not remember. The few pictures of his family were just . . . pictures, never memories. He could not get them back. The thought that his son would never know him, and that he would never see the boy run, smile, grow, watch him becoming a man—it was too much. He slumped back onto the cushions, exhausted with the telling. He looked up at Grant.

"And then it came," he said.

Grant stopped his notes. "What came?"

"I got a ticket, actually a notice, that her car was being sold. For storage," he said.

Grant leaned forward on the edge of his seat, his pencil poised, "From where?"

"Here! Well not *here*, but California, actually near here. Fairfax," he said.

"Fairfax! Are you serious?" Grant asked. "Christ, Fairfax! How the hell did she end up in Fairfax? When was this? How long ago?"

"Approximately four weeks ago; maybe five now," Williams added and explained that the notice advised that her car had been stored after being towed; that unless the towing and storage fees were paid, the car would be sold, at auction. It gave her name, the car license, but it had California plates. He had called the garage and the car had, by that time, been picked up by a man and woman. She fit the mother's description; she had a small boy with her when she picked up the car. They paid in cash. It was she, and the boy, his son, he was sure of it.

"How had they, the garage, found you, back East?" Grant inquired, "Something left in the car, I bet."

"Right," Williams replied. "When I called, they told me that they had found some mail, an old bill, something with an address, in the car, so they mailed her a Notice of Intent to Sell a Stored Vehicle. I had arranged to have her mail forwarded to me, right after she left, so I got it," he said.

"Sure," Grant replied, leaning backward, pensive, "They had to give notice of the planned sale, the law requires it, and they searched the car. You were lucky. They don't always do it correctly. Sometimes they just run an ad in any newspaper, and hope no one sees it. Then they have a car to sell. Sweet deal, if the car is any good," Grant concluded. "So what did you do next?" he asked.

Williams continued that he had hired a private investigator and traced the car, the woman, and the boy to a house in West Marin. They confirmed that she was living there and the situation was not good—no place for a small boy. He was the only child there. He described the area, Grant nodded.

"You're right, no place for kids, of any age. I know the area, not the exact house," Grant said. "I have had clients whose kids were busted for drug and alcohol offenses, 'crashing' they call it, in one of those run-down, usually abandoned, houses out there. It is called Lagunitas or it could be Wood-acre. You have the exact address, right?" Grant paused. "Amazing," Grant said. "Wow! What are the odds that you would have found her?" he mused. "Just amazing . . . imagine how all that had to come together. Must be meant to be. Could have gone the other way, and you never would have found him. Luck or fate? Lots of luck I think."

Grant explained that after WWII, people from San Francisco built cabins and spent weekends, some entire summers. When other locations eventually became more popular, many of the houses were abandoned. The hippies discovered the empty houses, close to the river, the ocean thirty minutes away. No cops, maybe an occasional sheriff. And the party started, as they say.

"Go on," Grant said.

Williams continued that he had arranged for an investigator to get into the house, and one night he got the boy out. He described the events. Grant was poised on the edge of his chair. He smiled broadly and shook his head when Williams described the incident at the river.

"What a story. It must be true, because it is too good, too wild, to be made up, unless you were writing a book or a screenplay. God, what a saga!" he remarked.

"So, I rented a car, "Williams said, "And we waited until I knew we could grab him, get him out of there. And we did. Last night. I have him, now. Safe. With me." His tone was firm, his look, satisfied. No, *triumphant*, Grant thought.

"You snatched him out of the house! So that's the kidnapping?" Grant asked.

"I guess so. Yes," Williams replied.

"My God! Where is he now?"

"In a house I rented, here in San Rafael. The one Angela helped me get."

"Not alone?"

"No, the lady next door, she watches kids. She has him, just so I could come here," he answered.

"And you want to get custody of your son, Jason? And do what with him? Take him back to Boston, or—?" he stated more than asked.

"Yes," Williams answered, "That's what I want, and that is far better than where he is now," he replied.

"O.K. Well, for openers," Grant paused, "there is nothing criminal about what you did. Maybe the investigator, but I doubt it, and no one is going to charge him anyway, not under these circumstances," Grant said. The intercom buzzed and Grant stood, stretched, and reached for the button. "Mr. Grant, it's almost 2:00 P.M., are you going to want something for lunch? Can I get you anything?" his receptionist asked.

"Thanks for the reminder, Rene. No, we're O.K., I think we'll take a break now. But, Rene," Grant added, "will you please alert Caron, we might be late tonight, and I will probably need her help after 5:00 P.M., if that's O.K. with her. I will fill her in after we get back from lunch."

He pushed the disconnect button and turned back to Williams.

"Tell you what, let's take a break. We can go to Corey's across the street, grab some lunch, and discuss how we are going to finance all this," Grant said. "This is going to be a contested matter, for sure, and it will require an evidentiary hearing. And it is not going to be cheap. I can explain the procedure involved, which will start tomorrow. O.K.?" He reached for his jacket. "Can you call whoever is watching Jason and tell them you may be late getting back today. We will need the entire afternoon, and maybe the evening, depending on the typing and how long the declarations will be."

Williams rose and stretched. "Sure, I have her number, and told her I might be late. How long do you think?" he asked.

"You can use my phone. With dinner and dictation, no later than maybe 10:00 P.M. Probably earlier. We have a lot of work to do."

~

As the afternoon wore on, Mara became increasingly upset. Together, the three women searched the surrounding area again, including several nearby empty houses and the creek in the back. Mara repeatedly walked up to the front of house and onto the road to see if they were coming. They had gone to the store, but Mattuzig had not seen them since yesterday, and he was not surprised that they didn't know where the boy was, "they never did," and Mara had stormed out of the store.

Phil had gone to check out the river. Convinced that John and the boy had gone on one of their adventures, Elaine reassured Mara that they would be back, surely by dark. But as the shadows lengthened, they realized that soon there would be nothing more they could do but wait for Phil to return. They were in the living room, Mara by the door watching, her unlit cigarette ignored, when Phil burst in.

"Look what I got," he shouted. He held up a small, dirty, familiar child's shoe.

Mara rushed to him and grabbed it. "My God, it's Jason's! Oh, my God! Where did you get it, Phil? Where?" she cried.

The others moved closer. Dean reached for the little shoe. Mara pulled it back.

"How do you know it's his?" Dean snarled.

"Don't be stupid, Dean," Elaine said. "It's his. She knows her own kid's shoes, for God's sake!"

"Phil, where did you find it?" Mara demanded.

"It's dry, so he hasn't been in the water. Thank God," Elaine observed.

"Shut the fuck up, Elaine. Where'd you find it, Phil?" Dean asked. They all stared at Phil.

"I was comin' back from the creek—"

"It's a river, you asshole," Dean sneered. Phil took a step back. Mara glared at Dean.

"—and I crossed over the road in front of the church, like I always do. I cut through the parking lot. It was empty. I saw it. I walked right by it, on the far side. Near the church. I knew it as soon as I picked it up. It's the kid's, isn't it?"

"You found it in the fuckin' parking lot?" Dean asked.

Mara ignored Dean. "Yes, Phil, it's Jason's, I'm sure. But why? Where exactly was it?" Mara asked.

"It was over by the church, on the far side of the lot. You know, if you walk up the front, from the highway. Right there," Phil answered.

"Not over by the store? Or by the wall? Sometimes they sit there," Elaine said.

"No," Phil replied. "It was by where the cars park."

"But the church is closed. They're only open on Sunday," Penny mused.

"Brilliant, Penny. That is so smart," Elaine scoffed. "Somebody put him in a car." She paused for a moment and stared at Mara. "And … they … took … him," she said slowly, her voice a whisper. Everyone looked at her.

"Who the hell is 'they'?" Dean snapped.

"Not 'they,'" Elaine met Dean's gaze. "It was John. John took him."

CHAPTER 4

GRANT SHIFTED HIS BRIEFCASE TO OPEN the door to the Courthouse Creamery, across the street from its namesake. Preserved in its art deco style, a glass pastry case, topped by a marble cashier's station, formed the hub of a long, horseshoe-shaped counter, each side of which ran to the rear of the restaurant. The black vinyl swivel stools were trimmed in chrome, and matching booths lined both walls. No one could recall a creamery being located on the premises, but it had been called that as long as Grant could remember. He slid into a booth opposite Williams. "All done," he said, and he pulled a sheaf of papers from his briefcase. "Caron came in early and finished what we did last night. I proofed it. Looks good," he said, handing the typed sheets to Williams. "You need to sign on the last page, here," he pointed.

"Do I need to read all this first?" Williams asked.

"No, but—"

"Excuse me, Mr. Grant, breakfast this morning?" Grant looked up at the waitress, in her starched black dress, white collar, and white cuffs, her spotless, starched, white, V-shaped apron tied with a bow. He smiled at her.

"Coffee, Iris. That will do it for me. Thanks," he replied. She held her pencil poised.

"Sir?" she looked at Williams, "Anything, or just a refill?"

"I'm good," Williams replied, his hand over his cup. She put the pencil back into her hair.

"Coffee it is, Mr. Grant. Black. The orange scones are awfully good today," she teased.

"Coffee. Black, Iris," he repeated. "We are due in court." She produced a cup and saucer and poured for Grant. "Thanks, Iris. How's your daughter doing?" Grant asked.

"She is just fine. All A's and B's so far. Thank you for asking." She turned and moved away, smoothing her apron with one hand, adjusting the pencil with the other.

Grant turned his attention to Williams. "I included everything you told me in your declaration. Sign there," Grant indicated. "Good," he said, accepting the document back. "That second set is your copy." He took a sip of his coffee and began, "Now, here is what will happen this morning."

Grant explained that each morning the court heard "urgent" cases at the end of the court's regular calendar. No one would appear for Mara because she would not have been served yet. All done on paper so far, the goal was to get an immediate order for temporary custody and a restraining order preventing the child's mother from taking him back, or away, when she realized what was happening. That temporary order would last until a later court hearing. Even though there was to be no opposition, they still would have to show a strong reason, "good cause" it was called, why the court should make such an order, depriving the mother of the right to her child, without first having a hearing.

Williams's recitation of her flight, the environment in which the boy was found, all detailed in the sworn declaration that Grant had prepared would be sufficient to get the custody order that would keep the boy safe with his father, for now. Once the order was signed, Grant continued, then Mara would have to be personally served with all the documents, and there would eventually be a hearing on the question of Jason's permanent custody. Until that hearing, she would have no rights to see him.

"How do we serve her?" Williams asked. "If she refuses to take the papers, then what happens?"

"Good questions," Grant replied. "Sometimes we use the sheriff, but if they are busy, I might use a private process server. Depends on the sheriff's workload, and I will check that out. So long as she is served, that's all we need, and if then she doesn't show, that's it. You get permanent custody. But she will show. She is not going to walk on the boy. I don't see that happening? Do you?" Grant asked.

"No, you're right. Somehow she will fight it," Williams agreed. "She will fight us."

"Let's go," Grant drained his coffee.

Outside, while they waited for the light, Grant remarked, "Looks like some sort of press conference, over there, on the courthouse steps," gesturing toward the building. Williams could see that a small crowd had gathered on the stairs. A TV crew was setting up. "You're right, wonder what it is?" Williams said. The light turned green.

"Tell you what. Let's go straight," Grant said. "We can go in through the sheriff's office in the basement. Here." Grant led Williams inside a chain link fence that encircled the courthouse parking lot. As they walked between two rows of parked patrol cars, a uniformed deputy exited a vehicle in front of them.

"Hey, Wade," Grant nodded.

"Mr. Grant. How are you, sir?" the officer approached, smiling, and shook Grant's hand.

"Something going on in front, Wade," Grant offered. "Maybe some political deal."

"Yes, I saw it. Come on, you know the way," the deputy said indicating an open door ahead. Together they walked down the slight incline and into the basement, the Office of the County Sheriff. A uniformed sergeant manned the chest-high booking desk. To the left, a heavy barred door led to the cell rows.

"Mr. Grant, here to spend some time today?" The desk sergeant's eyes sparkled.

"Not today, Sally. Not tomorrow. Not ever," Grant laughed.

The elevator was straight ahead; Grant pushed the button. He heard the elevator respond above.

"*Secret* entrance," he nodded to Williams. "I used it to get into the law library late at night, and to get out of the building after it was closed, when I was in law school," he explained. "In the old days, before the elevator, they used to hang people upstairs, and the body dropped down here." Williams's eyes widened. The deputy smiled and nodded. The elevator door opened, and the three entered.

"Floor, Mr. Grant?" Wade asked.

"Second, Wade, going to Judge Halsey. You still working West Marin, Wade? Civil stuff?" Grant asked the deputy.

"Sure am, sir," Wade replied.

"Great. Look, I may have a TRO for Lagunitas. Might be ready in a few minutes. Could you check the desk before you leave? I would like it served today." Grant said. "It's a custody matter," he nodded to Williams. "His son,"

"Sure thing, Mr. Grant. I have an easy patrol today, so I should be able to attempt service." He paused, "I'm getting off here, for the DA. I will be done in a half hour or so. I'll look for the papers on my way out. In fact, I can wait for you, sir," he concluded.

"Wade, that's terrific. I won't forget when the tickets for the Sheriff's Circus fundraiser come around next year," Grant grinned.

"Bribery. For a good cause," the deputy laughed, exiting the elevator.

"Two good causes," Grant said softly. He glanced at Williams, and the elevator door closed.

~

"Great. This looks great," Dean said. "What a dump."

Dean and Mara were sitting in the worn waiting room of the law offices of Ivan Turoff. The names of the attorneys sharing the offices were stenciled on hardboard plaques inserted into a worn and chipped wooden rack, affixed to the waiting room wall. Any pretense of success of an established law firm was left at the generic entry door. The two couches were leather, cracked seams showing, dangling threads, missing buttons. After a second knock, a receptionist had surfaced behind a sliding frosted window. A stained and peeling coffee table faced the couch and held an array of outdated magazines.

Dean slouched in his seat, one foot resting on the table. The Legal Aid Service of Marin County had referred Mara to this San Francisco attorney, whom they said was quite competent and was accepting cases pending in San Rafael in order to "expand" his practice. He was the only one on their list available for an emergency contested-custody matter. And he was free. Mara had a set of the legal papers, which had been served upon her at the house by a uniformed sheriff's deputy. Dean had freaked out when he opened the door and found the deputy standing on their porch, the patrol unit parked in front, overhead lights blinking.

"Mrs. Evans?" Turoff was short, not much over five feet tall, dressed in slacks and an open white shirt. A faded, narrow, paisley tie dangled from his open shirt collar; the third button down was missing. There was a tear in the collar of the white T-shirt that he wore underneath.

Mara stood. "I'm *Miss* Evans," she answered.

"Ivan Turoff," he replied. "Come in, please." He led them down a hall narrowed by cordons of shoulder-high precariously piled file boxes, each labeled with a large magic marker, 'Somebody v. so and so,' They passed a bathroom, its door open. Dean nodded to Mara. The bathtub was full of file boxes, stacked to the ceiling, the whole mass tilting toward the center.

As they followed the attorney, Mara noticed his unironed shirt and pants, and the worn-down heels of his shoes. In his office, the attorney cleared a pile of files from one of the two chairs. When he moved behind his desk, he had to stretch to step over more files on the floor. The desk was a motley tower of unsorted papers, legal tablets, and files. He cleared a small space in front of the mess.

"You brought your file? The documents you were served with?" he asked.

Mara had them in her lap. "This is Dean, my friend," she opened. "We lived together. Shared the house," she explained.

"Dean. Yes, his name is in the declarations of a ... Mr. Meagor," he replied.

"That asshole investigator. A complete lying asshole," Dean retorted.

Turoff, startled, leaned back. "You question his statement?" he looked at Dean.

"Damn right," Dean replied. "He is some kind of a private pig of an investigator," Dean said. "His stuff is all bullshit. He was wasted most of the time he was there. A real trippy dude, that guy." Dean slouched. Mara glanced at him and then at the attorney.

"And you are prepared to testify to that? With specifics? Is that right?" Turoff faced Dean.

"Absolutely. Put it in one of those declarations or affidavits of yours, whatever," Dean said.

"No, I mean *testify*. Take the stand, under oath, and tell that story?" Turoff was watching Mara.

"Absolutely, fuckin' A," Dean confirmed.

"O.K., that's a start," the attorney said. "All right, let me tell you what we have here, how this is going to work. I already have a copy of the Order to Show Cause for Custody and supporting papers. When you made this appointment, we called, and they sent the papers over to us yesterday," he said.

Turoff went on to explain that the boy's father already had obtained a Temporary Custody Order, preventing Mara from seeing the boy without court approval of the arrangements; that she could not see him alone, and she certainly could not take him anywhere. Mara had been told that she had no chance to get those orders set aside since she had—"absconded" were the words used in the papers—"fled with the child, without notifying his father, and she was now residing in filth and squalor. . . ."

Turoff launched into an explanation that this case would be heard by a judge, not a jury, and that it would involve an actual contested proceeding, a trial in all respects. Witnesses would be called and the parties themselves, Mara and Williams, were expected to testify. It might take several days.

"What about Jason?" Mara asked. "Would he be there . . . testify?"

"He is too young. Three or four, correct?" Turoff asked. "No, in view of his age, he would not, could not, be called by either side. And, it is very unlikely that the court would want to interview him either," he said. "Sometimes little kids are like warm puppies. They like best whoever petted or fed them last," he grinned.

Dean and Mara looked at each other. Dean shrugged. Turoff went on to explain that before the hearing, a county probation officer would conduct an investigation for the benefit of the court, which would include meetings with Mara and Williams; that the investigator might visit their living arrangements and would surely meet informally with the boy.

"Why all that?" Dean interrupted, sitting erect.

"Good question, Dean," Turoff continued that the probation department staff had trained child psychologists, experienced in custody matters. He explained that as hard as these cases are on the parents, it is, they believe, actually harder on the child, considering the later consequences. The investigator was an expert whose job is to evaluate the facts and make a "recommendation" for the court on custody.

"Then why have a trial, or a hearing?" Mara asked. "Just let them do it. I'm screwed!" Turoff continued that the investigator would file a comprehensive report, that she would be given a copy. But, he empha-sized, the report does not *determine* who gets custody; that is up to the judge—he can accept or reject the report, even ignore it completely if he chooses. The investigator is not *trying the case,* not resolving disputed facts. But her recommendation is vitally important; it is crucial to get a good report. It is very difficult for the party against whom the recommen-dation is made. The purpose of the hearing, he explained, was to have a chance to question the facts, the evidence, the motives of the parties. The guiding principle is not what the mother or the father, or anyone, wants for the child. The *only* question is What is in the best interests of the child?

Their meeting continued with Turoff taking extensive notes, filling pages of yellow legal pads. They would meet again, he told them. He wanted to go over the stories of the others to decide who ought to testify.

~

On the drive back to Marin, Dean, his feet propped on the dash in front of him, a cigarette in one hand, said, "That attorney is a dork, Mara. Did you see his diploma shit on the wall. It looks like he has only been doing this stuff for a year or two."

"What else can I do, Dean? I can't just walk on this," she said. "But, no attorney, no judge, is going to tell me how to live my life!" She slammed the steering wheel.

"Relax, Mara. I got a couple of ideas on how to handle this," he smiled at her through a cloud of smoke, exhaling from his nostrils.

She looked over at him. He glanced from the road ahead of her and nodded his head emphatically. Mara made no response. Her hands draped loosely over the steering wheel, she eased the bus into the curb lane and onto the Golden Gate Bridge. She stole a look to her right at the shining bay below, its surface dotted with sails and streaked by wakes.

"And least of all, not some uptight probation bitch!" She glanced at Dean, who nodded.

~

Sarah, eyes shut, closed the door carefully behind her, so that the glass panels in the door and in the walls dividing her office from those of her associates would not make that annoying rattling sound that she had grown to hate in the six years she had occupied this second-floor office. The Probation Department, Family and Custody Division, had outgrown the courthouse and was now located directly across the street from the court building. She looked at her reflection in the glass as she did each morning, and she saw a thirty-nine-year-old, still-single, intelligent, educated woman; reddish-brown hair pulled back in a tight bun. A finger went to a touch of gray; a high forehead; no makeup; shoulders square, figure hidden in the ankle length lightweight cotton mauve dress. Smoothing the dress over her hips, she revisited whether she should have included a belt or sash. She sat down.

Each object on her desk conformed to some invisible template. Yesterday's files were exactly where she had left them on the credenza behind her, the corners squared, each pile toeing an unseen line. In the center of her spotless blotter (she kept a hand blotter in the top drawer, right side, for the real work) was her list, typed at 4:50 P.M. the day before: a schedule of today's work: names, appointments, times, file references, all neatly arranged. She knew exactly what she would be doing at 11:10 A.M., at 2:15 P.M., at 4:00 P.M. Today's work should be done today, she believed, and it would be. At the head of the list, every day, she typed her title: "Sarah Redding, Prob. Ofcr—Chief, Custody Investigations." That title was replicated in the copper and black placard set in a polished wooden rail, sited directly in front of her list, facing whoever occupied the two wooden slat-backed chairs.

She reached for a file, resuming where she had left off. The rattling of the glass to her left indicated that Jesse Morehead, P.O., Custody Intake, had arrived. She knew if she looked up, he would be looking down at her, smiling. Jesse was assisted by Constance Smart, and together they did the initial interviews and field work, witness verification, home visits, confirmation of employment, medical record checks, the background information, that once concluded, hopefully, but not always, formed the basis of her report, the heart of which was a recommendation to the court—what was in the best interests of the child. Nothing else mattered. Her recommendation spelled victory for one party, defeat for the other, and her recommendations were adopted by the court precisely 90.6 percent of the time. Whoever had her recommendation would be granted custody. And Sarah knew it.

Sarah Redding was an only child, her parents long deceased, and she was single and childless. She took her work very seriously. She felt her door open, then close, and she looked up as the tall man lowered himself into one of the chairs. Jesse had a slim and, therefore, *new* file in his lap.

"Smart called in sick." he said.

"And it's not even a Monday, how unusual," Sarah replied, letting her chair lean back.

"Right," he grinned, his enormous perfectly square, blinding-white teeth framed by full, almost ashen black lips continually surprised her. She was sure he sensed it, but he was always the perfect gentleman.

"So," he said, "I've got the Snyder witnesses lined up today, most of the day, and three of them are in the City. So, I am gone all day. Hearing's next week."

"I know," she interrupted. "I have a draft report waiting confirmation of your witness statements."

"Right. Well, I am out of here, and they handed me this file on the way up, from Judge Halsey. I only glanced at it, but it is top priority, involving a runaway mother, a stolen child. The father stole the boy . . . three years old, I think . . . back. The father is here from back East, and he has an order for immediate sole custody from Judge Halsey. The memo from the court says 'Put It On Top,' and the file is stamped 'Expedite,'" he paused.

"And?" Sarah asked.

"And, I can't get to it. The father is here in town. The mother 'resides' in West Marin, in one of those old summer cabins, you know."

"And?"

"C'mon, Sarah," he said. "Give me a break and interview at least the parties, or this will never get done on time and it may have to be continued. I don't want to have to listen to Halsey, *Judge* Halsey, excuse me, about that."

The court was ever critical of the time it took to complete the child custody investigation process. Until the probation report regarding custody was filed with its all-important recommendation, the case would not be heard by the court, and, in the interim, weeks often, sometimes months, the lives of the parties, particularly the child, were on hold.

"This may be a snap," he continued. "The file says that there is a P.I. report. He apparently moved into the house and actually lived there. I only glanced at the dec's. That he grabbed the kid." He leaned forward, offering her the file. He did not put it down on the blotter.

"Well," she sighed, taking it. "I'll look at it. But you know, Jesse, how reluctant I am to do the field work. My job is to evaluate the case, and it is difficult to be objective when you have to deal with the parties firsthand. That is the point, isn't it?"

"Sure, I know how you look at these matters. But if this *is* one of those hippie pads, and they are, the mother anyway, raising a small boy there, *and* the P.I. lived there," he continued, "It may be all done for you," he shrugged, eyebrows raised.

"It's never 'all done for you.' If it was, anyone could do this job," she countered. "I'll start on it for you, but you please let me know when you are finished in the City. If Connie comes in, I will discuss it with her, all right?"

"Perfect," he said rising. "I'm on my way. The P.I.'s contact information is attached to the attorney's dec. You might start with him." She took the file and turned away, replacing the opened file back in its place on the rear credenza. With his finger, Jesse slid her name placard slightly to the left, off center.

"Who is doing this? You or me?" she replied turning back toward him, setting the new file now on her blotter.

"You are," he replied opening the door. The teeth again. He nodded.

"And, Grant, Will Grant, is the attorney for the father," his smile narrowed.

She met his stare. He closed the door. The glass rattled, just a bit. She re-centered her name plate and opened the file: *"In Re the Custody of Jason . . . ."*

~

As Grant walked to the front porch of the home Williams had rented, he admired the neatness of the neighborhood. *Almost over*, Grant thought, as he listened to the chimes within.

"Come in, Will," Williams opened the door. "Glad you could make it, but I am not sure about your timing," he smiled. "Miss Redding is here."

"Oh," Grant replied. "Let's check . . . see if she wants me to leave," he said. "How long has she been here?"

From the living room. Grant could see the probation officer outside in the patio area, sitting with Jason. Grant could hear the boy's animated demonstration on dump trucks through the open screen door.

"Miss Redding? Mr. Grant is here. He wants to know if that is a problem for you. He can come back later," Williams asked.

"No, not at all. I am finished," she said, standing. "I now know all about dump trucks and loaders and graders." She ran her hand through the boy's hair.

"... and 'dozers!" Jason added.

"And 'dozers," Sarah replied. "Yes. Let's not forget those 'dozers!"

They laughed, and she stepped back into the house. Jason remained on the patio surrounded by his toys.

"What is it with heavy equipment? A genetic thing?" Grant asked, laughing.

"Not mine," Williams replied.

"Well, he is quite a character," Sarah offered. "He loves to talk, and he is not afraid of adults," she said. "But then ... I better save this for my report."

"Right. We do not want to be accused of influencing your judgment," Grant smiled.

"I'm sure you wouldn't," she smiled back. "I'd better be going. Mr. Williams, please say goodbye to your grandmother for me. She has been a big help to you, I can see that," Sarah held out her hand. When he had obtained the order granting him custody, Williams had flown his grandmother out to help with the boy.

Williams shook Sarah's hand. "I could not have done it without her, but it has been hard on her. Especially the supervised visitations with Mara these past few weeks," he said. "They really wore her out."

"Well, thank goodness she was here and able to help. So much better than using a member of my office or the police to supervise those visits," Sarah explained. "And we had no problems. I know how concerned you were at the beginning that she might take off with Jason again."

She turned to Grant. "Mr. Grant, nice to see you again." He accepted her hand.

"I'll see you out to your car," Grant replied. He opened the door and followed her down to the curb. They paused.

"How is it coming?" he asked. "I don't mean your conclusion or recommendation. I mean the timing. Is it about done?"

"Actually, we are quite far along. I have an appointment with the mother, Miss Evans, set for the first of the week. You know I usually have my staff do these interviews. But, we were short-handed, and Judge Halsey had marked it 'Expedite.' So, once I started, I decided to stick with it. Depending on the interview with the mother, it might be completed in a week or so."

"Great," Grant replied. "That will fit with the court's date, and we will not have to re-set it. I am anxious to get this over with." He opened her car door. "I just don't like the idea of her with no roots or attachment to the community, the county. I don't want her to split," he said. Sarah got into her car, the window was down. "But then if she split, that would make it simple, wouldn't it?" he smiled at her as he closed her door.

"I am not so sure. Would it?" she smiled back. "See you in court, counselor," she said.

Grant watched her car make the turn at the end of the block, and he walked back into the house.

~

"Your ten o'clock is here, Miss Redding," the receptionist announced over her intercom.

"Put her in the small conference room, Lettie. Room 104. I'll be right down," Sarah responded. "Oh. Lettie, is she alone?" she added.

"She seems to be."

Sarah closed her file and sat back, readying her thoughts. She had read the police reports, the statements of the potential witnesses, most of them supplied by Will Grant's office. She had spent an afternoon at Williams's rented house, visiting with the boy; met with the grandmother. Sarah knew how it was going to end. She sighed, stood, and left her office, closing the door behind her. She winced when the glass rattled.

Room 104 was a private office space converted into a small conference room by outfitting it with a metal ceramic-topped table and six matching chairs, all made by the inmates of the nearby state prison. Two of the walls were lined with law books borrowed from the Public Defender's Office. As she entered, Sarah unconsciously turned on the room lights normally left off to conserve electricity. A small hand-lettered sign, dirty from use, read 'Turn me Off.'

Mara was standing at the far end of the room, leaning against the table. She turned to face the woman, an unlit cigarette in her mouth.

"I'm sorry," Sarah approached, her hand outstretched, "there is no smoking in here," she nodded to a sign near the door. "I am Sarah Redding," she said, accepting the other woman's hand.

Mara removed her cigarette and set it down on the table. Both women watched the cigarette roll toward the edge, until it stopped.

"Please sit down," Sarah said. She took a chair opposite Mara, who then sat and leaned back, arms folded in front.

"Well, I am pleased to meet you, Miss Evans," Sarah said as she opened her file, meeting the other woman's gaze. She could be quite attractive, Sarah thought. Mara was dressed in a dark T-shirt, tucked into army fatigue pants. The young woman's hair was pulled back, tied in a ponytail. She wore no makeup, and her eyes looked tired, far away. Sarah thought she might have been crying. She looked older than her years.

"I am the chief of Custody Investigations," Sarah began slowly. "I will be preparing a formal report for the court regarding you, your son, and the circumstances regarding his living situation." She paused.

"I understand," Mara said. She leaned forward, a hand under her chin, supporting her head, the other hand toyed with her cigarette.

"Good," Sarah continued. "Now I have several questions for you, and this is the time for you to tell me your side of the story. But before we begin, you have representation—an attorney—correct?" Sarah asked.

"Yes, I do. Or, I will at the hearing. But, I . . . he . . . couldn't be here today," Mara shifted.

"Well, I have to conclude this investigation. Do you want to reschedule, so that he can be with you while we talk, or are you comfortable going ahead . . . today?" Sarah asked.

"No," Mara responded. "Let's go ahead. It's O.K. with me to go ahead without him. I mean, if I don't like it, I can just leave, right?" she asked.

"Well, yes. Technically, you could do that, but," Sarah fingered her hair, "that would delay things."

"Let's do it, then," Mara replied. She leaned forward, both arms on the table. She rolled the cigarette back and forth with a finger.

For the next hour they talked. Sarah took Mara through the entire history of her pregnancy, the birth of her son, why she came to California, how she ended up in West Marin. She thought Mara forthright, and she was puzzled at her candor in the face of what she surely must realize was going to result in the loss of the custody of her son.

"You know that your present living situation is not conducive to raising a small child," Sarah said gently.

Mara replied, "Yes, I realize that I have put my life ahead of his. That I was selfish. But, I was so mixed up and I saw my life ... getting away," she paused. "I just wanted, you know, to experience stuff. ..." She continued, "I never expected to get pregnant. I mean I was headed to college and stuff. It was such a mess." She caught her breath, her eyes softened. "I want the best for Jason. This has been a big awakening for me."

"So?" Sarah said.

"So, here is the deal," Mara replied, straightening in her chair, confident, leaning in. "I have this chance to get a place, a room actually, for Jace and me in San Francisco."

"Where?"

"Near the Haight. I know ... not *in* it, but nearby. Ashbury something. With a family who needs a sitter. They have other kids, one anyway," Mara added.

"I will need the details—names, addresses, references, everything, the particulars" Sarah responded. "Because I will need to contact them, make a house visit."

"Oh, great! I'm sure they will love that!" Mara sat straight up. "Probation driving up in a marked car, investigating. That will get me the job, for sure," she waved a hand toward the ceiling and shrugged, angrily.

"Look, Mara," Sarah leaned back. "We, the county, have to be sure that Jason is in an appropriate place."

"How can I ever do that?" Mara replied. "With you following me around?"

"If you are sincere. If you truly have a plan," Sarah said. "We will work with you. Job, babysitter, school. We can help you, but it has to be definite," she finished.

"You will *help* me?" Mara asked.

"Yes, of course. The law prefers that small children remain with their mother. But, up to this time, in your case, that appears not to have been the best arrangement, in the best interests of your son," Sarah paused.

"So, can you just put it down, in the report, that I have a place lined up? And, that I have a lead on a job, part-time, in a dress shop nearby? Can you put all that in?"

They reviewed Mara's plans, and Sarah noted all the details. Though Mara seemed sincere, after years of hearing such stories, Sarah was skeptical. Mara was in big trouble and likely to lose her child; her *plans,* if there were any, were out of desperation, Sarah thought, which was usually the case. But part of her, the nonprofessional, felt sorry for Mara. She had a beautiful child and was throwing him away, for what? To have some fun!? To do some drugs, have sex? Hang out in the woods? Her son might have drowned if that investigator had not saved him. Not likely, she thought. What is *wrong* with these people? Sarah closed her file and stood.

"I think I have it all," she said.

"If you give Rob, his father, custody, I will never see him again," Mara said, standing. "He will take him back East, to his home, and I will never see Jason again. They will never let me! Never!" She glared at the probation officer. She picked up her cigarette and pointed at Sarah. "How could *you* do that? How could *you,* a woman, let that happen?"

Sarah was quiet. She stifled her thoughts: *It's not about me, lady. It's you who put yourself and your child in this situation. You, who exercised poor judgment. My job is to fix it! To protect your child, from you, if necessary.*

"I do not make the decisions, Miss Evans. The court does," Sarah replied evenly. "I have all your explanations, your ideas, your plans. They will be in my report, and you—your attorney—will get a copy," she said. "If you firm up your job and living plans, and they do sound appropriate, let me know," she said. "But, do it very soon. We have ways of checking these things without upsetting the others involved. You need not worry if you have or can make the arrangements you mentioned. If that happens, I would be favorably inclined to consider those options," she said. "No one wants to separate a mother—or a father—from their child. Unless there is no alternative. That may be up to you, at least in part. Understood?"

Mara made no response, and Sarah turned to leave. As she opened the door to the hall, she heard, "Miss Redding?"

Sarah turned. Mara appeared distraught, her bravado gone.

"I know I screwed up," Mara said, her voice breaking. "I just want a chance to fix it. I didn't know you could, or would, help me," she said, "I thought you people were the enemy."

Sarah looked at her, "We are not, Mara. We are not your enemy. But *you* have to help us help you. Do you understand?"

"Yes, Miss Redding," Mara replied, "I do now. Thank you."

Sarah squared her shoulders, turned, and walked from the room. She forgot to turn off the lights.

~

Back in her office, Sarah looked up as her door opened. Jesse leaned against the jamb.

"That was the hippie case?" he asked. "I saw her leaving as I came in. How did it go?" his eyebrows rose.

"The usual. 'I have plans. I can change. I didn't mean it.'" Sarah replied, her chin resting on her hands. She straightened, leaned back.

"So, what you gonna' do?" Jesse smiled his smile.

"What I always do, Mr. Morehead. Make a recommendation based on what is in the best interests of the child," she sighed.

CHAPTER 5

"ALL RISE. THE HONORABLE HOMER J. HALSEY, Judge of the Superior Court."

The trial to determine the custody of Jason Evans, a.k.a. Jason Williams, commenced promptly at 9:00 A.M. in the second-floor courtroom. They all rose as the judge took the bench: Grant, at the left side of the long counsel table, Williams to his right. Next to Williams, attorney Ivan Turoff, and to his right, Mara.

The witnesses were seated in the first two rows behind the attorneys, separated by a gated railing.

"Please be seated," the bailiff intoned. The judge opened a file.

"We are here *In Re the Matter of the Custody of Jason Evans,*" the judge looked up at the parties seated in front of him. "The record will reflect that all parties are present with their counsel?"

"Yes, Your Honor. Will Grant for Petitioner, Mr. Robert Williams. Mr. Williams is present," Grant replied. The judge nodded at Grant and looked to the other attorney.

Turoff stood. "Ivan Turoff, Your Honor, representing the mother, Miss Tamara Evans."

The judge regarded Turoff. "Mr. Turoff, I do not believe I have had the pleasure. Welcome to Department 3," he smiled at the lawyer.

"Thank you, Your Honor," Turoff replied.

"All right. This is a hearing on the issue of the custody of Jason Evans, who is . . . three, almost four, years of age." The judge consulted papers neither attorney could see. "I have read the moving papers filed by each side, and the Probation Report, including the recommendation of Miss Redding."

He looked up. "Good morning, Miss Redding," he nodded at the probation officer who was seated in the first row, behind Grant.

"Mr. Grant, your client is the moving party, you may proceed," the judge said.

"Thank you. I will call my client, Your Honor." Grant looked and nodded at Williams, who stood, walked quickly to the witness stand, and took his seat, below and to the right of the judge. He was sworn in by the court clerk and responded with his name and address. Grant stood behind his chair, sliding it forward until it touched the table. He rested his hands on the chair back. A file was open on the table in front of him. He preferred to work standing; not all judges would allow it, but he knew that Judge Halsey had no rule against it. He smiled, a brief softening of his face. Williams was seated almost directly in front of Grant.

"Mr. Williams," Grant opened. "Your full name is Robert Bradford Williams, is that correct? May I call you Rob?" Williams nodded. "Rob, you are the father of Jason, correct?" Grant asked.

"I am," he replied.

"And you are requesting that this court grant you sole, physical custody of your son, with the intention of returning with him to Massachusetts to reside there with you and your grandmother . . . the boy's great-grandmother, is that also correct?" Grant looked to the judge.

Rob looked directly at the judge. *Look him in the eye,* Grant had instructed.

"Yes, sir, that is my plan."

Grant heard a sob to his right: Mara, he knew without looking, and a murmur from those behind him. The judge looked over and behind Grant.

"There will be no comments from spectators in my courtroom. None!" he said. "Continue," to Grant.

All morning, Rob remained on the stand. Grant talked him through the history of his relationship with Mara; the birth of Jason; the advent of problems; his decision to seek custody, before she disappeared; and the search for, and recovery of, the boy. As they had rehearsed, Grant phrased his questions so that they often served as a springboard for lengthy, fact-filled answers by Williams. This allowed him to tell the entire story as it evolved, in a personal, emotional fashion. Initially. Turoff objected to the manner of Grant's questioning, protesting that it was "leading" or that it "called for a narrative," both appropriate legal objections, but the court quickly overruled him, making it clear that the judge was interested in assessing Williams as a father and a witness, and that the court wanted to move quickly through material, much of which was probably undisputed. Turoff, knowing that his further objections would only irritate the jurist, acquiesced in the procedure and sat back, waiting his turn for cross-examination of the witness.

By the midmorning break, Grant had concluded his examination of Rob, and after a brief recess, it was Turoff's turn with Williams, who remained on the stand. Turoff, unlike Grant, remained seated, and his questioning focused on the father's plans for moving Jason back to the East Coast: how he would provide for his care once there; and then he raised the issue of, and contact with, the boy's mother, Mara.

"So, what is your plan for visitation by my client? After you remove the boy from this jurisdiction, where she presently resides, and you take him to Connecticut?" he asked.

"I am not removing him. I am taking him home. That was, and is, his home," Rob countered. "And it is Massachusetts."

"Right, Massachusetts. I always get those eastern states mixed up," Turoff responded testily.

Grant leaned forward, and he turned to look at the other attorney, "That's an interesting admission."

"Is that an objection!?" Turoff snapped, without looking up.

Grant sat back.

"You have the question," the judge inquired of Rob. "Go ahead and answer."

Rob replied. "Yes, Your Honor. I will comply with whatever the court decides with regard to her visiting Jason. I understand," he continued, "that if I am granted custody and take him home, that there is some procedure for the local, Massachusetts, court to oversee her visitation. Whatever this court, or that court says, that's what I will do."

"So, she would have to go there, to Massachusetts, to see her son. Who is going to pay for that?" Turoff demanded.

"Not me," Rob replied softly, looking down at Grant.

"From a practical standpoint then, she would never get to see her son. Is that it? Is that your *plan*?" Turoff stated, his voice rising. "You think that's fair?"

"Argumentative, Your Honor," Grant objected evenly, to give Rob some time to think.

"I'll allow it," the judge replied. "But watch your tone, Mr. Turoff," he warned.

"It is not *my* idea, Mr. Turoff," Rob replied. "It was *her* idea to disappear and come out here. She is the one who picked here to live. All I want is my son to be raised in a loving and safe environment."

"But how? How is she to . . . ? Never mind! Strike that," Turoff stammered. He stopped and fumbled through his notes. After a moment, during which he stared at Rob, he continued:

"It was *your* idea to sneak someone into her home! To spy on her and her house—or her roommates. To kidnap the boy in the dead of night, violating the law, instead of seeking a custody order using the courts! " He was almost shouting.

Grant was on his feet, but before he could speak, the judge held up his hand. "Either withdraw that or rephrase it, Mr. Turoff. And calm down, sir. I think we all know that we would not be here if this gentleman had not, well, acted to protect his own interest and that of his son, as he saw it." Grant sat down.

"Your next question, Mr. Turoff, please," the judge said.

Turoff huddled with Mara. She was visibly upset. Turoff put a hand on her arm and shook his head.

"No further questions," he said, settling back into his chair. His head was down; his eyes were glued to his open file.

"Redirect, Mr. Grant?"

"None, Your Honor."

"Fine," the judge said. "We will take our noon recess. Please be back, ready to go, at 1:15 P.M. And, gentlemen, I have nothing else this afternoon, so we will go until 5:00 P.M. today. Please plan your witnesses accordingly." Judge Halsey stood and left the bench, his robes billowing behind.

~

Both sides crossed the street to the Creamery. The physical division of the restaurant with its two long counters allowed adverse parties to occupy booths on opposite sides of the dining area, out of earshot of the other. The restaurant had been a favorite of litigants and their counsel for years, a tradition. The waitresses were sensitive to the time constraints of the attorneys and discreet to their clients. Grant entered first and went to his usual booth on the right. John Meagor was waiting. Rob followed with Sarah and Jason, who had been waiting with his grandmother in an adjacent jury room. She had excused herself from their lunch.

Turoff and Mara, with their witnesses, entered a few moments later. When Turoff spotted Grant and his party, he led the others to a booth to the left, toward the rear of the restaurant.

Grant turned to Sarah, "Ok, why don't you take Jason to wash his hands. That will give us a couple of minutes."

"Good idea," she replied. "Let's go to the little boy's room, Jason."

"I don't have to pee," Jason replied, looking at John. John smiled and patted his head.

"Come on, you know the rules. We wash our hands, or no lunch."

"Aww," Jason replied. He held the woman's hand as they walked away.

The others sat, Grant and Rob opposite John.

"Ok, before they come back, here is what happens this afternoon," Grant said. He explained, after they ordered sandwiches and beverages, that he had finished with Rob, and that John, the investigator, was his next witness. He reminded the young man that he was not to worry about his willing participation in the sex and drug incidents. They had reviewed and role-played the expected cross-examination, using one of Grant's associates as Mara's counsel.

"It's all in the report," Grant said. "None of it is going to surprise this judge, who has already read it." He explained that Turoff would attempt to attack John's credibility, to discredit him. Grant reassured the young man that he had nothing to fear.

"Good," John replied. "Because I was, I am still, worried. You never know, there I will be under oath, on the witness stand, admitting doing drugs and stuff."

"John, you were the rescuer," Grant said. "Don't lose sight of that. The court knows that you had to find some way to gain their confidence. This judge knows what goes on in that valley. It is not a problem," he assured him. "I am not even sure that the court will want to hear much about it. What you did does not change the issue, that it was no place for a child. And that's what this case is about. They," he nodded across the room, "are in huge trouble," Grant continued. "Whatever they say about you, John, they have no plans for taking care of the boy, and they have to know that is the key. Mara has no job, no place to live, despite what she says in Sarah's report. There is no way they are going to win this, and they know it."

"I'm glad you are all so confident. The whole thing freaks me," Rob said.

"Rob, you did fine this morning. Just like we planned and rehearsed," Grant replied.

"The judge was clearly impressed with your efforts to get your son back. I cannot imagine him releasing Jason to his mother . . . to go where? And you offer him a loving home, even if it is out of state. That's the problem for Mara. She uprooted him, brought him here to suit her own plans," Grant said.

"Oh, oh, here they come." John stood to allow Sarah and Jason to squeeze into the booth. The waitress brought their food. While they ate, Grant went over the plans for the afternoon. John concentrated on distracting Jason, and together they worked on coloring the place mat that the waitress had given the boy.

~

Meanwhile, Turoff, Mara, and her housemates filled a large semicircular booth at the rear of the restaurant. After they had ordered, the lawyer reviewed the morning's events.

"There was not much I could do with Williams," he explained. "It is what it is. The key is whether they, Grant and his client, can convince this judge to allow the father to take the boy two thousand miles away from you, Mara, effectively depriving you of any access to your son, in the practical sense," he said. "Unless of course *you* move also."

"But what about that probation officer's recommendation? When do we get to that? What do we do? How does Mara get around that?" Elaine asked.

"Right," Mara seconded her. "What do we, or *I*, do about that? She doesn't like me, I know it," her voice strained.

"Well, we just have to deal with it," Turoff responded. "It is just a recommendation after all. The judge is not obligated to follow it."

"Shit! Fat chance!" Dean retorted loud enough for Turoff to flinch and glance across the room. "That bitch has it in for you and for all of us—that

Sarah. She didn't even want to interview me, Elaine or Penny. She's only got half the story," he hissed. They continued to talk.

Mara glanced across the room when Jason returned from the bathroom. He looked so cute, she thought. The others were all dressed better than she and her friends. Even her attorney looked outclassed. She felt a sinking feeling and pushed her food away. She listened to snatches of her attorney's conversation, her mind wandering to the quiet stream, the green forest. *How,* she wondered, *how did he ever find us? What does it mean? How will this end? Why …? I just wish it would all go away somehow. If I could just disappear. Be gone?*

"They're leaving," Turoff said. "We better go." He slid out of the booth.

"Cool it, counselor," Dean sneered. "They can't start without us," he said.

Turoff ignored the remark, picked up his briefcase, and headed for the door, the others trailed behind. He noticed that Grant was already across the street, starting up the courthouse steps.

While they waited for the light to change, Mara looked across the street as Jason, his hand held by the probation officer, skipped up the steps. She was overwhelmed by a mixture of feelings—regret? Envy? Guilt? *No!,* she thought, as she stepped from the curb. *It's anger—I am pissed.* Angry that she had lost control. That her fate was to be decided by others and she could not let that happen. She glanced ahead at them, and she vowed that she would fix it, somehow, some way.

~

"Meagor. John Meagor," in response to the clerk's question. "5448 Ashby Avenue, Berkeley, California."

"You may be seated."

He opened his dark brown, herringbone sports jacket. He wore a blue button-down shirt, regimental striped tie, with dark slacks. Gone were the shoulder-length locks. Grant stood to the side of the counsel table, his legal tablet resting on the edge.

"Mr. Meagor. John, please state your age, occupation, and trace your educational experience for us." These early questions were designed to allow the young man to get comfortable on the witness stand and to develop a rhythm to his testimony.

"I am twenty-four. I graduated from UC Berkeley with an undergraduate degree …"

Grant tilted his head in the direction of the judge, reminding that John should make eye contact with the jurist, as they had rehearsed.

"... in English, a year ago," John shifted slightly, to face the judge, "I was admitted to law school and just completed my first year. My uncle owned, owns still, a small private investigative firm, in San Francisco, EKI Investigations. I went to work for him during this past summer, between semesters."

"And what were your duties at the investigation firm?" Grant asked.

"I sort of did everything. Helped out in the office, answered phones, served process papers. I got registered as a process server, so I could do that," he continued. "Because I had time, I took the ones that were hard to serve, that involved a stakeout, things like that."

"Was the firm, EKI, actually licensed as a private investigative firm?" Grant asked.

"Yes, sir," he replied, stating the firm name and the license number.

"But you were not personally licensed?"

"No, sir," John said. "I was not, and I am not now. I am presently a law student at the University of San Francisco, School of Law."

"All right, now tell us how you became involved in this case, if you will." Grant picked up the yellow legal tablet, and he leaned casually against the counsel table.

Comfortable now, John testified that the firm had been contacted by their client (Grant had instructed him to refer to Rob as "the client"), who was searching for his missing son and the boy's mother; he took the initial call. He recounted that Rob had traced her to Marin through the garage that had towed her car.

"My uncle, Burt, and I, took the background story. I actually wrote it up and located the house where we confirmed she was living," he explained.

"And what did you do next?" Grant asked.

"Well, we decided we needed to recover the boy, so that the client could get physical custody, and then go through the courts, like this," John said. "We figured that we would try to get in the house, by making friends with them somehow, and then came up with the idea of me trying to get invited in," he paused.

"And why you?" Grant asked.

"Well, I was the right age and I had, then, kind of this radical hair, down to my collar, so I sort of volunteered."

"Had you any experience in undercover work?"

"No," John answered. "We figured that if I could become one of them, that would be easier than just trying to grab the boy, and it would be less traumatic on him. That was the idea," he said.

"Continue," Grant said

"Some of my friends knew Marin, and they told me the river, Paper Mill River, was a big hangout spot. So, I got set up and found them easily, on the second day out. I got lucky," he explained. "I had pictures of Miss Evans and Jason; he had all that dark hair. That confirmed that we had the right people."

"All right. You rescued Jason from that river, is that correct? Saved him from drowning?" Grant asked.

"Yes, sir. I did," he answered.

"You gave a complete statement to the sheriff's office after you and Rob, your client, recovered Jason, and you prepared a separate report for your own office. Is that also correct?"

"Yes, sir. The sheriff's office took my report the next morning, and I started my in-house report that day, completing it the next day," he said.

"All right, with reference to that report and starting with the rescue at the river, please take us, if you will, through the events . . ."

Both reports, attached to and summarized in the Probation Custody Report, had been given to Mara and her attorney. Grant walked John through the events in which he had been a part. Turoff, knowing the story full well, and considering that little was to be gained by attempting to keep out what was already part of the record, made few objections. At times, Grant felt as if *he* was testifying. When he thought he could get away with it, he asked leading, fact-filled questions, soliciting Meagor's agreement. While clearly objectionable, Turoff did not object. They moved quickly through his testimony. The judge had early on turned to closely watch Meagor. Riveted, Grant thought.

Pausing, Grant sat down. He looked up after a moment. "Mr. Meagor, John, do you have any brothers or sisters, younger ones?"

"Well, my sister has a young boy, my nephew. He is almost five years of age."

"I see," Grant leaned back. He looked over at Turoff, who met his gaze. Without breaking eye contact with Turoff, Grant asked, "John would you let—allow—your five-year-old nephew to reside in . . ."

Turoff glowered and cut him off: "Objection, Your Honor!"

"Sustained," the court immediately responded.

Grant turned to his witness. "Mr. Meagor, from your experience in the house, with the group, the events in which you participated or witnessed, do you have an opinion as to whether that living situation is, or was, a suitable one for a child of Jason's age?"

"Objection, Your Honor!" Turoff was on his feet.

"The grounds, Mr. Turoff?" the court asked, looking at the attorney.

"Lack of foundation, incompetent, biased, lacks expertise, and calls for an expert opinion," Turoff paused.

"Well, let us look at your grounds, Mr. Turoff," the judge focused on the attorney. "Foundation: he was certainly there, living with the participants, with adequate opportunity to observe what went on, in fact he played an active role." The judge glanced at his notes and looked up at Turoff, continuing, "Competence: he was present and able to observe the things to which he testified. Same thing." The judge paused. "Biased? Not a basis for objection, and I presume that he was biased, after all that is why he was there, but that is not an appropriate objection." He hesitated, reflecting, and said, "Which brings us to the issue of expertise and expert opinion. Mr. Turoff's objection is sustained on the grounds calling for expertise." He looked up at Turoff, who was smiling. "However . . ." Grant swore that there was a trace of satisfaction in the judge's expression, " . . . an opinion on the fitness of a home, for raising a child, or the extent, or lack thereof, of care for a small child, that is a matter of *common* observation, not unlike, say, left out in the rain, as it were. Such an opinion does *not* call for expertise in the matter, and I can accord it the weight to which it is entitled. And, we do have Miss Redding's thoughts on the same subject. So, Mr. Turoff, your objection to the coming testimony is overruled. I will allow it," the judge concluded and directed his attention to the witness.

Turoff glowered.

"Mr. Meagor? Do you have the question in mind?" Grant asked.

Meagor nodded. "It was no place for a child, Your Honor. Any child," he responded. "Not Jason. Not my nephew," he looked down at Turoff. Grant said nothing; he sat back, satisfied.

"Anything further of this witness, Mr. Grant?"

"None, Your Honor."

"Your witness, Mr. Turoff," the court nodded.

~

Turoff intended to conduct his examination while seated at the counsel table, and he leaned forward, a yellow tablet in front of him. Grant could see that his first page was filled with short blurbs, reminders. He wondered how many more pages he had prepared.

"Mr. Meagor," Turoff began. "You are not a licensed investigator? Not licensed by the state, or anyone, I take it?"

Grant had decided to make Turoff work for it, and he wanted to protect Meagor. Earlier, Turoff had gone relatively easy on Rob, rarely objecting; it would have been bad strategy for Turoff to attack the boy's father, who had not been at the house. Yet, Grant had decided that this was the place to draw the line. Meagor was the heart of his case. Turoff would have to earn his points, the hard way.

"Objection, Your Honor, relevance," Grant announced firmly.

The judge looked at Grant, his face impassive. "Sustained."

Grant glanced at Turoff, waiting. "Well, you have no special training, do you?" Turoff followed.

"Objection, relevance," Grant repeated.

"Sustained," the judge's voice matched Grant's tone and volume.

"But Your Honor," Turoff said, one hand raised, "this is preliminary, just to show that the witness had no right to be in their house, spying on them; no right to testify what is good or not good for the boy . . ."

Grant was on his feet now, and he turned toward the attorney, waiting for a pause, for his turn to object, but before he could speak, the court interrupted, "Mr. Turoff, Mr. Meagor was invited into the house by the occupants themselves, as I recall his testimony. They had possession of that residence. Whether they had any *right* to be there is another question, but it is not before me, the issue of possession of the house. As I recall they invited him to . . . dinner, wasn't it?" he consulted his notes. "Yes, as a sort of a 'thank you' for saving your client's child's life, it seems to me?" he looked at the attorney, his eyebrows questioning.

"But he has no expertise on child behavior," Turoff lamented, his voice strained.

"Well, that is true, he did not relate any such training. I recall he is a law student," the judge looked at Grant.

"That's correct," Grant replied. "And besides, Your Honor, he only testified to what he personally observed in so far as the boy was concerned. He did not give an expert opinion, Judge," Grant concluded.

"I think that is accurate, Mr. Turoff. We have been over this," the jurist leaned back. "He did make that observation in answer to a question that he thought it was no place to raise, or keep, a child," the judge continued. "I took that as a personal observation, not an expert opinion, Mr. Turoff. And I will give it weight accordingly. The objection is sustained. You may continue," the judge nodded at the attorney.

Grant sat down. His goal was to keep the other attorney off balance, to upset the rhythm of his questions; to make him worry about the form of each and every question. Turoff was lost in his notes. The sag of his shoulders was a realization that it was not going to be easy.

Turoff continued, "You were hired by Mr. Williams to steal his child back? Is that correct?"

Grant smiled, but let the question go.

"Not to *steal* him, but to try to get him back to his father, so that this . . ." indicating the court proceedings, ". . . could happen. Yes," he replied.

Grant sensed Rob stiffen next to him, and he leaned and whispered, "We let him go, Rob. John can handle himself," he cautioned.

"But you did *steal* him, didn't you?" Turoff pressed.

"I'm not sure *stealing* is the right word," Meagor replied, looking at Grant.

"You took him out of a darkened house, after everyone was asleep, in the middle of the night, isn't that correct . . . to a waiting car, and never told anyone?"

"That is correct," John replied confidently, "except I did tell someone, sir," he replied.

"Really! Whom?"

"His father," John replied, "He was in the car when I took the boy, that night. And the next day, actually later that day, in the morning, we told the sheriff's office. I, we, went to the sheriff's office, the client and I, and we made a report telling them exactly what happened and that our client would be seeking a custody order, which," nodding to Grant, "they did."

There are times when an attorney asks one too many questions, Grant thought. *This was one of them.*

Turoff now adopted a knowing, sarcastic tone. "All right, Mr. Meagor. While you were in the house you did drugs, did you not?"

Without hesitation, Meagor answered, "Yes, I did. It was marijuana, sir."

Perfect, thought Grant. *Just like we discussed, including the emphasis on the "sir" part.*

The candor and the simplicity of the witness's reply seemed to startle the attorney. He looked at Meagor. "Well?"

"'Well' is neither a sentence, nor a question, Your Honor," Grant interjected.

"Nor is that a proper objection, Mr. Grant," the judge said. "Continue, Mr. Turoff. Let's move on."

"You admit that you did drugs? Is that your testimony?" Turoff asked.

Again a simple, "Yes, sir."

"Illegal drugs?"

"Yes, sir, marijuana."

"And it was *your* marijuana, wasn't it? You brought it in, you supplied it, didn't you?"

"Yes, sir."

"And where did . . ."

Meagor didn't wait for Turoff to complete his question. He answered, "From some of my friends, in Berkeley. I bought it from them."

"Tell us, tell this court, the names of the persons who sold you these drugs, Mr. Meagor," challenging. "Give us the names!"

Grant edged forward on his seat, waiting. They had planned this, in case.

"Objection! Your Honor," Grant offered calmly as he rose from his seat. "Relevance and outside the scope of direct examination." Meagor had not answered the question as instructed by Grant. He had waited for Grant's objection, expecting it, and now he waited for the ruling from the court.

"The man is a felon, Judge. A criminal! " Turoff was on his feet.

"Mr. Grant?" the judge asked.

"Mr. Meagor is not on trial, Judge. He stands charged with nothing. He has admitted to using and purchasing the pot, to give him credibility with the boy's mother and her ... *associates,* rightly suspecting that to have it would gain him entry," Grant said. "The names or identities of those from whom he purchased it would not advance the issues in this *custody* case," he concluded.

"Sustained. Continue, Mr. Turoff?"

Grant stole a look at Mara. She was slumped in her chair. He could only imagine what the others, her friends, must be thinking, but he was reluctant to turn around and look. They had not said a word since they had been admonished by the court.

Turoff continued, standing, leaning slightly forward against the table.

"And you engaged in sexual activity in the presence of the boy, didn't you?" triumph in his voice.

John looked down at Grant as he responded, "Yes, that was my testimony. It happened. I didn't know he was there. I ..."

"In front of this child, you participated, willingly, in a graphic sex act. Isn't that your testimony?" Turoff demanded; he knew the answer. "And, you have the audacity, the unmitigated gall to come into this court ..."

Grant heard a chair snap back up in the gallery behind him and then rapid steps out of the courtroom. The judge was looking over his head, frowning. Grant swiveled around just in time to see Penny violently push the door open and exit the courtroom. Her friends looked shocked. Grant half smiled at Dean. Elaine's head was down, studying the floor.

Turning back, Grant spoke as he rose to his feet, "Objection, Your Honor, objection," Grant interrupted. "He is badgering the witness, attacking him, actually." Grant was anxious to protect his witness, and Turoff was on a roll, going a little too far and too fast.

"Overruled. Your witness is doing quite well, Mr. Grant. I think he can handle himself." The judge nodded at the young man and turned to Turoff.

"Let us see if we can do this, perhaps, an easier way, Mr. Turoff," the court interrupted. "So let *me* ask *you,* Mr. Turoff. Tell me where you are headed with this line of questioning. I think I know, but why don't you make an offer of proof." Grant sat back, satisfied that he had slowed things down and that he had bought time for Meagor to compose himself. No matter how many times they had gone over this moment, Grant knew it was stressful for the young man, particularly since he was headed back to law school, and he would one day apply for admission to the State Bar to practice law.

"Certainly, Your Honor," Turoff replied, reeking confidence. "I intend to show that this witness committed a variety of crimes, perhaps felonies, Your Honor, in this matter, in getting into the house to begin with. His actions once there included illegal drugs, overt sexual actions, themselves contributing to the delinquency of this minor child. Intentional kidnapping and . . ."

The court interrupted him: "Toward what end, for what purpose, Mr. Turoff? What is this line of questioning intended to *prove?*" the jurist leaned forward, fixing his gaze on the attorney.

"To discredit his entire testimony, Judge, including his statements in the investigation report. He has violated the law to such an extent, well, he is not to be believed, Your Honor," he paused, "It should all go out. His testimony should be stricken. I so move." Clearly winded, Turoff paused.

The judge sat back, pensive. He looked at Rob, out at the others seated in the gallery. Dean was grinning.

"I thought so. So let's see if I understand you and this line of questioning," the court said.

"Your Honor," Grant interrupted, leaning toward the bench, "I do not see any relevance to this line of questioning, I—"

"I have it, Mr. Grant. It is *my* turn," the judge said sternly. "Mr. Turoff, I understand your offer of proof, that you are intent on discrediting the witness with this line of questioning and in order to seek a ruling which would exclude his testimony, presumably all of it. Is that a fair summary?" he paused.

"Exactly, Your Honor," Turoff replied, satisfaction evident in his clipped tone.

"All right. With that offer, the objection is sustained. Not on the badgering, but on the ground of relevance, gentlemen." Turoff reddened. The courtroom was still. "While I do not condone the witness's behavior, and I suspect that he is perhaps not proud of it, nevertheless it is the situation, the *environment,* in which Miss Evans and her friends placed a young child. An *environment* into which the witness was invited, openly, by them. He did not create it. Let me finish, Mr. Turoff," the judge raised his hand, acknowledging the coming protest.

The court continued: "This is not a criminal case; the witness is not charged with any crime. I express no opinion on the criminality of his behavior, but I refuse to discount or discredit his testimony. Firsthand, independent, eye-witness testimony. You know these custody cases often involve *accusations* of conduct, conduct which is difficult to prove, very often never proven. But that is not this case. Mr. Meagor had a legitimate and lawful purpose in mind, and he took, I believe, a serious risk. So, gentlemen, let us move on. I will neither strike his testimony," he looked at Grant, "nor will I entertain any further questioning inclined to erode Mr. Meagor's testimony as suggested, Mr. Turoff," the court explained. "His actions, his conduct, it is what it is, and remains what it was. What he saw and what he experienced, and I will consider it as such. Recess, gentlemen and ladies. Ten minutes." He rose, nodded to his bailiff, and stepped down from his bench.

~

While the others waited in the nearby jury room outside the court, during the afternoon break, Grant went into the men's room, around the corner in the main hall of the second floor. He entered through the double doors. Dean stood at the far right of the three urinals, opposite two closed stalls. Grant took the urinal to the far left; he said nothing. Dean glanced at him, sighed audibly, and then laughed.

"Gotcha!" he snorted.

Grant said nothing.

"The big hot shot lawyer, huh?" Dean taunted, casting a sideways glance at Grant.

Grant was silent.

Dean, finished, backed up. Grant could see his movements; he sensed the coming hostility. From behind, he heard as Dean continued:

"The big hot shot, going to take her boy away from her, is that the deal? Punish her?"Grant finished, stepped to the wash basin, watching Dean in the mirror behind him. Dean had not moved.

"So, you sneak your pretty-boy private eye into our pad. He brings in his private stash, swipes garbage for the kid to eat, drinks our booze, rapes our women, and kidnaps Mara's kid. Bet you're proud of pullin' that shit off," Dean snarled. "Well, you wait 'til we get to testify. We'll set it straight, tell that asshole judge what really went down! That may just fuck up your little custody party, huh!?" Dean paused.

Grant reached for the paper towels, still watching Dean in the mirror. "My turn? Are you finished?" he said, slowly wiping his hands. "Because if you are—"

"Fuck you, asshole," Dean snorted. He had not moved.

"Let me know when you are done. Done?" No reply. Grant turned to face him, inches separated them.

"This is what *you* are going to do, Dean," as he patiently wiped his hands. "If you are called as a witness—you or any of you—you will tell the truth, the whole truth, and nothing but the truth, so help you God, or whomever. And if you do not—because you and I know the truth," he continued, "then I will walk you through the parties, the booze, *your* possession of *your* drugs, using them in front of the boy, and maybe suggest that you had some 'fun,' maybe gave the kid some, or let him get a 'contact high' blowing smoke at him . . ."

Dean was frozen in place; Grant thought that he was not even breathing

". . . and I will have your answers typed up, get a transcript, and I will walk it downstairs and have my friend the D.A. prepare a criminal complaint, while 'we wait,' for child neglect, contributing to the delinquency of a minor, drugs in the presence of a minor, felonious child endangerment, that's a good one, and have you arrested before you can get your sorry ass out of this courthouse." Dean blanched.

Dean's eyes registered a mix of hatred and alarm. He still had not moved.

"And you can sit in that dark, damp jail cell downstairs, for six months, all by your disgusting self, trying to figure a way to raise bail, maybe longer, until your case comes to trial, and that's before you are convicted," he paused. "You 'ahdda' that, you worthless bag of shit!"

Grant tossed his paper towels, now compressed to the size of a golf ball, in one smooth arc into the trash can beside Dean. And as he did so, a voice behind Dean said, "That's 'two!'"

"And Dean," Grant continued, a smile crossing his face, "you ought to pay attention to whomever is in a public bathroom before you spout off your perjury plans," Grant nodded over Dean's shoulder at the uniformed bailiff who was emerging from the nearby bathroom stall.

Grant brushed past the startled Dean and out the double doors. As he entered the hallway, he felt a hand on his shoulder, and from behind, "What's this 'ahdda' stuff?" the bailiff asked.

Grant smiled and laughed softly. "Some 'shit' left over from my tour of duty in Korea. Bubbles up from time to time. House-boy talk, it means 'understand?' but it's not very polite," and the two of them turned the corner toward the courtroom.

"I 'ahdda,'" was the deputy's soft reply. He patted Grant on the shoulder.

~

Back in the courtroom, all parties present, Grant walked quickly to his seat. As he approached the counsel table, Williams looked up. Grant wondered if the heat of his confrontation with Dean showed on his face. Williams said nothing. Grant motioned to John that he should resume the witness stand. Grant leaned over to Williams and said quietly, "Turoff will finish his cross- of John, then we call Sarah Redding, the P.O. She's next." Williams nodded. He picked up his copy of her probation report and began to read.

"All rise!"

"Remain seated," the judge announced and, taking his seat, he looked immediately at Turoff. "Mr. Turoff, you were cross-examining the witness, and I had ruled on your motion when we recessed. You may continue."

Turoff studied his notes. He returned the judge's look. "In view of the court's ruling, Your Honor, we have no further questions of the witness at this time. But, Your Honor, we reserve the right to recall Mr. Meagor as our own witness, during our part of the case," he concluded.

"Certainly, that is your right, Mr. Turoff," the court replied. Turning back to Grant, the judge asked, "Mr. Grant, any redirect?" Grant was satisfied with his witness's testimony. "No redirect, Your Honor," he replied.

The judge swiveled toward Meagor. "You may be recalled later in this proceeding, young man." He looked at the attorneys. "The witness is to remain available," the judge instructed. "You may step down." Then he looked at Grant. "Mr. Grant, your next witness?"

"We will call Sarah Redding, Your Honor," Grant replied. "Miss Redding?" he turned to the rear of the courtroom, where she was seated. His eyes met Dean's. Grant winked, once.

Sarah Redding came forward. Grant opened the gate in the railing for her, and she took the witness stand. The clerk administered the oath. Grant began by asking her detailed questions about her education, training, and professional experience, until the court interrupted.

"Mr. Grant? Counsel?" this latter to Turoff. "Miss Redding is well known to this court, as are her qualifications. Perhaps, gentlemen, we can stipulate to her competence, to her expertise, and save some time." His tone left no doubt that they should avoid any testimony that the court might consider unnecessary.

"Certainly, Your Honor," Grant said.

"Mr. Turoff, I know you are from out of the county, but . . . ?"

Frowning, but with no real alternative but to annoy the judge, Turoff replied, "Yes, Your Honor. So stipulated." Mara stared at him, obviously displeased.

"Good. Let's move along," he nodded at Grant.

In response to Grant's questions, Redding identified her report.

The court inquired on its own, "Miss Redding, do I understand that you, personally, conducted the interviews as part of this investigation. Isn't that rather unusual?" the jurist asked her.

"Yes, it is, Your Honor," Sarah explained, turning to face the judge. "But the urgency of this matter, the fact that the court had marked the file 'Expedite,' and that we are short on staff . . . since I had started on it, it was more efficient for me to see it through, and I did so, Your Honor."

"Well, that makes the recommendation just that much more well-founded, I suppose," the court commented.

After highlighting the key areas of her investigation, Grant asked, "And what is your recommendation, Miss Redding?"

Addressing the court directly, she replied, "As my report indicates in the section titled 'Recommendation,' that the father be granted sole and exclusive custody of Jason, with the mother . . ." Sarah saw the scowl settle on Mara's face that quickly changed to anger, denial; she continued, ". . . to be granted visitation only after she has established herself in some safe residence and secured employment, and then only under strict supervision. She is not to be left alone with her son, ever," she finished.

At these words, Mara slumped and began to sob. The unintelligible mumble from the row of Mara's witnesses, which sounded like Dean's "bullshit" to Grant, was immediately gaveled silent by the judge. "There will be no comments from anyone. Understand!?" Grant did not turn around.

"And the reasons for that recommendation? They are enumerated in your report, correct?" Grant was standing now, behind his chair.

"Yes, they are," she replied.

"And, if you had to prioritize those reasons? Could you?" he asked.

"Objection, Your Honor!" Turoff interrupted. "He is leading her, Judge! And the report speaks for itself."

"Overruled. He only asked if she *could*, Mr. Turoff," the court answered. "Continue," he nodded to Grant.

Grant looked at Sarah. "Yes, certainly," she replied.

"Please do so," Granted asked.

"Objection!"

"I'll allow it, Mr. Turoff," the court answered. "You may cross-examine. I think it is important for her to tell us what she thinks, how she came to her conclusion. You can answer, Miss Redding."

"The single-most important thing I considered, Your Honor, is Miss Evans's choice of lifestyle, and the fact that her commitment to that chosen style of living, if you can call it that, presents a clear and present danger, not to just the emotional . . ."

"Oh, God, that's—!" Mara's voice rose and broke. "This is—!" her voice resonated throughout the room.

"Miss Evans," the court interrupted, leaning forward, one outstretched hand pointing directly at the woman, "If you persist in these outbursts, I will have the bailiff remove you. I mean it," he warned. "I suggest to you that your comportment in this courtroom is probably as important as the content of this report! Mr. Turoff, control your client," he looked at the attorney, "or I will," he said. Turoff turned to Mara, who shrugged him off. She stared defiantly up at the court. Turoff remained silent.

Turning to Sarah, the judge nodded, "Please continue, Miss Redding."

"Yes, Your Honor. Not just to the emotional health of this young boy, but she represents an actual danger. A physical danger to him as well. I don't mean that she would intentionally harm him, but in my view," she continued, "she is putting, and will continue to put, herself, her personal desires, whatever they might be, not only ahead of any concern for him, but she is making, and will continue to make, lifestyle choices without considering the effects on, or the consequences to, this little boy. Essentially, she is not, and in my judgment is presently incapable of, responsibly parenting him," she concluded.

"Thank you, Miss Redding," Grant said. He turned to Turoff, "Your witness."

"A moment please, Your Honor," Turoff replied. He bent over, and Grant could see and hear the strain and disagreement in the whispered conference between the attorney and his client.

"No!" they all heard the attorney blurt.

Grant caught part of Turoff's plea, ". . . you will get your chance to tell your side of the story."

Mara slammed her hand down on the counsel table. Turoff recoiled. She sat back glaring at Turoff and then at the court. Turoff directed his attention to the bench. "No questions at this time, Your Honor. Reserve," he said quietly.

"Redirect?" the judge looked at Grant.

"None, Your Honor," Grant replied.

Closing his file, the judge looked at Sarah and smiled.

"Thank you, Miss Redding. You are excused for now; you know the procedure."

Sarah nodded.

"That will do it for today, gentlemen and ladies. We resume at 9:00 A.M. tomorrow. Your time estimates, gentlemen? Do they remain the same?" the judge inquired.

Grant turned to the rear of the courtroom, eyeing Dean and Elaine. "I think so, judge." He paused. "We will need the three days, minimum."

"Mr. Turoff?"

"I believe so, Judge. We are just getting started and . . ."

"Well, I don't want to press you, but I would appreciate your consideration of the court's time, and let's try to avoid any duplication?" he said. "Good. We are adjourned." Taking his file, he stepped down from the bench.

Grant picked up his papers and, with Rob, he held the door for Sarah as they exited the courtroom. He glanced over his shoulder at Turoff and Mara still huddled at the counsel table, in a heated discussion. Dean and the others had joined them. *They know that they are in trouble,* he mused. As he entered the hallway, Penny passed him headed back into the courtroom. She avoided his look.

~

Turoff and Mara continued to argue at the counsel table. Turoff arranged his file in his briefcase. Mara sat slumped. Dean came forward, slamming the gate shut behind him.

"Fuck her, that bitch!" he scowled.

"Not in here, for God's sake!" Turoff looked around. "The bailiff will tell the judge. Just knock it off, Dean."

Dean mumbled something; Penny and Elaine joined them.

"This is a mess," Elaine offered.

"Thanks a lot, Elaine," Mara straightened and then stood.

Turoff snapped his briefcase shut as the bailiff reentered the courtroom.

"You all done, because I am locking up," he said, an order, not a question. "If you need a place to talk, the jury room just outside stays open; you can use it." He walked to and opened the gate. He smiled as Dean walked past. Dean avoided his look. Turoff led them out.

In the jury room, Turoff flicked on the lights. The others entered and settled into chairs around the table.

"That John," Mara began. "He lied his way into my house, lied to my Jace, lied to me. He smoked our pot, stole garbage, had sex with Penny! Shit! How can anyone believe him? It's pure crap."

"And it was *his* weed!" Dean snarled. They ignored him.

Mara stared at her attorney, eyes defiant, jaw clenched. The others looked at her.

"I will have all morning, tomorrow, to attack his story, Mara," Turoff responded. "I told you we will get our chance, and you guys all get to tell your side of it. We will get our turn." He continued, "I know it is tough sitting there taking it, but the judge knows that we have equal time. Just let's hang in there." He searched their faces. "Please."

"I'm not so sure," Elaine said. "Whether we like or not, he *is* telling the truth. And that probation report, it sure seems to hurt us."

"What do you mean *us?*" Dean snarled, leaning forward, inches from Elaine. "Mara! Mara is the one who is getting fucked by that hot shit lawyer and that pig bitch of a social worker. What does *she* know?"

"A lot. She knows a lot. All of it," Elaine said softly, glancing at the others. The attorney was quiet, listening. "Look, Mara," Elaine continued, "Why don't you talk to them. Try to make a deal. Some sort of sharing or visitation. Maybe your ex- can have him, like, in the summer or something." She paused. "I mean, if I wasn't under a summons, or whatever you call it . . . "

"Subpoena, by attorney Grant," Turoff interrupted. "You are required to be here and testify if he calls you as a witness."

"Subpoena, whatever, I would not be here. What can I say against John, he saw all of us."

"Deal? Good luck with that shit," Dean leaned back in his chair. "They ain't talkin', I can see that. Didn't you tell us if *they* got the report that was the ballgame?"

"Yes," the attorney replied, "The probation report, her recommendation, that *is* a problem. But the judge has to consider the facts, and if Mara comes across as sincere, as she is," he looked at her. "no court, no judge wants to deprive a mother of her child. Let's just stay calm and let it play out. The report is a *recommendation,* that's all, not a decision. We're a long way from the end. We can poke some holes in the P.I.'s testimony. Obviously, he has, had, an agenda. He is hardly impartial," he said. "He was hired to kidnap the boy, and he committed a handful of felonies doing it."

"And, if Penney testifies he raped her . . . ?" Dean said softly, his brows raised, eyes narrowed, focusing on Penny.

"What!?" Penny exploded. "What are you saying?" Penny interrupted. "Who told you that?"

"O.k., so maybe it didn't happen *exactly* that way," Dean retreated. "I thought you told us you were asleep or something, one of the times, or . . . ?"

"Damn you, Dean! Damn you!" Penny blurted. "I never told you that, and it didn't happen. Damn!" her voice rose. The other women stiffened. "I know what perjury is, and I am not going into that courtroom and lie for Mara, or you, or anyone. No way!"

"Relax," Dean touched her arm. Penny recoiled.

"No one is going to testify falsely here," Turoff added. "I'm not risking my ticket by having you commit perjury." He stared at Dean.

Dean stared at Penny. "I guess I misunderstood, I just thought you wanted to help Mara." His voice dripped with sarcasm.

"That's it! That does it, Dean. I am out of here!" Penny stood and pushed her chair back.

Turoff held up his hand. "Let's just calm down. None of this is going to happen. Let's just do it as we planned. We tell our side," the attorney looked slowly at each of them. "The court will decide, and it is really very difficult to take a child away from his mother," he continued.

"No one is taking Jason away from me," Mara stated. "No one is going to run my life. No one is going to tell me what I can do or not do! Not you. Not Dean!" Mara straightened. Her jaw was set, fists clenched white. She looked at each of them. "And certainly not this judge! You'll see!" She paused and then, standing: "I am out of here." She stalked from the jury room.

CHAPTER 6

IT WAS 9:05 A.M. "MR. GRANT, your next witness?"

He looked over at Rob and replied, "We call Miss Evans, Your Honor, under Section 776 of the Evidence Code." As Grant stood, he looked over at Turoff and Mara. She looked startled. *Turoff forgot to tell her,* Grant thought, *that I could call her as my own witness. I do not have to wait until he examines her and then cross-. I get her first, and obviously unprepared. This should be very interesting.*

"A moment, Your Honor," Turoff said.

"*One* moment, Mr. Turoff. I would like to finish today, or at least get close, if that is possible," the court answered, glancing at both parties. Neither Grant nor Turoff replied.

Turoff bent over and huddled with Mara, deep in conversation. Grant stepped behind his own chair and looked out at the witnesses in the first row. Dean scowled; the two women impassive as they focused on Mara and her attorney.

"Can he do this? You didn't tell me!" Everyone heard. She was furious. Turoff tried to calm her.

"Mr. Turoff? Let's proceed, shall we?" the court said.

Turoff sat back, Mara ashen. Turoff nodded to her and pointed to the witness chair. As she stood, she whispered to her lawyer; his face turned crimson and he cringed.

He didn't warn her! He forgot. Grant was certain. *So she is unprepared and surprised. Good!*

Mara scowled at Grant as she moved to the witness stand. The clerk administered the oath.

"Miss Evans . . ." Grant began.

"One moment, Mr. Grant," the court interjected. The judge leaned toward her. "Miss Evans, you have been called by Mr. Grant, as what we, the law, calls a *hostile* witness. This does not mean that you *are* hostile, but the law considers you as an adverse witness. Do you understand?" he paused.

"No, I do not, Your Honor. My attorney . . ."

"All right. I will explain it to you." The court glanced at Turoff, who was bent over, studying his notes. Grant stood behind his chair, hands crossed behind his back.

"The other side, that is, Mr. Grant, has the right to call you as their own witness, before Mr. Turoff would call you to testify. Mr. Grant can put questions to you in a format that he could not normally do with his own witnesses. There may be very little difference that you will notice to that, but he has a freer rein, if you will, in the way he asks you questions," he said. "Your attorney still has the right to examine you when Mr. Grant is finished, or he can wait and call you as his own witness during his, your, part of the case. That's his choice," the jurist paused and looked at Turoff. "Though I would hope that as long as Miss Evans is up here, perhaps we can get it all done then, in the interest of time." He looked at Turoff, "Is that a fair summary, counsel?" Turoff nodded.

"Mr. Grant, you may proceed."

Grant had not moved since Mara took the stand. Hands behind his back, without notes, he began.

"Miss Evans, your full name and residence address, for the record, please."

"Tamara Evans. Tamara Marie Evans," she replied

Grant waited. Nothing. "Your residence address?"

Turoff stared at Mara. Silence. Grant waited.

The court intervened. "Ms. Evans, your residence address, please?"

"Uh, well, you see, Your Honor," she paused, "at the moment I am looking for a place that would work for Jason and me. But until I know what is happening here, it is hard for me."

"I understand your hesitancy, Miss Evans," Grant helped. "So, just start by telling us where *you* are living now," he said.

"Well, I am staying with my friend, but only temporarily."

"What is the address of the place where you are staying with your friend?" he asked. "Where did you spend last night? Let's use that as a starting place."

"Objection, He is badgering my client, Your Honor!" Turoff was perched on the edge of his chair.

"Overruled, Mr. Turoff," the judge answered without a pause. "This is as if it were cross-examination, Mr. Turoff, and Mr. Grant knows full well my boundaries," he nodded at Grant, both to underscore his point, and that Grant should continue.

"The address, please, Miss Evans."

She sat up, erect, and met Grant's eyes. "I don't know the address. It's in San Francisco. It's a place, my friend's . . . they have friends there. I had my own room," she stared at Grant.

Grant picked up his tablet. "I'm sure you did, Miss Evans," he said, his eyes never leaving hers. "Maybe you can tell us what part of the City it is in?" he asked.

"I am afraid not, Mr. Grant," she said with momentary confidence. "I do not know the City very well, as you know. But it's near some big park."

"Basement, ground floor, second floor, third floor?" Grant reeled them off, the corners of his mouth barely lifting.

"Excuse me?" she answered.

"What floor was your room on . . . last night . . . in the City?"

"Why, the second floor, I think. Yes, the second floor. I had the room next to Penny," she nodded toward the first row.

"Fine, thank you," Grant said, turning to look at Penny. "We can ask *her* about it then, in a few minutes," he paused. Penny's look told him that Mara was lying and that Penny was not going to cover for her. His back still to Mara, he traded looks with Penny and watched her catch her breath when he asked, "What is the name of Jason's pediatrician?" He slowly turned back to face Mara, awaiting her answer.

"His what?"

"His pediatrician, his physician, his doctor," Grant pressed, his voice low.

"He has not been sick, never," she said.

"What shots has he had . . . ever?" he asked.

"Shots? Well, he has not needed them."

"When was his last physical, Miss Evans, please?" he asked.

"I told you he has not been sick, never. Except for a cold or a bug. He never needed a doctor," her voice was strong, but unsure. "What are you getting at?" she asked.

"Miss Evans, *I* get to ask the questions. *You* get to answer them. That's the way this works," Grant said.

"Your Honor!" Turoff interrupted.

"Mr. Grant, let's move on," the judge replied.

"Let me see if we can sum this up, in the interest of time," Grant said. "Since you *left* the East Coast, up to this moment, has Jason been seen by any doctor, dentist, medical practitioner, any medical personnel? And before you answer, I want the dates, places, names, and the reasons, please?" Grant moved forward, his tablet resting on the back of his chair, his pen poised.

Mara glanced at Turoff. He made no response. She settled, just a bit, in her seat. "No," was her soft reply.

"No, *what?*" Grant urged.

"No. He has not needed to see anyone," Mara replied.

"And is that your standard? He does not ever see a doctor or anyone, until what? He *needs* to?" Grant asked gently.

Grant waited; the judge watched her. She made no reply. Grant moved slowly to his left, toward the end of the counsel table. Still no answer. "How much does Jason weigh?" he asked.

Silence.

"What is his shoe size? What is his favorite book? Does he have any books? Any toys?" Grant paused briefly after each question.

"What are the names of his friends? Does he have any friends, other kids his age? With whom does he play?"

Nothing. Mara simply stared.

Grant turned and moved back to his seat, and as he did his eyes met Rob's. Grant shrugged, a slight tilt of his head. Rob's face was a mask—lips drawn, cheeks hollow. Grant picked up his file.

Turning back again to the witness, he asked, "How do you intend to support yourself, Miss Evans?"

"Well . . . well . . .," she replied, seemingly relieved to be done with the Jason questions. "I have a chance to work in a woman's shoe shop, part-time, maybe more. Depends," was her answer.

"And where is this shoe shop?"

"In the City. Oh . . . on Haight Street," she said.

"Oh," Grant responded, "Is it downstairs from where you are living? Are you living above the store, in your friend's place?" he asked.

"I'm not living in the Haight!" she said.

"Oh. Never mind. The name of the shoe shop is what?" Grant waited.

"Gosh, I forget the name," Mara said with obvious sarcasm.

"You haven't started yet? I thought you said . . ."

"No, Mr. Grant. I said 'I have a chance.' I have not started yet."

"Excuse me, Miss Evans. I have that wrong then. The name of the owner who is going to give you this chance . . . is?" Grant smiled slightly.

"Uh, I don't remember now. Could I ask Penny?" She nodded at the young woman in the first row.

"No, that's all right. You forget, right? I'll ask Penny, later." Grant turned to smile at Penny again. "I just want *your* recollection, Miss Evans. So, let me see if I have this so far." He turned to face Mara and took a step closer. Grant had the probation report in his hand; he knew that she knew what he was holding. He glanced down at it, and then taking his time, set it down on the table.

"As of this moment in time, you have no job. Correct?" Nothing.

"No place to live for yourself. No place for you and Jason. Correct?" Nothing.

"No plans on how you intend to care for the boy, and no funds for his care?"

Mara jumped in at this. "But he'll have to pay child support, Mr. Grant. Then I *will* have funds for Jason!" she interrupted. "Won't I?"

"Yes, Miss Evans, you will. And then you can find a physician to give the boy regular physicals, can't you?" he asked. "And you had that help in Boston, didn't you, before you hit the road!" he paused.

"Objection!" Turoff.

"Sustained," the judge replied, his raised eyebrows served as a warning for Grant to be careful.

"All right. Miss Evans, let's turn to the beginning and talk about you and Jason, and your friends, here in California, shall we?"

For the next hour, Grant questioned her regarding the events outlined in the probation report. Often he got her to concede the accuracy of those events as related by John Meagor, and if she did not agree, at least she did not contradict them. Just before the afternoon recess, he asked her, "What did you think Rob was doing while you were gone, on your trip?"

"I don't know," she said.

"Did it ever occur to you to call, write, anything, to let him know at least that his son was alive or dead?" he asked. She gave no answer, consistent with the pattern she had adopted when she did not like his questions. Grant had decided rather than argue with her or attempt to force a reply, that her non-answer was as telling, as damaging, as what she might say, probably more so.

"And if you didn't care about Rob, what about Jason? What did you tell him had happened to his father? To his great-grandmother? Did Jason think that they had abandoned him?" Grant pressed, his voice rising. "You didn't care, did you? Not about Jason; my client, his father; the boy's only relatives. It was all about you, *only* about you, and your what . . . your adventure?" She made no sound.

The court looked at Turoff, who made no objection to this highly objectionable manner of questioning, and then at a pause said, "Mr. Grant, you might slow down and give the witness an opportunity to answer." Grant did not reply.

"Miss Evans, Jason is just in the way. In *your* way, isn't he?" Grant asked, and he paused looking at the jurist. Nothing. After a moment, "You do not spend any time with, or *do* anything with, him? Do you?"

"That is not true," she answered finally, her voice straining for control. "I did things with him. We'd go to the beach at the river . . ." she paused, remembering.

"And?" Grant waited. "What else? As mother and son. What else?"

Barely audible she muttered, her head back, defiant, "Lots of things. You know . . ."

"Lots of things," Grant continued for her. "Like dumpster diving late at night?"

"Objection, Your Honor! Objection! He is interrupting the witness, not allowing her to complete her answer!" Turoff was trying to buy time for her.

"Withdrawn, Your Honor," Grant said. "Nothing further!" Grant slammed his note pad down on the table.

The judge frowned his displeasure and said, "We will take our noon recess now." To Mara, "Miss, you may step down. It is 11:55 A.M. All back here, 1:30 P.M." he announced. He stood and paused looking over the heads of those seated at the counsel table. "The witnesses, under subpoena, you are directed to return to this court as before. You remain under subpoena. 1:30 P.M."

When Grant bent to pick up his file, he heard a gasp from Mara's friends, seated behind him, including a barely audible, ". . . the son of bitch . . ." from Dean. Grant turned to see Mattuzig walking into the courtroom. He was unshaven, his suit coat did not match his pants, neither fit and both were dirty. He wore a T-shirt and no tie. He nodded at Dean and the women, a smirk of satisfaction on his face.

"I guess I'm in the right place," he said to no one in particular.

~

As they had the day before, both sides were back in the Creamery for lunch, separated by the counter. Mara and the others took the same booth at the rear of the restaurant.

"You order, I can't eat," Mara said. The others gave their orders to the waiter who placed water glasses in front of each. "I don't know how much more of this crap I can take." Mara sat next to Dean and opposite the attorney and Elaine. Penny had squeezed in on the end.

Mara sipped her water and said, "Well, you screwed that up big time. What, 'out of order,' he called it?"

"I am sure we discussed that, Mara," Turoff replied defensively.

"Bull! We never did! You know I was surprised," she countered. "So were you. What a mess you've made of this." She stared at the attorney, her eyes a mixture of defeat and defiance; her jaw clenched. The others looked at her and said nothing

"Look, I know you are upset," Turoff started, "but I get to put you back on the stand as part of our case. So we, you, still get to tell it your way."

Mara interrupted, "But they have, the judge has, already heard, 'their way!'" She snapped. "And that John, he lied his way through it."

"And now what's with that retard Mattuzig?" Dean said. "How the fuck did they get him here?"

"He is going to be trouble for us, I think," Penny said softly. "He never liked us." They discussed the morning's testimony until their lunch was delivered. As they ate in silence, Mara brooded and kept looking across the room at Jason and the others. At one point Jason was standing on the seat of the booth, and he looked directly over at her. She thought that he smiled, but then she decided that he had laughed at something said at his table. Turoff was speaking to her.

"Look, I will call you as my first witness, like we discussed," Turoff said in an attempt to calm her down. "Then Elaine, and Penny..."

"Not me. Do not call me," Penny interjected. "I am not getting up there and let that Grant work me over, like he did Mara. No way," she said.

"Thanks, Penny, for your support," Mara replied sarcastically.

Dean was silent. They picked at their food. Mara glanced over at Jason. She could not see him at the table. She wanted to be out of there, have this over with. She wanted to be done, with them, with this process, free again, on her own. She had stayed too long she decided. Well, she could fix that. She heard Turoff explaining that the others had to help her, but she no longer cared.

"Mara?" Turoff touched her arm. "Are you O.K.? You know that you're on next," he said.

"I know!" she replied, distant. She pushed against Dean. "Let me out, Dean. Move!" she snapped.

As Dean stood, she pushed past him.

"They're done," Elaine nodded at the others preparing to leave. Grant was at the register. Mara paused, and she looked at the attorney and then at her son.

"We better go," Turoff said as he slid from the booth.

~

Outside, they stood together in two groups, waiting for the light to change, sharing sideways glances, shuffling, cold stares, in mutual and impatient discomfort. Mara moved forward and touched the probation officer's shoulder.

"Can I take his hand?" Mara asked Sarah quietly. "As we cross the street?"

Sarah surprised, made room for her, and they stepped off the curb. The others parted ways for them; no one spoke.

"Come on, Jason. Watch the curb," Mara said gently as they stepped up onto the opposite curb. "You look so nice. I love your shorts and your new tenni's.

"Daddy got them for me," Jason replied. He looked at his shoes and smiled at Mara. "I like them too. John says they are 'cool.'"

"They are," Mara replied, the picture of self-control. They stepped up onto the plaza. The group had divided into two trails as they mounted the courthouse steps. At the top, Grant moved to the front, next to the boy. He reached around them and opened the tall courthouse door.

"After you, little man," he said, holding the door. The boy ducked under his arm and stepped inside, leading his mother still holding his hand. As Mara passed close to Grant, she hesitated. The chill of her stare startled him.

What was it he thought as she moved inside: *hatred? Maybe. But also fear and determination, somehow mixed. Well, that's what courts are for,* he shrugged, following her as the others entered. *And not much longer lady, it's all over today. You wrote your own ending.* Grant felt no sympathy for her or her predicament. *It sure is easier to be an attorney than one of the parties,* he thought.

The lobby rose over two floors. The second floor was accessed by either the elevator, set against the side wall in front of which they had all paused, or by two sets of curving stairs, one on each ascending wall. A landing at the top afforded a view of the floor below

"Can I push the buttons, mommy?" Jason asked. Grant noticed the elevator was down in the basement jail below.

"Sure, Jason. It's coming up in a second," Mara replied.

"Oh, boy. I like the buttons," the boy replied. "Especially the door ones."

Grant, sensing that Rob was uncomfortable, said, "Tell you what, the elevator won't hold us all anyway. Let's take the stairs," indicating a set of stairs opposite the elevator.

Sarah nodded to Grant that she would stay with the boy, and Grant crossed to the stairs and started up. Rob and John followed.

At the top of the stairs Grant paused, shifting his briefcase. He looked down at Mara and Jason with the others, waiting for the elevator.

"They must have some prisoners coming up, Rob. The elevator is still downstairs in the jail," he explained. "It may take a couple of minutes." Mara was speaking to her attorney in front of the elevator. Behind her, Dean and the women stood off to one side. Sarah had Jason by both hands, as they rocked in front of the elevator door. She looked up at Grant and met his eyes.

Grant turned away and with the others walked down the long hall. At the end, as he turned the corner, he looked back and saw Dean, Elaine, and the others, too far away to make them all out, exiting the elevator on their floor.

"They are behind us," Grant said to Rob. They entered their courtroom. The judge was on the bench, and Grant looked up at the clock behind him—1:25 P.M. They were not late.

"We had a short matter. A modification of a sentence," the judge said, looking up as Grant and Rob came forward to the counsel table. "I squeezed them in ahead of you, so we would not have to interrupt your case, Grant," the judge said.

"Thank you, Your Honor," Grant replied. "I thought we were on time." He stepped through the gate.

"You are," the jurist said, swiveling in his chair, side to side. "Well, we can resume. Are you all here? I don't see Mr. Turoff."

At the counsel table now, Grant replied, "They are right behind us, Judge. They waited for the elevator." He turned as he heard the courtroom door open.

"Come on in, Mr. Turoff," the Court directed. Turoff looked startled to see the jurist on the bench. "Relax," the judge said, "You're not late. *I'm* early."

"Yes, Your Honor," Turoff said as he moved towards his seat. He nodded to the others to take their seats as before in the first row. Dean, Elaine, and Penny filed in and sat.

"Your client?" the court inquired. "Mr. Turoff?"

"They stopped for the restroom, Your Honor. The little boy, Jason . . ." Turoff replied. "He is with Miss Evans, his *guard*, the probation officer."

The judge frowned at this reference to Sarah.

Grant settled in his chair, his file arranged before him. He heard the courtroom door open, and he casually swiveled around as the court looked up. Sarah had entered, alone. She stopped short of the railing,

"They are not here?" she asked surprised. "They must be right behind me," she turned as she approached the bench.

"Excuse me?" the court asked.

"I'm sorry, Your Honor," Sarah said looking down at Grant. "Are we late?"

"No, no, you are not late, Miss Redding," the court explained. "Where are the others?"

Grant looked at his client and at the faces of the others. Nothing. He turned to face Sarah. She had paused at the railing.

"They . . . We all stopped at the restroom, Your Honor, for Jason. He wanted to have his mother help him, and they went into one of the restrooms, the old single ones across from the elevator," she said. Looking at Turoff, she continued, "You were standing there. I told you . . ." she said. Turoff only looked at her. "Well, Your Honor, I took advantage of the opportunity myself, but I had to wait a minute." She stared at Turoff, "*You* were standing there . . ." but her voice was uncertain. Turoff's face was a blank.

"I just assumed that they had gone on ahead," she said. "That you, they, were ahead of me. They are not here, are they?" she asked.

"They are not, Miss Redding," the court answered her. "Mr. Turoff?"

"We just walked down the hall, Your Honor. I thought Miss Redding had things under control." Turoff had turned in his chair to face the jurist.

Sarah replied, "I'll check the restroom and the hall, Your Honor. Maybe they just had some difficulty," Sarah said. "They should be right here."

"Please do, Miss Redding," the judge replied. Sarah turned and left the court, the door swinging behind her.

Grant turned and studied the yellow sheets in front of him. Rob, seated next to him, rocked gently back and forth. No one spoke as the moments passed. Grant saw the judge look up as the door opened behind him.

"I can't find them," the strain in Sarah's voice reached out to Grant; it touched him. The hair rose on the back of his neck, and he felt his chest tighten. He turned.

Sarah was suddenly pale. "I checked the bathroom: theirs, and the one I used, to be sure. I even went downstairs. I came back up by the rear stairs, Your Honor, in case they might have gotten confused. I didn't see them anywhere."

Grant was standing, his chair pushed back. He studied the faces of Mara's friends. Nothing, at first. But as awareness arrived, he noticed the first traces of what would be a smirk on Dean's face, the mouth, the narrowing eyes. *Shit, he knows, the little bastard,* Grant thought.

Grant looked over at Rob. His was absolutely pale, ghostly, all color gone. His jaw was tight clenched, muscles jutting on either side.

"Your Honor," Grant turned.

"Mr. Turoff. Where is your client and where is the boy? Do you know, sir?" the judge's tone left no doubt of the urgency of his question.

Turoff rose, slowly, "Your Honor, I have no idea. She, Miss Redding, must be mistaken. We should check again. She has to be here, Your Honor," Turoff replied.

"I'll take that as a 'No,'" the judge said, his anger evident. "Bailiff, you accompany Miss Redding, Mr. Grant, and Mr. Turoff, and the four of you check the restrooms, the hallway, search the whole damn courthouse! I want them back here. Now! In handcuffs if necessary! Understand!?"

"Yes, Your Honor," the bailiff replied, heading for the door. He stopped and held the gate for Grant and Turoff. Sarah was already through the door.

Dean and the two women had risen to follow them, and the court stopped them, saying, "The three of you sit back down. One move and I will take you into custody for contempt. Not a move, understand? Until I say so!" They sat. "Go!" the judge waved at the attorneys.

Grant looked back at his client seated at the counsel table. He looked stunned in the certain growing knowledge that something had gone terribly wrong.

The courthouse was compact, and it took the four of them only a few minutes to check the court floor and its restrooms, then the lower floor and the parking lot. They looked into the other courtrooms, with hearings in progress, just in case. They checked the reception areas of the county offices. They walked around the entire building. No one spoke except once or twice to make a suggestion.

Grant, throughout, had that sick, sinking feeling of someone caught in a wreck, in slow motion, helpless, out of control. *What did I do to deserve this,* he thought, *scouring the court building for my client's missing child, in the middle of a custody case? He knew they were gone. Gone! The case he could not lose, lost! "Kidnapped" right out of the goddamn courthouse. My God!*

~

The judge was standing at the railing, speaking to Dean and the witnesses as Grant pushed open the courtroom door and entered, followed by Turoff,

Sarah, and the bailiff. Grant held the gate for Turoff as the two attorneys returned to the counsel table. Rob had been slumped down in a front-row seat, and he looked up as they entered. Grant's expression told him all that he needed to know. Sarah took a seat next to Rob.

"Gone, Your Honor. Not a clue," Grant announced, facing the jurist, who straightened and looked at Grant.

"I suspected as much," the judge said. "Be seated, gentlemen." The judge stepped up and walked behind his raised bench. He sat and leaned forward. He nodded to his reporter.

"Madam reporter, we are on the record. All counsel are present: Mr. Grant. Mr. Turoff. All parties, save one, are present. Ms. Evans and her son, Jason, the subject of this custody proceeding, are absent." He paused then slowly continued. "This morning at the conclusion of our session, we were in recess until 1:30 P.M. for lunch. At the break this morning all parties were told to return to this courtroom at 1:30 P.M. for further proceedings, including those under subpoena," he continued.

"The subpoenaed witnesses are here," indicating Dean and the others. "It is now 2:15 P.M. Ms. Evans is *not* here. She was present when we adjourned for lunch. I understand that her son, Jason, though not in the courtroom, was with the parties at lunch. Is that correct, gentlemen?"

"Yes, Your Honor," Grant and Turoff answered in unison. The judge nodded.

"The court has been advised that Ms. Evans and her son have not been seen since, after returning to this building from lunch, after they used the restroom. At the court's direction, a search was made of the building. They have not been found." He paused. "Accurate so far, gentlemen?"

"Yes, Your Honor," Grant stated. Turoff nodded his assent.

"All right, we shall proceed," the judge said. "When we recessed, Mr. Grant had concluded his examination of Ms. Evans pursuant to Evidence Code 776. Am I correct, Mr. Grant?"

"Yes, sir."

"Then, Mr. Turoff, you could have examined your client at that time or waited until your case in chief. But you cannot do that now."

"No, Your Honor," Turoff's voice a whisper. The court reporter leaned into his answer to be sure she heard it.

"Then, it is your turn Mr. Grant. Any further witnesses or evidence?"

"None, Your Honor, except to suggest to the court that Miss Evans's flight ought to constitute evidence against her, pursuant to Evidence Code . . ." Grant said.

"Taken, Mr. Grant. I do not need the citation," the judge interrupted. "Rest? Grant?"

"We rest, Your Honor. We are prepared to submit it," Grant said.

"Now, then, Mr. Turoff," turning to the attorney, the judge leaned back. "Let me inquire, whether you have any witnesses to call or evidence to present at this time. I realize that your client is not here. But that is her choice. This hearing goes on anyway. Clear?" the judge waited.

Turoff replied, "Well, yes, Your Honor. This, I mean, this is rather irregular. But, no, I have no witnesses to call," he turned and looked at his witnesses in the front row. "No, none. No evidence to offer," Turoff said, turning to face the court.

"Submitted, Mr. Turoff?" the court inquired.

"Submitted," Turoff replied, his voice forlorn.

"Good! That takes care of that. Now, sir, Mr. Turoff, do you know the present whereabouts of your client? Or her son?" the court asked.

Obviously startled by the directness of the question, Turoff fidgeted and said simply, "No, Your Honor."

"And, I presume that you had no knowledge or warning of her decision to absent herself from these proceedings this afternoon?"

Turoff hesitated, aware that the question might be objectionable, an invasion of the attorney-client privilege. The court sensed his ambivalence.

"None," he said quietly.

"All right," the judge now erect, his glance indicating to the reporter and clerk that they should note the ruling he was about to make. "I am going to suspend these proceedings. They are neither concluded, nor in recess. Based on what has transpired here today, I will take judicial notice of Miss Redding's thorough report and the testimony received." He paused. "Petitioner, the father, is awarded sole physical and legal custody of his son, Jason Evans, a.k.a., Jason Williams, forthwith. I direct that whenever and wherever he is found that he, the boy, is to be taken into custody by law enforcement and Child Protective Services, for return to his father. We will need your client's addresses, Mr. Grant," he paused. Grant nodded. The judge continued, "Miss Evans is to have no, I repeat no, visiting rights or right to custody, pending further proceedings of this court. Understood, gentlemen?" the court paused.

"Yes, Your Honor," both intoned. Grant stretched. Turoff sank deeper into his chair. "Further," the judge nodded to his reporter and the clerk, "I find Miss Evans to be in direct contempt of this court and its proceedings. I direct that a warrant for her arrest shall be issued forthwith. Bail will be set ... No. No bail. This is to be a 'no bail' warrant." His stare challenged Turoff to object. "In addition," the judge continued, "the bailiff will prepare a report to which will be attached a transcript of these proceedings, and that report, Frank," the judge looked over at his bailiff "is to be delivered today to the Office of the District Attorney with the recommendation of this court that a criminal complaint for kidnapping, child stealing, whatever the penal code provides, as warranted by these events, these facts, is to be issued, accompanied by an appropriate warrant for her arrest. All local and appropriate law enforcement agencies are to be notified, Frank," he hesitated, and then he continued.

"I want them back in my court: Miss Evans and the boy. No one is above the law. No one!" he said, and now leaning forward, he addressed Grant's client directly.

"Mr. Williams, I offer you my profound apologies, sir, for what has transpired here today. You came into this court, *my* court, into *my* county, at considerable trouble and expense on this, a matter of critical importance, fearing for the welfare of your son, as a father should. Seeking truth and justice. We, this court and this system, have let you down, and for that I apologize, sir. I will do everything in my power to correct this situation for you," he concluded, his forehead creased.

Rob looked at the judge; his face was colorless; he bore the weight of the entire proceeding. "Thank you for that, Your Honor. I know it is not your fault. I trust the system, but I am not sure that we will ever find my son, now ... I mean, this is the second time she has done this, and ..." he sobbed, his head sank.

The judge waited and when after a moment, Rob raised his head, the jurist met his gaze and continued, "Sir, there will be a day of reckoning for her, I assure you. Miss Evans cannot hide, not with a small child, not forever . . . hopefully, not for long. Wherever she goes, she will have to lie about who she is, for herself and the boy, and that is not easy to do, because, Mr. Williams," he paused, "the problem with a lie is that there is *so* much to remember. And she *will* make a mistake. You know, one lie begets another and another, and they pile up like so many stones, until one day they have become a sign post, pointing to the truth . . . and that truth will out . . . it will out." The judge's face and his tone ached with sympathy and compassion for this young father as he continued: "Justice is one of those truths, whether quickly dealt or long in coming." He paused, "I firmly believe," Mr. Williams, "in fate—in destiny—that what is right will somehow come to pass for you. I do not know when, or where, or how, but that destiny may suddenly one day land at your feet. And when it does, sir, it will be no coincidence. It is inevitable . . . justice is inevitable, and you should believe and trust in that. You will have your son, I know it," he concluded.

In all the years that Grant had known the judge, he had never seen him so impassioned and so convincing. *I hope so, too*, Grant thought.

"I hope you are right, Your Honor, at least on the 'not for long' part," Williams responded. "I hope we can find them. I don't know how long I can keep doing . . . this," he sighed.

"For your son, Mr. Williams, I think as long as it takes," he replied solemnly.

The judge looked over at Grant and nodded. Reaching down, he closed his file and said, "That does it, gentlemen. Oh, one last thought. Mr. . . . Dean, is it?" The judge focused his attention on Dean and the women in the first row of the seating area, none of whom had moved: ". . . and ladies. If you encounter Miss Evans or see the boy, or learn where they are, I admonish you that if you fail to report that to the authorities, then you are as guilty of her crimes as she. Do you understand that?" he paused. The three of them were standing now, ready to leave; they said nothing; their faces showed no expression. Turoff followed them out of the courtroom.

As Grant gathered his things, the judge, almost to the door of his chambers, stopped and bent over to speak to his bailiff. He looked back out at Grant and said, "Grant, see you in my chambers."

His briefcase closed, Grant paused, "Rob, you and John wait for me in the hall, I will be just a moment."

Grant followed the judge into his chambers. The judge ran his hand tenderly over a bronze statue of *The Thinker* sitting on a corner of his desk, before settling into his chair.

"Keeps me 'thinking,'" he nodded at the statue. "My son-in-law gave it to me when I was sworn in. It's not quite as worn down as St. Peter's foot," he smiled. "Nasty business, Grant," he said. "You have any inkling? Any clue? I thought not," when Grant shook his head. "Well," he continued, "our Miss Redding has learned something. God, after all the cases she has worked. I bet she is a wreck. Look, I called the sheriff and asked him to put out the word, from the court, from me, that they're to stay on this. But you know how this works, or how it doesn't. There are no resources to chase parental custody kidnaps. They always flee the court's jurisdiction. She's probably gone to San Francisco or north already. God knows. And the other counties don't have the manpower. Neither do the Feds . . . nor the FBI. It's a mess," the jurist sighed. "This does not happen in my courtroom. No, by God, it does not—not in all my years on this bench." He leaned forward, "Grant, whatever I can do, I promise you my full support. We'll find her someday. A woman and a boy, they can't hide for long."

"Judge, I hope you are right, for his sake, but what are the odds? If we don't catch her in the next day or so . . . Look what she did when she moved here. Williams got lucky when he found her the first time," Grant said.

"Do you know your philosophers, Will?" the judge asked. "It wasn't lucky that your client found her here, or that he picked you." He paused. "No, I think it was destined to be, and we've not heard the end of this, not yet." He leaned forward, his chin resting on both hands, elbows on his desk. "Centuries ago, Plutarch told us that coincidences occur all the time: seemingly improbable occurrences of fate . . . destiny . . . lives intersecting. We, you and I and Mr. Williams, *we*, have not seen the last of Miss Evans or of that boy, Grant, mark my words."

The judge stood, rounded his desk and held out his hand. "There is nothing you could have done, Will," the judge said. "Someday, hopefully soon, but someday, probably when you least expect it, you will call me, and you or your client will have found her, and he *will* have his son back. And justice will, as they say, 'out.' I truly believe, Will, that justice is inevitable. Someday we will have procedures that will allow us to actually enforce the law in these types of cases."

Grant shook his hand. As he reached the door, he looked back and said, "I hope so, Your Honor. I truly hope so."

By the time Grant returned to the courtroom, everyone had left, except Rob, waiting for him in the hallway. They exited the rear of the building. Neither spoke. Grant turned at the corner, and as they approached the sheriff's parking lot, he slowed at the driveway entrance. He stopped and looked inward toward the jail entrance they had used the other day. He looked at Rob. He felt the hair stand up the back of his neck.

"That's it," he said, gesturing. "Come on." He walked across and down into the sheriff's office. Rob followed. At the booking desk, the deputy, Sally, smiled. "Mr. Grant. How are you today?" she asked.

"I've been better, Sally. Look, about an hour or so ago, did a woman, twentyish, blonde with a small boy come in here?" nodding toward the elevator.

"Sure did, Mr. Grant. I was just going outside to put some report forms into the patrol vehicles, and the elevator door opened, right there. You know it happens once in a while, too often, actually," she replied. "People don't realize that the ground floor is the jail. They get confused when the door opens and they see where they are," she smiled.

"What happened?" Grant asked.

"The woman said that he, the boy, was pushing the buttons, and she asked if they could get out this way," Sally continued. "I said 'Sure,' and I led them to the parking lot," nodding to the door which Grant and Rob just entered.

Rob met Grant's look. "And what else, Sally? Where did they go?" Grant asked.

"They followed me outside, and I showed them the gate and the street. The little boy was sure cute," she said, "had on new shoes. I like it when parents dress their kids better than themselves. We don't see a lot of that down here," Sally smiled.

"Did you see where they went?" Grant asked.

"Gee. No, I didn't, Mr. Grant," Sally said. "The last I saw, she had him by the hand and the two of them walked out to the street. Is there a problem?"

"I'm afraid so, Sally. But it's nothing you did or didn't do. Thanks." Grant finished.

He turned, put one hand on Rob's shoulder, and the two men walked slowly out of the building.

~

Back at the office, once Grant briefed his staff, a pall settled over the office. His associate attorneys, one by one, stopped by to commiserate. No one had any idea what ought to be done.

Grant slumped in his chair, Rob sat across from him.

Finally Grant said, "Rob, I am at a loss. I have never heard of anything like this happening, and it sure as hell has never happened to me or to anyone I know. How we could have left her alone with him. Sarah . . . ? "

"What now?" Rob asked. Grant tilted forward, and he sat erect.

"Well, I have asked my secretary to get a copy of the court's minute order, the version prepared by the clerk, regarding custody. I'll have to make up the formal order that the judge just made. We send it to him for signature. We will do that today. It will be back in a day or so, tomorrow, if we walk it around," Grant explained. "But the arrest warrant, that is something entirely up to the court and to the system. The judge has already issued that, and it will go to the sheriff's office. It is probably there already. They'll put it out on the radio police net, and maybe we'll get lucky."

"How about the federal authorities? Will they get involved?" Rob asked.

Grant explained that until it was determined that she had taken the boy across state lines, that federal agencies had no jurisdiction, and no interest. He went on to explain that it was worse than that. The several local cities and sheriff's offices, each of them independent, were on different radio frequencies, and they were not linked up (*maybe someday,* he said), so any APB, an "all-points bulletin," would probably go out by telephone, followed by mail, though some of the local jurisdictions had begun to use fax machines. It was going to be damn tough to get the warrant information out locally, fast enough for anyone to spot her if she was on the move. Her head start might prove to be insurmountable. Unless they got lucky.

"But what do . . . ? What can *we* do?"

"Nothing, I'm afraid. Not a thing," Grant replied. "Except wait. We know they cleaned out the house already. They haven't been there for weeks."

"What about that place she said she was living, in San Francisco?"

"We can send an investigator, or you and I can go. But she's not going back to any place we know about," Grant replied. "She's on the run."

"*They* are on the run, you mean," he interrupted.

"Right," Grant corrected. "*They.*"

Rob stood. He extended his hand to Grant, "You did everything you could do, Will. It's not your fault. It's no one's. It just is what it is," he said.

Grant came around his desk. He took the man's hand. He put his other hand on his shoulder. "Go home. Here. Don't leave town, not yet. Let's give it a few days. I would hate to have you leave and then find them. If in a week or so we have nothing, no clue, then you can decide," he said. "Will that work for you?"

"I guess it has to. I have the house. Mom, my grandmother, will probably want to go home. But I can stick it out," he said. "I don't want to call it quits, until I know. If that happens. Know what I mean?" He sighed. "I'm not sure *what* I mean, Will."

"I understand. You will know," Grant replied, walking him to the door.

"I'll call you the minute I hear anything."

"Will, thanks for everything." He turned, and Grant watched him walk slowly down the hall, his head up, but his shoulders sagging.

Grant heard the office door close behind him, and he remained standing in the door to his office for a moment. Behind him, his intercom buzzed. "Mr. Grant? It's the sheriff's office!" Rene announced. Granted felt his body tense.

"Rene, get Rob back here!" he shouted. "He just left. Take the stairs if you have to, but get him back here, Rene! Now."

Grant spun and picked up his phone. "Grant," he answered.

"Mr. Grant, this is Deputy Arnold, at the Marin County Sheriff's Office."

"Right. This is Grant. What have you got?"

"Well, yes, sir," the deputy replied. "At 16:10 hours today, I received a call from Deputy Wade. He was off duty actually. But calling in on a land line . . ."

"For Christ's sake, Arnold, did they find her!?" Grant blurted. The officer's patient professionalism was maddening.

"No sir. Not *her*. But her car, a VW bus, is in the bank parking lot, near your office on B Street. Deputy Wade said to tell you he is sitting on it until you can get there," he continued.

Grant looked up as Rob entered his office. "They got the car!" Grant said. He sat on his desk, the phone still to his ear. "Go on . . ."

"Yes sir. Deputy Wade is sitting in his truck, a blue quarter-ton Ford. He said to tell you that he is in civies, sir," he continued.

"Thanks, Arnold. Tell him that we are on the way. Thanks!" He set the phone down.

"C'mon, Rob. Maybe we got a break after all." He led the startled, silent man to the elevator, but before he pushed the button, he moved to the nearby door. "Stairs. Let's take the stairs. Faster." In a few minutes they reached the lot. They slowed their pace as they neared. "God! There it is," Granted stopped, pointing. The car was parked in a diagonal spot, facing the ice cream store, opposite the rear entrance to the bank. It was empty. Grant moved to the car and ran his hand over the rear engine compartment: cold. Then he saw headlights blink once, at the rear of the lot. He gestured to Rob, and they walked quickly across to the waiting deputy. Wade got out of his vehicle as they approached. They stood to the driver's side, his truck between them and the VW.

"Mr. Grant. That was fast," he smiled.

"You knew it would be," Grant said, shaking hands. "This is Rob, the father, I don't think you have met, "Grant said.

"Deputy, my pleasure," Rob said. "We did meet, shared an elevator the other day, right?"

"Yes, sir, good to see you again," Wade said.

"Good work!" Rob added.

"Thank you, sir. I heard the call go out on the warrant, and I remembered right away that I had served her with the TRO, the restraining order. The bus was in front of the house the day I served her, and I recognized it right away today, when I drove here, into the bank lot," he nodded toward the car. "I'm off duty and was doing some banking. I saw it, and I drove past to be sure no one saw me. It was empty, and I've watched it ever since. No one has been near it," he nodded at the vehicle. It was three spaces from the sidewalk, parked in the direction of the exit to the lot. There were cars on either side of it, and while they watched, a woman emerged from the bank and got into one of the cars parked next to it. She backed out and exited the lot.

"Look, Wade, I know you can't stake this out, but we ought to," he looked at Rob. "It's all we have going for us. They . . . someone has to come and get it. Probably not Mara, but they may lead us to her. So, here is what we need to do . . ." Grant went on.

CHAPTER 7

FOR FIVE DAYS, ROB WATCHED the car, day and all night. After the first two nights of dozing in a rented car, he was stressed and exhausted. Grant arranged for his process server to take a shift to relieve him. During the day, Rob took meal and bathroom breaks at Issak's Grill, which was directly across the street from the parked car. He changed rental cars, make and model, every day. When he could, he parked in the lot, away from the VW; otherwise on the street.

The exit from the parking lot was a right turn onto a fronting one-way, two-lane street. At the end of the next block, a left turn led directly onto the freeway. The only other "escape" route was a right turn at the end of the short first block, onto another three-lane, one-way street, usually heavy with traffic, which led in the opposite direction and across town. Rob's plan was to follow the car, whichever route it took, regardless of who was driving, even Mara. Rob and Grant hoped that whoever was driving would lead them to the boy, and then they could contact the police.

Grant knew the manager of the bank lot where the VW had been parked, and the manager quickly accepted Grant's explanation and agreed to leave the VW bus alone, though there was a one-hour limit for customers. And so they watched. In the interim, there was no word from the sheriff's office; Grant checked daily. Rob had a certified copy of the court order giving him sole custody of Jason, and Grant had provided a list of the phone numbers to call for help: the sheriff's office, local police departments, Grant's office, depending on where and when they caught up with her.

At night Rob parked in the rear of the lot along with locals who lived in apartments nearby. There were always enough cars so that his would not stand out. Or, he parked in front of Issak's along with the few cars that remained on the street after the meters expired.

~

It was dark when Grant approached Rob's parked car. He stepped off the curb and knocked on the driver's side window. Rob leaned over and smiled as Grant got in.

"Company?" Grant said.

"Sure," he replied. "Anything new?"

"Not a word. I just checked with the desk sergeant. He had already called around to the other police stations to be sure that they are putting the APB out at each shift change," Grant said. "The sheriff is on it. As much as he can be. I think he's taking this personally since she 'escaped' from *his* courthouse, in the middle of a trial. Not something he wanted to have happen on his watch. But it's all we can do," Grant continued. "You know, the police are too stretched. Our best bet is that some officer on patrol will recognize the car, or that she will be stopped for a traffic violation. But that's a long shot."

Rob stretched his back, pulling on the steering wheel. "Well, I don't know. I'm not sure how much more of this I can take."

"Have you eaten?" Grant asked. "I could spell you."

"No, that's O.K., Issak is taking care of me. He always makes sure I have something when he closes."

"He makes a great Reuben," Grant smiled.

"Tell me about it," Rob grinned, pointing at his stomach. "I've had three or four of them since this started. Real heart stoppers," he laughed, "even with Rolaids. Issak is great. I use his restroom, and he watches for me," he nodded to the grill visible in the restaurant window. "You know, today, two people, a guy and woman, stopped and walked around the car. I thought I had something. They looked inside and left. I didn't recognize them."

"Who knows, maybe someone who works nearby and got curious, since it's been there so long."

"Probably."

They sat in silence. Grant studied the other man's face and after a moment said, "Rob, you started to tell me once how you met Mara, how this all happened."

Rob smiled, "How much time have you got?" he asked.

"I told Kay I'd be late, that I was checking on you. She understands," Grant replied. "So, go ahead."

"Well," Rob slouched in the seat, shifting his position. He stretched one leg over the hump in the middle of the car floor. "It's quite a story. Sometimes I ask myself 'Who painted me into *this* picture?'" He paused, looking out at the darkness.

"About a year before Jason was born, I went to a football game with a guy, Mike Gadney, I knew him slightly. A last-minute thing, he had an extra ticket . . ."

~

"We had met at Mike's home that morning. I left my car, and he drove to the game. After, we had a couple of beers at his frat house. It was already dark by the time we got back to pick up my car. Mike slowed for the turn into his driveway. The lighted house was visible through the trees. There were cars parked in front, and I could hear the music."

"My sister's having a party," Mike Gadney explained, "I forget the reason. Maybe just because it's Saturday." Mike's smile flashed in the dash lights on the darkened windshield. "Actually, it might've been a brunch, so they've got a head start," he laughed. "They're getting it on in the game room, sounds like," Mike offered, as he stopped the car behind the house.

The house was a mansion, the game room included a pool table, full bar, and huge TV set. As my eyes adjusted to the dim light and the cigarette smoke, I noticed couples dancing and others sprawled on sofas and chairs; some were seated at the bar. I didn't recognize anyone except Mike's sister, Nancy.

"There's someone I want you to meet," Nancy Gadney said, taking my arm. "I told her about you. She doesn't have a date." She led me to an oversize upholstered chair in the corner. "Tammy," she said, "This is Rob. I told you about him, remember?"

She was slouched in the oversize chair, her legs over one arm. She looked up at me, over the bottle of beer in her hand, like it was a gun sight, pointing it at me. She said nothing.

"Hi," I said, and I extended my hand. She shifted the beer to her other hand, and reached for mine and held it for a moment, and then with no

warning, she pulled me, hard. I caught myself as she swung her legs over the arm of the chair and stood. Blonde hair, worn down, she was almost my height.

"Here," Nancy smiled as I took the cold bottle that I didn't remember ordering. "See if you can catch up."

I looked at Tammy. She was clad neck to toe in a black fuzzy leotard. In the dim light it accentuated her figure—raised breasts, narrow waist, slender long legs. She was barefoot. She stepped around me, still holding my hand, and I turned with her, thinking that maybe she wanted to dance. My back now to the chair, she placed a finger on my chest, her eyes never left mine, and with one push, she dropped me backwards into the soft chair. I struggled to hang onto my beer. In one fluid motion, she settled into my lap, her legs across the arm of the chair. Her free hand went behind my neck, and she slowly pulled my head to hers and kissed me full on the mouth. I could feel her tongue searching for mine. Her perfume, clean, powdery. I couldn't breathe. She leaned back slightly, her eyes scanning mine, as she raised the bottle to her mouth. I watched her long throat as she swallowed. Lowering the bottle, she continued to stare at me. Then for the first time she spoke: "Hi," she smiled, her voice was soft, husky, challenging. I didn't know whether to . . . shit or go blind, or what.

Rob looked up as their car filled with the lights of a passing truck. He was silent for a moment. Grant felt that they both had been holding their breath.

Well, for the next couple of hours, maybe two, we sat in that chair, she on my lap. At one point, she put her head on my shoulder and went to sleep. I guess she passed out. I had only the one beer; she had maybe two more. I don't know what she had to drink before I got there, the others were having Singapore Slings, rum, different stuff. We just never got out of that chair. She made out with me a couple of times, in between beers. It was sort of weird. Here I had this beautiful, stacked, sexy girl, her warm soft body plopped in my lap, dressed in what looked and felt like PJs, who was obviously wasted, that I had never met . . . But she was, or had been, drunk enough. There was no way I could catch up with her, or the others for that matter. So, I was sort of stuck.

Finally, I had to go to the bathroom. I got her off my lap. On my way back, I stopped in the kitchen. Nancy said, "looks like she likes you."

"Right," I said, "but she's hammered."

"She did have something to drink," Nancy laughed. "That's for sure. But so what, just roll with it," she laughed again, her eyebrows raised.

"It's not working for me," I said. "I don't feel right about it."

"Well," Nancy said, "why don't you get her out of here? She is staying at the Malones, Lisa's parents, you know where that is?"

"Sure," I said.

So, that sounded like a plan, or I was just going to split, but I was curious what she might be like when she woke up, if you know what I mean. So, I went in and asked if she wanted to get out of there. She never answered, she just stood up, took my arm, and we went out to my car. I opened the door for her, and she said she had a suitcase with her stuff inside, so I went back in and found it. When I got back in the car, she was asleep against the door. I drove to a drive-in coffee place and got two black coffees and some donuts: chocolate old-fashioned, that ought to do it, I thought. I woke her up, and we sat there drinking the coffee for a while. She came around a little bit, nibbled on the donut, and then said she didn't feel very well, would I take her home. I knew where, so I drove. She fell asleep, and I had to grab her coffee. I pulled up in front of the house. The Malones lived in an expensive area. It's now maybe 11:30 P.M. The front door was lit, and I could see a few lights on downstairs. I figured I'd just get her to the front door, open it, or ring the bell, and beat it. I'd never been to the house; never met the parents, just their daughter. So, I stopped short of the house, next to this big privet hedge, and cut the lights. She was asleep, but she stirred when I shut off the engine.

"We're here, I'll give you a hand," I told her, and I got out of the car. As I walked behind the car I glanced at the house for a second, listening to hear if anybody was awake or might see us, because the last thing I wanted was to have to explain. I walked around to her side, and her door was already open up against the hedge and she was gone. I mean gone, like, not there. I thought maybe she had fallen back on the seat, but nothing. I looked up at the house. Maybe she had started to walk toward the door, but I couldn't see her and she wasn't on the ground. I thought what the hell. Then I heard a noise, kind of a moan, coming from, like, below me, way below. I couldn't see a thing. I

stepped through the hedge, the bank dropped off out of sight. It was dark, but I figured that she must have fallen down the hill. Shit, I thought, I can't leave her there. It was cold, but had not yet snowed. She moaned, "help me," and I was sure the house would light up. I said, "O.K., I am here."

I picked my way down the slope; it was like a canyon. She was a long way down. The ground was covered with dead leaves, and every step there was this loud crunch, I was sure they would hear me. I sort of slid down to her. She was on her back, in the leaves. She could have been really hurt, or unconscious. But she said she was O.K., so I sort of half carried and dragged her back up the hill. It seemed like it took forever. The whole time I'm looking at the house, expecting it to light up, like . . . And we were making so much noise . . . that I was certain they would hear us. I had to tell her to shut up a couple of times. I was not very nice. But I was pissed and scared. What if she was hurt."

"You're not making this up, right?" Grant interrupted. "This actually happened?"

"No, it really happened, trust me. This is a true story; *the* true story," he shifted in his seat. "It gets better, or worse, depending on your point of view," he said. "So . . . " he continued.

"There we are back up to the driveway. We had made so much noise I thought I was dead, that the people in the house would show up any second. But nothing. I leaned her against the rear of my car. "O.K.," I asked her, "are you hurt?" She mumbled no, that she was O.K., but that she did hurt in a few places, stickers and stuff. Then I saw the leotard. She had leaves stuck in her—everywhere. The whole place is full of those pin oaks, with pointed leaves. Her hair, front, back. She looked like some giant pin cushion. And every time she moved, the needles stuck her. If I was not so freaked, I would have laughed. I started to ease her toward the house, and she was now more alert, I guess, from the fall or the leaves. As we got closer to the front door, she stopped and told me she was staying in the pool house behind, down the drive, and she was not going in that front door. That was O.K. with me so long as we got past the door and the lighted area. And we did. I helped her, but she was walking O.K. and if I touched her, took her arm, the needles pricked her, so we sort of walked together. We got to this gate away from the house and I opened it and

she led me into this separate unit, a guest or pool house. There was a light on, a small table lamp, and I could see it was a bedroom or sitting room. I kind of stood there not sure what to do, and she headed for the bathroom and turned on the light. She was a mess, I mean her whole outfit was stuck with leaves, and in her hair. She started to cry, and I asked if there was anything I could do. She just looked at me in the mirror, crying. My suitcase, she said, it's in the car. Her shoulders slumped. 'I'll get it,' and I left, just glad to be out of there. I got back to the car; the same house lights were on. The driveway was sloped, so I just released the handbrake and coasted down to the gate, parked off to the side. I went back in and she . . ."

"Somebody walking through the lot," Rob pointed past Grant. Grant turned.

"Two. A guy and a woman," Grant replied.

Rob leaned forward to look around Grant. The two figures approached the car, and the man paused. He reached out and traced something with his finger in the dust on the engine compartment. They heard his soft laugh and her inaudible reply, then the two resumed walking, toward the main street and away.

"Happens a lot," Rob said. "Keeps me on my toes . . . you never know." He settled back. "Where was I?"

"You just got back to the room, after getting the suitcase." Grant said.

"Right . . ."

I went inside, and she was in the bathroom trying to pick out the leaves. She was still crying, and I felt sorry for her, almost guilty; but then I hadn't done anything. I put the suitcase down, and I walked to the open bathroom door.

"Can I help?"

"They stick, and they hurt," she said, "and I think I cut myself," looking at her shoulder. Our eyes met in the mirror. "Can you?" She asked.

I stepped forward and looked at her shoulder. I moved a torn flap of fabric. She winced. "Just a cut, a small one," I said. "But we ought to get a look at it. Little bit of blood. And it's torn, your outfit is. On your elbow here and on your leg."

"Oh, my God," she cried, and she began to sob.

"You have to get out of this thing, the leotard," I said.

"Yes, the damn leaves are killing me, I feel like a pin cushion."

"I know. Look, there's a robe here, why don't you get this off. I'll close the door, and then maybe we can get something on that cut, and you can see if there are any more."

"I can't get this off, my arm hurts too much." She watched me in the mirror, still.

"O.K., look, I'll turn off the light and help you pull this off, you can put the robe on."

"Do it," she said. I did.

It actually unzipped from the back, and we eased it off her sore shoulder and she stepped out of it, her back to me. In the darkened bathroom, I couldn't see much, actually nothing. She got the robe on and told me to turn on the light. I did. We examined her shoulder, and there was some antiseptic ointment stuff in the cabinet. I put it on the cut. We checked her back. Lot of little dents from the leaves. Then we noticed her knee was cut, deeper than the others. She started to cry again, and I said "why don't you sit down in there," meaning the room behind me. I turned the bathroom light off. She sat on the edge of the bed, and I got a Band-Aid and the ointment stuff, and I knelt down and fixed her up. I was afraid she would see my hands shaking when I couldn't tear that little strip off the Band-Aid. She never said anything, but when I finished and looked up, she was staring at me. "I don't even know your name," she said sadly. "Rob," I told her, and I stood up. She held out her hand. I took it.

"We got the leaves anyway," I said. I couldn't think of anything else to say. "Except for your hair." She touched her hair. "Oh." I leaned toward her to get some of the bigger pieces. "There's a brush in my purse." I got it and she started to brush it herself, but her arm and shoulder hurt. I took the brush and sat on the bed next to her, she turned away, and I slowly brushed her hair. I had never done anything like that before. I don't have a sister. But I did it. Slowly, uncertain, gently, so I would not pull her hair. I brushed it, picking out the twigs and pieces of leaves. I lifted her hair off her neck. I held her hair in my hand, it spilled over onto my arm. I ran the brush slowly through her hair down to my hand, over my arm and down, again, again, again. My hand rested on her warm neck, next to a small S-shaped scar, hidden by her hair.

She sighed, relaxed. "Feel better?" She nodded. I figured this was probably a good way to calm her down, so I took my time. "I think I'm done here."

She turned and ran her hand through her hair. It was this blonde terrific hair, smooth. I had never brushed a girl's—a woman's—hair before. "Do the front," she said softly, turning to face me. I worked on the front, one hand on top of her head, pushing her hair toward the side, the back, holding it from falling over her face, the side of my hand brushing her cheek, warm, soft. I brushed and I picked out the leaves, pieces of them, stuff, pushing the hair with the brush. Long strokes. She watched me, and I watched her watching me. Her face in the shadow of the table lamp behind me, and then illuminated, as I moved back and forth in the light. She was really beautiful. I looked into her eyes, and my mouth felt dry, but I was perspiring. I realized that I was aroused, and it sort of surprised me. You know, the drama, the first aid. She sensed it, I guess. She smiled, maybe for the first time, just at the corners of her mouth and in her eyes. She took my hand, the one with the brush, and lowered it, and she took the brush from me, let it drop to the floor. I looked down at it on the floor, it wobbled, back and forth. She put my hand inside her robe, onto her breast. I stopped breathing. I looked at her. She was soft, warm, the tears had stopped, her hair fell back over part of her face, and with my other hand I pushed it back behind her ear. I leaned forward, and I knew it was O.K. to kiss her as she leaned back. I did, and she kissed me and then she pushed my face down gently into her open robe, to her breasts.

"... and I was done."

"What do you mean 'done'?" Grant surprised himself. "Done. What?"

"I had never done anything like this ... I didn't have much experience in this stuff. Some backseat stuff, you know. But this was different, unexpected, almost on autopilot once it, we, started. I don't even remember taking off my clothes. It sort of took on a life of its own."

After a moment, Grant said, softly, "No rubber? No condom, right?"

"Right, Will. That's right."

~

The next afternoon, while Grant waited to cross at the light, he scanned the near and far sides of the street. He crossed and stepped up onto the curb. Since the court hearing, he could not stop looking for Mara: on the street, driving, everywhere. Twice he had made U-turns, thinking he had seen her pass. Rob was parked in front of Issak's, in the *car du jour:* today, a green, aged pickup. He rapped on the fender, and Rob smiled in the side mirror.

"Want a bite?" Grant asked, glancing across the street; the VW bus was there.

"Sure, a burger, medium rare, hold the pickle," Rob replied softly. "And *no* grilled onions."

Grant nodded, and he stepped into the usual noon-hour buzz of the popular restaurant.

"Issak," Grant said, taking a stool near the window, directly behind the busy cook. "How's it going?"

"Nothing new with your buddy. He's still out there. So's the car." He pointed a greasy spatula at the VW bus.

"I understand he's recruited you as a lookout when he is . . . indisposed," Grant grinned.

"A nice kid that one. I'm happy to help," the older man replied. He wiped his sweaty forehead with the back of one hand, which he then wiped on his stained apron. "Sad times when a father is kept from his son. Sad times," Issak murmured. "What you guys want? Something to eat? A Reuben maybe?" He knew better.

"No, not today. We'll take two Issak burgers. Hold the—" Grant stopped. The bus was slowly backing up.

"It's moving! My God, the car is moving," Grant said, as he looked out at Rob. He slid off the stool and out the door, eyes locked on the slowly moving bus. At the car he shouted, "Move over! I know the streets better than you!" He slid behind the wheel as Rob quickly moved; Grant slammed the door. Rob had the engine going.

"He killed it," Rob said and they watched as the driver of the bus leaned forward, struggling to keep the engine revved. Grant eased the pickup back, so that they could quickly turn out of their parking space, between two parked cars. They waited. Several cars passed, momentarily blocking their view.

Grant said, "All right, Rob, once again, here is what can happen. Once he exits the lot, he can go down the short block and then take a right on 3rd Street, at the corner, and head west," Grant nodded, "or he can go straight down B Street here in front of us, and at the end of the next block, take a left and he's headed for the freeway, only four blocks away. Either way he has the traffic lights to deal with and we have to make them, too."

"Right, like we discussed," Rob replied, staring at the vehicle. "I can't see who it is. What do you—? He's got it going again! Here he comes."

The VW eased back out of the space, then crawled forward toward the driveway and paused, waiting for a break in the midday traffic.

"I can't see who is driving, but it looks like a guy," Rob repeated.

Grant gently revved the engine of the idling truck, his foot poised on the clutch. He stole a glance at the gas gauge—three-quarters full.

"My money's on Dean," Grant replied. "O.K. Here he comes. Remember, we just follow him."

The VW had crossed the sidewalk when suddenly their view of the bus was gone, totally blocked, as if it had suddenly vanished. A delivery truck had pulled up next to their pickup, and double-parked, trapping them in their parking space. They could not move, and now all they could see was the delivery truck's door—*Tamalpais Produce . . . Fresh . . .* —parked so close to them that Rob could not open his passenger's side door. Instantly Grant leapt from the pickup and raced to the front of their vehicle. He saw the VW make a right turn, now out in the street, moving slowly away from them, behind several slow-moving cars. Grant turned back and the produce truck driver was at the rear of his truck, pulling out a large cardboard box of lettuce.

Grant screamed, "Hey! We need to get out of here! Now!"

The man looked up, the box on his shoulder, and as he stepped up to the curb, he took his measure of the lawyer: "Relax buddy, I'll only be a minute," he crossed the sidewalk and disappeared down an alley.

Desperate, Grant turned to look at the VW. It was now halfway down the street, stopped at the light in the curb lane, right turn signal blinking.

"He's going right. Move this truck, somehow," he shouted at Rob, and he stepped out into the street. He dodged two cars and ran toward the lot. As he crossed the driveway, he glanced down the street to his left. The light was green, the VW had moved to the corner and was out of sight, blocked by the buildings. Grant raced across the open lot and angled left toward the street, and as he ran between the parked cars, he caught sight of the bus moving slowly in the traffic. *I'll never catch it, and if I do, then what?* he thought, heart pounding. Grant stopped when he reached the sidewalk on the far side of the lot. The VW was in the center lane of the three-lane street, stopped for a red light, first in line in the waiting traffic. Grant heard a screech of tires, and he looked to his left to see the produce truck careen around the corner, heading toward him, crates and boxes spilling from the open rear door. Rob braked sharply in front of him. Grant jumped in the passenger side.

"There! Right there! Just ahead," Grant pointed, slightly ahead and one lane to the left of them.

"I see him. Think he saw us? Or you?" Rob asked.

"I don't know. He hasn't looked this way, and we didn't make eye contact, at least not that I saw. He's heading west. We can slip in behind him, behind these cars, once the light changes," Grant said, looking to the rear. "You O.K.?"

"Oh, sure, fine. I just added car, make that *truck*, theft to my resume," he said, teeth clenched, staring at the VW.

"Light's going to change," Grant said, "Here we go."

The cars in front of them began to move, and Rob eased out the clutch. The VW had not moved.

"We don't want to pass him," Grant cautioned.

They paused. The car behind them braked sharply, a horn blasted. Traffic was stopped behind the bus, and Rob and Grant were only two cars behind it. More horns. Rob eased forward. He did not want to pass the VW. Suddenly, the bus made a violent lurch and turned hard left, across the moving traffic behind it and to its left. Tires screeched, horns blared. Now the VW was heading downhill on the street to their left, going the wrong way on a one-way street and away from them.

"Shit, he's going the wrong way down that street!" Rob shouted. He glanced to his left and to his rear. "I can't get over there!" The two lanes of cars to their left, no longer held up by the stopped VW, were filled with cars, moving quickly through the intersection.

"He's screwed us, if he doesn't get into a head-on. Go, straight!" Grant shouted and pointed ahead. As they crossed the intersection, Grant looked down the street the VW had taken. He saw the rear of the vehicle as it turned left, headed the opposite way now, away from them, toward the freeway, out of town.

"We have to circle back. Take the next left, here," Grant directed. Rob changed lanes and made the turn at the corner. "Now left, at the light. Go! It's green, almost," as they made the turn and cut in front of an oncoming car, causing it to brake wildly and skid into another lane.

"Green ahead of us!" Grant urged. "We're going the same way as he is now," he said. "He's headed out of town. Only three more blocks to the on-ramp."

"I don't see him," Rob said. "Do you?"

"No. He's got a pretty good head start. Our only hope is to see if we can spot or catch him on the freeway. We need to get lucky," he glanced at the other man.

They made or ran the remaining lights. Grant did not want to look back. At least he had not heard a crash.

"Bear right, up the ramp," Grant indicated, and Rob aimed the truck toward the freeway.

They entered the freeway, two on-ramp lanes merged into four freeway lanes. An interstate, the highway was divided from the northbound lanes by two sets of guardrails.

"Oh, oh. Traffic's slow ahead," Grant warned, the strain showing in his voice.

"I see it," Rob replied as he slowed for the vehicles stopped in front of them.

Grant looked over at Rob's taut face and reddened brow. "We have to make a decision here, Rob, if we don't see him. Whether to stay right and take the off-ramp at the next exit, or to stay on this highway and see if we catch up." The pickup eased forward, the traffic all but stopped in their lane. "If we take that exit ramp, it is a fly-over, we are going to the East Bay and we will have a tough time spotting him. But if he goes south and stays on the freeway we have a better chance to see him, even if he exits somewhere." Grant paused, looking at the traffic. "I don't think he would risk putting himself in that mess. Get over to the left, the fast lane, we're going south."

Rob eased the pickup over one lane, then another, toward the guardrail, into the line of creeping cars and trucks.

"Maybe he got into a wreck," Rob sighed, looking at Grant.

"No such luck," Grant replied.

Ahead they could see that an eighteen-wheeler had pulled to the far right, blocking two of the lanes. The driver was out, directing traffic. All the lanes were backing up now. They came to a crawl. Rob eased into the innermost lane, drawing an angry horn blast from the car behind. He could feel the wind from the unimpeded oncoming traffic flowing the other way, just across the narrow divider barriers.

"Oh, man, we are screwed now. We will never find him," Rob groaned.

As they approached the overpass, which they had elected not to take, they could see vehicles entering the northbound lanes coming toward them, moving slowly to merge into the traffic flow opposite them. And then they saw it coming.

"Oh, no!" Rob shouted. "There he is! Here he comes. Look!"

Now, Grant saw the bus, changing lanes, coming toward them on the other side of the dividers, gathering speed. As it approached, separated from them only by the guardrails, so close they heard the distinctive VW horn. Dean was clearly visible now, his left arm extended out the window, his fist clenched, and as he passed only a few feet away, on the other side of the barrier, he opened that fist in the universal one-finger salute. And he was gone.

After they exited the freeway, they stopped at the first place that had a telephone. They called the sheriff's office and reported the incident. Grant explained Dean's route. The sheriff's office promised to put it out on the radio, but they had heard nothing. Grant called the produce company and made arrangements to return their truck, explaining what had happened.

~

The following afternoon, in the backyard of Rob's rented house, Grant took a long pull on his beer and looked at Rob, sitting across from him.

"I took care of the produce truck. They were not very happy, but I paid for the stuff that fell out, and Issak knew the owners of the produce company and somehow convinced them that it was their fault for double parking and blocking us. I couldn't stay at the office. Can't concentrate," Grant said. "I kept seeing that SOB flipping us off. God, I can't stand that guy. If it had been Phil or one of the women . . . Anybody, but him," he said.

"Yeah," Rob replied. "But what gets me is that it was twice. They got away twice."

"They're not that smart," Grant offered. "Not to grab that car in broad daylight. But it worked. And that U-turn move off the freeway, that *was* classic."

"They're damned lucky is all," Rob said. "We just came up empty on luck. So, the question is, now what?"

"Well, I guess that depends on you and your schedule," Grant answered. "There is no telling what might happen," he said. "Like we discussed when she took off from the courthouse, you can stay and wait or you can go home, but they might nab her the next day."

"Yeah, but when we had the car covered, it seemed like we might have a shot," Rob replied. "Now? I don't know. We have nothing to go on." He stood and walked around the patio, gazing out at the open space behind.

"They have the APB out on the car, and it's not like it is your average black sedan." Grant offered, leaning forward, elbows on his knees. He sipped his beer. "It won't hide, Rob. Not that car and that color. Unless they dump it."

"I just don't know," Rob turned to face Grant. Frustration lined his face. "I can't do this forever, Grant. I don't know."

"Well," Grant leaned back, "you don't have to be here. If they find her and the boy, they will take her into custody and place the boy with Child Protective Services temporarily, or a foster home, until you can get back here," he said. "And they know to call me."

"Oh, that's great. Foster home or something like it! Strangers! My God, what is all this doing to my son?" he said.

"I know," Grant replied. "But what else is there? Stay here? But that won't find them. Or go home and get on with your life, and hope that they turn up." Grant's tone indicated his own indecision "Look. This is not some common criminal on the run, Rob, who can hide out with other bad guys," he paused. He walked out onto the lawn, collecting his thoughts. He turned and stated methodically, "There are two of them, a woman and a young boy—a *child*. She can only do so much explaining the child: his name, his birthplace. She has to have a social security number, someday soon a job." He continued, "The boy will have to be looked after, go to school, people ask questions, all sorts of questions. Even of people with nothing to hide."

Rob turned his hands on his hips, "And she has the whole damn country to hide in, Will. And a head start to … we don't know where!" he shouted.

"Christ, Grant, I appreciate your thoughts, but this is over! Over! I am never going to see Jason again. Never!" His voice broke.

Grant put his arm around the man. His throat was dry.

"Rob, like the judge said, you have to believe this. You absolutely have to. Someday, somehow, she will slip up, or we, you, will get lucky," Grant's voice was soft but firm, certain. "She's not going to be able to hide forever. She can't. She'll get a speeding ticket, get in a wreck, get a job; the boy will get sick, will need a doctor, will be at school . . . something will happen, when or where you least expect it, I just know—I feel—it. (*Grant recalled the judge's remarks about destiny.*) That day will come, and then you are getting your boy back. I know it, and for your sanity you have to believe that." He stepped away.

"Grant, I really appreciate all you have done. I could not have asked for a better lawyer," Rob replied, "but—"

"Look," Grant interrupted him. "Every time I see a curly-haired boy in front of me on the street, in a passing car, until we find him, I will hurry ahead, stop, or turn around to see if it's him. I promise you."

"I know," Rob continued. "But I have to get off this roller coaster and get on with my life. Whatever, or wherever, they are." He ran his hand through his hair. "That's it. I'm going home, tomorrow or the next day, as soon as I can. Maybe I'll drive across country," he said.

They walked back into the house to the front door. Outside, Grant admired the neat houses with their manicured lawns. A perfect place to raise a kid he thought. He turned, and he shook Rob's outstretched hand. "Look, the balance of my bill, for all this, forget it," Grant smiled. "A going-away present."

Rob's eyes narrowed, his face tense, "Thanks, Grant. I truly appreciate the offer. But I want a bill for everything you have done—for everything. This is your livelihood, and you and your office have been great," he said. "Besides, I may need you again someday, I hope. Soon."

Grant did not reply. He started down the path toward his car.

"Grant!" Rob's tone stopped him. Grant looked back. "Not for the stake out! Or for the car chase! O.K.?" Rob was smiling broadly.

"Or your life story," Grant laughed and turned to his car. Inside the house, they both heard the phone ring, Grant paused. "Probably Angela," Rob said.

"I called her about giving up the house. See ya, Will. I'll call before I leave." He turned and went back inside.

Grant stepped over the grass strip, off the curb, opened his car door, and he slid behind the wheel. He leaned back against the headrest for a moment, shook his head, straightened, and put his key into the ignition. He heard the house door slam, and he looked over. Rob was almost to the car, and in the next second he yanked open the door. Grant knew, without Rob saying a word.

"Where?" Grant shouted, starting the engine.

"Fairfax!" Rob was out of breath. "They found the car in a garage in Fairfax!"

"Not Jason?"

"Just the car, so far."

Grant glanced over his shoulder, made a U-turn, and the tires squealed as he accelerated away.

~

In a few moments, they were speeding down the parkway. Rob explained that the sheriff's office had called for Grant to report that they had found the VW within the hour, in Dick's Garage in Fairfax, the same shop to which the car had been towed months before, leading Rob to Mara and his son. The garage owner had denied any knowledge of the whereabouts of the woman or the boy.

A rusted military Quonset hut, the garage was located one block off the main road. They pulled up in front, and Grant parked to the side of the structure. Axles, radiators, transmissions, many deep in the uncut weeds, lined the side yard. A car frame, parts of a boat trailer, leaned against the outside wall. They got out of the car and walked around to the front. The VW bus was parked at an angle, halfway back inside the dimly lit building. The floor was grease stained and hardened by years of wear; the air heavy with oil and solvent odors. The shop was packed with parts of various vehicles and construction equipment, hardly room to walk down a narrow center aisle.

At the rear of the shop, a man was hunched over, working an acetylene torch. Hood down, concentrating, he had not seen them enter. Grant moved to the front of the man, avoiding looking at the torch and the cascading sparks. Just as he was trying to decide how to get his attention, the man looked up. The torch popped as he killed the gas; he raised his hood and looked at Grant.

"Mr. Lynch?" Grant asked.

"Yeah," the man replied, as he set the torch down and slowly straightened up.

"I'm Will Grant, and this is my client," Grant said. "We would like to ask you about that VW bus," Grant pointed.

"You want to buy it?"

"No, not really," Grant said softly, sensing hostility.

"Then I told the cops everything I knew. Ask them. I'm busy," head back defiant. "I didn't cheat nobody. I paid fair price for that heap, and I don't have no time for explaining it to everybody who comes along." He bent down and picked up the torch, the igniter in his other hand.

"Hang on," Grant said. "We just want to know about the woman who brought it in. It was a woman, right?"

"Right. In a big hurry," he replied.

"Ok. Well, we're interested in finding her. We think she has her son with her, and this is the boy's father. She has sort of kidnapped the boy," Grant said.

"How in the hell do you kidnap your own kid?" he snorted.

"It is a long story, complicated. We just want to know if you can describe her. Did she leave her name?" Grant continued.

"Sure, she gave me the pink to the car. She signed off on it," he said. "I did it all legal. I told the cops, they were satisfied," he said. "I paid too much for it probably, gave her $300 was what she wanted."

"Did she have my son, a boy with her?" Rob asked.

"Sure. Cute kid. Dark hair, like hers" he replied.

Grant looked at Rob. "Not a blonde? Didn't she have blonde hair?"

The man smiled at them. "Do I look like I'm fuckin' blind?" He held up the torch and the igniter, one in each hand. "Dark hair, both of them. Must have the wrong ones, huh?" He started to turn away. "I'm busy, got to get that frame done today."

"Dyed her hair," Grant said to Rob, whose shoulders drooped at this complication.

Grant stopped the man, "Did she say where they were going? How did they leave?" Grant pressed.

"I just gave her the cash, and she and boy walked out of here. That's it," he said. "I followed them up front," indicating, ". . . last I saw they were walkin' down the road, headed that way," nodding back toward the downtown. "Didn't say nothin', and I didn't ask."

"When? When was this?" Grant asked.

"Couple of hours ago, this morning. Before lunch," he answered.

Grant glanced at his watch: 3:10 P.M. He looked at Rob. Rob backed up and walked away, his fists clenched, opening, closing.

Grant asked for and was given the pink slip to the VW bus. It was Mara's name, and she had signed off. No address was filled in the blank for the seller. The garage man allowed them to check the inside of the car; they found nothing. They thanked him, and he followed them as they left the building.

Suddenly Rob turned back to the man. "You knew her and the car, didn't you?" he asked, his eyes meeting the garage man's.

"Wha'dda ya mean," he replied.

"You *know* what I mean," Rob replied, his eyes challenging. "You towed that car a couple of months ago. Towed it here, and that woman, the blonde, she picked it up before you could lien sale it!"

"Well, so . . . ?" he replied.

"So," Rob moved closer, "If you know where she went, or if she comes back, I want to know. You got that?" he demanded. Grant was startled at the rage in Rob's voice.

"I don't know nothin', I paid her fair," he snarled.

"Give him one of your cards, Grant," Rob snorted. Grant handed one to him. "You call him, my attorney, if you learn anything. Got it?" Rob demanded. "She has my son, and I want him back!" Rob nodding, turned away. "Let's go, Grant!"

As he neared Grant's car, Rob turned and looked up at the road, imagining the way they had gone. He paused for a long moment. His eyes met Grant's across the car roof, then he lowered his head and got into the car. Grant backed out, and they pulled away from the shop. Rob, silent, stared ahead at the traffic as they merged onto the roadway.

In a few moments, they were in the central part of the town, and Grant slowed for pedestrians crossing the boulevard. Rob looked to his right, across the wide median that separated the roadway from the main shopping street of the small town, lined with stores: a bakery, a café, a bus stop, and a barber shop. Everyone was so young; they looked so relaxed, carefree. He was exhausted. Grant picked up speed, and Rob watched a Greyhound bus, its distinctive logo, a hound in full racing stride, pull out and move into the row of traffic behind them. The blue destination placard read "Downtown S.F. 7th Street."

He turned to Grant and sighed. "It's over Grant, over. I can't do this anymore."

Grant eased into the traffic. He glanced in his rearview mirror at the cars and the bus behind.

"Like the judge said, Rob, someday . . . someday. You never know. I don't think this is over, not yet. For now, for the short run maybe, but . . ."

"Oh, I know what he said, Grant, I appreciate it—his concern. But this is my life, not his, and I have to make some decisions. I have never been much for that karma or fate stuff. It has never worked for me. As for justice, truth, that stuff, it sure isn't helping me now."

Grant looked at him. "I know, Rob, but someday . . . someday, I just feel it, and you should never give up hope. Stranger things have happened to you. This whole case has been strange. I just think, well, maybe 'feel' is a better word, that this is not the end of it. Based on what has happened so far, it is sort of inevitable, maybe. At least I hope so."

Rob met his glance, nodded, and then shrugged.

Grant checked his rearview mirror. The bus was gone.

~

At 8:00 P.M. the lobby of the 7th Street bus depot in downtown San Francisco, two blocks off Market Street, was almost empty, the commute hour long over. From her seat at the rear of the station, behind a stained-tile pillar, Mara could watch the entrance, and she was near the rear door that led outside to the bus loading area.

Earlier, the wrinkled, tired ticket agent had asked through foul smoke breath, "Where to, young lady?"

"Tucson, please," Mara replied. "Two tickets," she pointed down to the boy at her side.

"How old is he?" rising from her steel stool to look down at the boy. "'Cuz if he's under four, he rides for free, in his own seat. He looks like three and a half to me," her knowing smile showing stained, split teeth.

"Yes, he's three."

"You got two choices, honey. Express via the freeway, nonstop, leaves . . .," looking at a chart overhead, ". . . 5:00 A.M. tomorrow morning. Or-r-r, the sl-o-o-w-w-w boat, local, with stops in the valley, at 9:00 P.M., tonight. That's a long haul for the little guy, but it's lots cheaper."

Mara purchased a one-way ticket for the 9:00 P.M. bus and waited.

An assortment of bums, travelers, street people, and the commuter rush had come and gone. No one paid her any attention. Jason slept on two cracked plastic seats next to her, his feet extending through the chrome arms of one seat onto the other. Tufts of filthy stuffing bled from the cushions; the entire depot redolent of time, bodies, stale food; reeking of despair, she thought. The floor was alligatored with dirt-filled cracks, chips, and missing pieces. She could not imagine ever picking up anything off the floor. The lighting fixtures were missing half the light bulbs. Even the tiled walls were grimy. The bathrooms were indescribable and smelled worse.

Earlier that day after they had sold the car, they walked the several blocks into town, using the side streets to avoid the heavier trafficked and open boulevard. In town, they had lingered in one of the coffee shops, seated to the rear, facing the street entrance. Mara knew that the Greyhound bus was the only public transportation, and the next bus to the City was at 3:30 P.M. that afternoon. So, she had waited, hiding behind a newspaper. Many young people hung out, some all day long, in and around the coffee shop, and so long as she bought a roll or a sandwich and refilled her coffee, the lone waitress paid no attention.

She had watched as the Greyhound bus pulled up to the stop outside the coffee shop, and when she was sure that everyone had gotten off, she timed it so that she and Jason would simply walk out of the restaurant and step onto the bus. Just as she had set foot on the sidewalk, she almost bumped into a police officer who was walking down the street, a young, scruffy, complaining juvenile in tow. The policeman had looked right at Mara without any recognition.

Without hesitating, she stepped around the officer and onto the bus. She purchased a ticket to San Francisco from the driver, confirming that this bus was headed to the City. When she took her seat, Jason beside her, she felt as if everyone was looking at her, and she knew that was stupid. But she could not shake the feeling. It gave her a chill, and she held Jason next to her as she hunched down in the seat. She saw their reflection in the bus window: her dark hair worn up and pulled back, his a crew cut, the long curls gone. She watched her smile slowly develop in the reflective glass.

The bus door hissed its closure, and they pulled away into a line of slow-moving traffic. She glanced up the aisle at the long row of cars ahead of the bus. She put her head back, took a deep breath, and dropped off to sleep. One hour and eighteen minutes later, the bus ended its run at the 7th Street depot in the heart of the City, four minutes late.

She had gone immediately inside the terminal, so that Jason could use the restroom, the ladies side. The smell made her gag. Back in the lobby, she had scanned the "Scheduled Departures/Destinations" from a large board affixed to one wall, which she could easily study from the seat she had selected, off to one side, away from the entrance. She kept telling herself that in this city of thousands of people, the law had more important things to do than look for her and Jason, but ... The next out of town bus was north to Portland, at 5:40 P.M., and another went south to Los Angeles at 7:00 P.M. Other cities were listed, but the departure times read: "See Ticket Agent." Not north, she thought. So, she waited and watched. Hungry, Jason moaned and they went next door to a coffee shop. She took a bus schedule with her and studied it while Jason ate pancakes with whipped cream. She had no luggage, and her only money was from the car sale. Arizona, she had decided. It will be warm and far enough away. They returned to the terminal and bought her ticket.

She fingered the bus ticket in her jacket and wondered: Were they looking for her? Sure. But how? Do they check bus stations?

"9:00 P.M. Number 808 to Tucson, local run, now boarding," the station agent's voice cracked, "Gate 5."

Mara looked up. The agent had the microphone in her hand, smoke trailing from her nose, and she was nodding Mara toward the rear door. Mara stood and pulled Jason from his seats.

"Come on, Jace, We're going. Come on, wake up."

She helped him to his feet. The agent was watching her, and Mara saw her shake her head. *She will remember me, she thought. She knows.*

Jason, now on his feet, took her hand, and she went outside to the buses. The cool night air, a trace of fog in the overhead lights, she counted the bus ramps overhead to number five. All the spaces were full, and passengers bumped past them. She stepped off the curb over to their bus. The driver took her ticket. He eyed her, she thought, and she kept her head down. He ran his hand against the grain of Jason's crew cut hair.

"Goin' all the way?" he asked. His words suggested more than her destination, Mara thought. She nodded as she stepped up and aboard.

"Sit up front, lady. The boy can watch the lights and the dials. Kids like that, keeps 'em from getting bored," she heard him over her shoulder.

She reached the aisle. The bus was only half full. Most of the passengers were seated toward the front in aisle seats. She headed to the rear and took a seat on the driver's side, guiding Jason to the inside seat. As soon as she sat down, she was exhausted, and she trembled. Jason curled up and was asleep almost immediately, his head against the window. She found a pillow in the chair back and arranged it behind his head, against the cold glass. She put her head back, closed her eyes. She heard the door close and latch.

"O.K., people," the driver studied his passengers in his oversize rearview mirror. "This is trip 808. It ends in Tucson via the central valley with stops along the way, lots of them," he paused for effect. "This bus comes equipped with a restroom in the rear; it is non-operational." Mara heard at least one loud sigh. "We will be stopping at a few bus stations, and several restaurants where there are no bus stations. At those stops, those who need to can use the facilities if they hurry. We will not wait for anyone, and I will announce the departure time on arrival. We will stop at . . ." Mara tuned him out. ". . . so lay back and enjoy the ride," he concluded. Mara was certain that he was staring at her in the mirror. She turned away. The bus jerked rearward as it backed out, and in a few moments they entered the street traffic.

She had no plan. But she was in charge. Not the court, not that damn judge, not her stupid attorney, not that bitch of a probation officer. God, how she hated her. No one is going to tell me what to do. No one, she thought. Wherever this damn bus takes us, and whatever happens when I get there, anywhere, I will decide. No plan, but things will work out. I got this far, and out of that courtroom, and I am free. Her actions had become her plan. And they would do. She was asleep before the bus turned onto the Bay Bridge headed away.

~

Instinctively Mara felt, she *knew,* something had changed. And that change had awakened her. She sat upright, alert, and she noticed that the bus was stopped; the hypnotic drone of the engine silenced. She reached out for Jace, but his head was in her lap, safe. She heard the whoosh as the door opened, and passengers were now standing, muttering, impatient, stiffly shuffling forward and exiting the bus. The aisle began to clear.

"Getting off, honey? We're stopping here for awhile," an old lady leaned over, her breath warm and soft on Mara's cheek. "Driver called it a C&P break. Coffee and pit—bathroom—stop," she chuckled. "Want me to watch the little guy while you stretch your legs?"

"No, we're fine. I'll stay here, "Mara replied, awake now, watching the passengers move away from the parked bus.

"O.K. Up to you, just offerin'," the lady replied, straightening up and running her tired hand over Jace's hair. "We'll be here a half hour or so, he says, so if you change your mind, let me know. I don't mind. He's a cute one." She moved down the aisle, which was now clear, and eased herself down the stairs. The entire bus was empty. She remembered the driver had said something about stopping, but this was not a bus station.

She looked at her watch. 2:00 A.M. She had been asleep for hours and had no idea where they were. She looked out the window to the side of the bus, clearing the fogged glass with a hand. She could see no signs indicating their location. Through the windshield she could see in front of the parked bus a brightly lit diner, the only building. She watched the old woman, the last person to enter the restaurant. She could see shapes of the passengers inside the restaurant. Rising, she eased the sleeping boy across the seat, and she stood and stretched her cramped back and legs. A single car flew past them, its headlights briefly traced the interior of the bus from front to rear, and then the darkness chased the light.

She heard Jace stir and groan softly. Not anxious to sit back down, she took a few steps. There were papers, magazines, a softback book, a sweater, and bags on some on the seats. She thought of looking for a purse or something that might have money in it, but then, *Not smart! Who else would have taken it? I'm the only one on the bus!*

As she walked back to her seat, bending and straightening, leaning on the chair backs to stretch, she noticed a gas station directly across the two-lane highway, and she was puzzled that she had not noticed it before. A row of dimly lit pumps was set back from the paved roadway, and an office to the right showed one dim light. She put her hand to the window to cut the reflection from the overhead lights left on in some of the seats. A VW bug was parked at an angle to the left of the gas station, probably near the restrooms, she thought. *If I have to go, I'll go there where I won't be as noticeable as in that brightly lit restaurant, full of people.*

She sat down, and Jace leaned against her, searching for the pillow of her lap, and then she heard them coming from the rear. The deep throaty rumble of a motorcycle. Or were there two? Down shifting, exhaust backing, throttles gunned, she looked up in time to see the two bikes almost directly opposite her, turn into the gas station and park near the VW, to the side and rear of the gas station. She watched the men remove their helmets and unzip their leathers. They were talking, *laughing,* she thought, but she could not hear what they were saying. All of a sudden, one staggered a bit, and leaning over, supporting himself on the handlebars of his bike, he doubled up and vomited. The other man jumped back in an exaggerated move. She could imagine what they were saying. The sick one gagged, vomited again, and straightened up, both hands on his knees, shaking his head. His partner was moving around him now, one hand on the other's shoulder, laughing. He slapped him on the back, and the man stood and threw a half-hearted punch at the other. They were both laughing now, alongside the VW. The taller of the two touched the hatch of the rear-engine car. They bent over and looked inside the car and then they moved around the corner of the building out of view, she guessed to the bathroom.

Mara leaned back against her headrest, eyes shut. Through her closed eyelids, she could see the lights from the occasional passing car. Jason stirred and sat up, and she realized she had dozed off. She looked at her watch. They had been stopped for only maybe twenty minutes. "Forty minutes, no more, no less," the driver had warned.

"Have to go pee pee, mommy," Jace moaned, squirming.

"You sure, Jace? You're just not saying that?" she replied. She looked at her watch. They had time.

"Have to go, now," the strain in his voice was all the proof she needed.

"O.K. We have to get off, then." As she spoke she heard the rasp of one and then the other motorcycle. She glanced over at the gas station. Both men were back on their bikes, engines running, headlights on. One stood, straightening his leather pants, pulling at his crotch. She could see the other laughing at him, pointing, and the man gave the other a thumbs up sign and then sat on his saddle. He took a long pull on his cigarette and flicked it at the other, sparks flying. His companion ducked, avoiding the glowing butt, and laughed. They revved the bikes and, spewing dirt and gravel, in a roar they both took off the way they had come.

"O.K, Jace, let's go," Mara said. She took the boy's hand and led him off the bus. They walked behind the vehicle, which screened them from the diner. She checked for oncoming cars and quickly crossed the highway. She was correct, there were two bathrooms behind the station. "Watch it," she said to Jason as she stepped around the vomit; she could smell it.

There were two rusted, battered bathroom doors, and for a moment she thought of taking him to the side and just letting him pee in the darkness. The door on the right had a piece of blue masking tape in the shape of a large "X" across it and a piece of tape over the door handle and lock. *Out of order,* obviously. She leaned into the other door; it moved but did not yield. She turned the knob, it opened. *Nice of them,* she thought, *to close the door all the way.* She stepped inside, and the odors stopped her cold. It was pitch black. As she felt to one side of the doorway for a light switch, the momentary glare from a passing truck illuminated the wall enough for her to find it. One dim bulb high overhead reduced the blackness to a murky gloom. *The bus station was a palace after this,,* she thought. It was the men's room, and Jace could see the urinal which was set at floor level.

"Need help?" she asked.

"No, John showed me, I can do it myself," he said, his back to her. She grimaced at the mention of the investigator. She looked around. Cracked paint mottled the walls. The floor was wet, muddy, and the smell overwhelming. Scarred black, the endless drip of the faucet had worn a small crater in the sink, and water escaped through a crack, wetting the entire floor. No towels, no soap, nothing. *Whatever happened to the "Service Station," she thought?* She noticed that the one stall had a door and for a moment considered relieving herself. The door was closed and they were certainly alone. There was no handle or lock on the stall door, so she reached up and pulled on the top of the door. Another flash of light hit the high ceiling, walked instantly down the wall behind her, and she cast just enough of a shadow that she was blinded for a moment. She blinked, and when she opened her eyes she saw, but could not for an instant comprehend, that there was a body in the toilet in front of her.

She choked back a scream, the bile rising in her throat. She put out one arm to lean against the stall door.

Face down, her head and one shoulder wedged in the toilet, bare buttocks gaping at Mara, was the body of a woman, her slacks and panties dangled from one ankle onto the wet floor. A trail of bright red blood trickled down the back of one thigh. Her upper back was forced up against the back of the toilet. Mara gagged and staggered.

"What's wrong, mommy?" she heard the voice of the boy, as if from far away.

"Nothing!" she was sure she had screamed. "Nothing! Stay there, Jace. Do not move!"

She leaned against stall and heard him flush the urinal. He loved to pull the levers, she recalled. "Pull it a few times, if you want, Jace. Lots of times. Mommy will be a minute. Stay there!" The sound of her voice surprised her. She heard him pull the handle, once, twice, and heard the water and the pressure in the pipes. As she wondered what she should do, she felt rather than saw the water begin to rise in the toilet in front of her, and as the toilet began to fill with water, the body dislodged and rose or slipped slowly, just enough so that the shoulders came free. The slight shift in weight caused the woman's body to tilt over onto the right side of the toilet, and it wedged between the toilet and the wall. Mara could now see part of her face. One of the woman's legs flinched slightly and touched the top of Mara's foot.

Mara screamed. "Pull the water, Jace! Flush it faster if you want!" she yelled at him.

"Mommy, what's wrong?" the boy asked.

"Mommy just sneezed, I'm all right. Stay there, Jace!"

"But, you yelled."

"No, I did not. I sneezed!" she shouted. "I'm all right," Mara said.

She looked down at the woman, no older than she, maybe younger. A scarf was knotted around her neck. Her face was blue, bloodless. *Dead?* She knew it. *Maybe? Those biker bastards. I have to get out of here, or I'll be caught up in this and then . . .* Her panic of a moment now turned to fear for herself. She moved her foot from under the woman's leg, and as she started to back out, she saw something in the corner to the side of the toilet. She leaned forward. A purse? Just beyond the woman's head. She knew instantly that she had to get it, if only to look. She leaned down, stretching forward, but she could not reach it without touching the woman. She put one hand on the back of the toilet and leaned down and forward, reaching. Her face came within inches, and then almost touched, the face of the dead woman, one glazed, sightless, open eye directly on her. She closed her own eyes and reached. Her face brushed the still warm face of the dead woman, and she felt the purse and yanked it free. She stepped back.

"What's that, mommy?" She heard Jason ask. He was at the entrance to the stall behind her, but Mara's body blocked his view. She stepped back and out against him, pushing him away from the stall. She slammed the door shut with her foot as she backed up.

"It looks like somebody's shoe, mommy. Did somebody forget their shoe?"

Mara looked down. The dead woman's foot now extended out and under the stall door. She tried to push it back with her own. It moved, but when she released her foot, the woman's foot eased slowly out again. She turned Jason away.

"Look, honey," she urged him away, toward the bathroom door. "Someone forgot their purse. Mommy found it," she said. "Let's see who it belongs to," and she moved him away from the stall and closer to the light, keeping the boy in front of her. She opened the leather bag and felt a wallet and then, car keys. She pulled the keys out. The leather tab had a metal disk: "My Bug" it read.

Mara grasped the keys. Action was once again her only plan. She reached for and opened the bathroom door. The small blue car was right there. In one fluid motion she pushed Jason outside and towards the parked car. The door was unlocked, and she threw Jason into the passenger seat. She moved quickly around the car, fell behind the steering wheel, and slammed her door. The engine caught on the first try. The gas gauge read "Full." *Thanks for that,* she thought. She jammed the gear shift down and back, searching for reverse, found it, and riding the clutch, backed out in a sharp curve. Cutting the wheel with one hand and shifting with the other, she slammed it into first gear, checked for oncoming vehicles, and entered the highway, headed south. As she passed the bus, she noticed the line of passengers beginning to board. *They'll miss me, that old lady will, but so what . . .* she thought. *I'll be long gone to . . . where?*

In her rearview mirror, the two large headlights of bus slowly receded, became one, and vanished.

Part 2

1998

CHAPTER 8

THE FLIGHT ATTENDANT TOUCHED HIM GENTLY on the shoulder.

"Excuse me, Mr. Ames. I am sorry to bother you, but we need your help."

Scott stretched his six-feet-plus frame. The cabin of the plane was almost totally dark.

She continued, "A mother, she is flying alone, has a problem with her young child, and we were hoping to move them both to this exit-row seat, so that we can help. They would be closer to us here," she nodded to the galley, "and to the restroom. And then she would not disturb the other passengers. We wonder if you would be good enough to consider moving to another seat. I am very sorry, Mr. Ames," she smiled.

He had wangled the exit row at check-in for the extra leg room, and he hated to give it up.

"Sure, I guess so. Sure," he said, and he felt for the seat button, but she beat him to it. His seat rose to the upright position.

Standing, he said, "I need to get my stuff."

"Never mind, that will not be necessary," the attendant said. "We will get it for you when we deplane. This way," she stepped back and gestured toward the forward cabin.

Well, that is a plus, he thought. *Business class is a step up.* He glanced at his watch. It was past midnight. They had left San Francisco for the all-night flight to Washington, D.C.'s Dulles Airport on this Thursday night, now Friday morning. He followed the attendant as she parted the curtain to the first-class section, and ahead he saw another attendant, one hand resting on an empty, forward-most, aisle seat. *1B.* He faked a frown. The passengers, including the occupant of seat 1A, were asleep.

"I hope this is not too much of an inconvenience, Mr. Ames."

Well," he grinned, settling into the wide luxury seat, and buckling up, "I guess it will do."

"We thought so," she whispered, smiled warmly back at him, and handed him a pillow and a blanket. "Can I get you anything?"

"No, thank you. I'm set, and I need the sleep."

"Very well, but I assure you we will make up for it at breakfast. O.K.?" She gave the back of his seat a pat, then walked down the aisle. She glanced back at the handsome young man and then blushed as she noticed the other attendant rolling her eyes, brows raised.

"Cute," the attendant said to her.

"Better than cute."

They both smiled. "Uh, huh!" the other woman nodded. "Get thee back to coach!" She held the curtain aside for her to step back to the rear section of the plane.

Scott tilted his seat all the way back. The leg rest rose from under his seat, and he stretched out. *That first class leg space*, he thought. *Nice!* His feet touched the bulkhead in front of him, so he eased back just enough until they cleared it. As he settled in, his thoughts wandered back to the events that got him here.

His company, just himself and his assistant, Ross, had applied to the government for funds to support their habitat restoration projects on the coastal rivers of Northern California, the ancient home to spawning salmon and steelhead, both threatened with extinction. Scott had actually forgotten about the grant request until he received a letter saying that he was a finalist in competing for funds from private industry: the National Filter and Environmental Corporation, based in Washington, D.C. Correspondence and telephone calls had led to an interview, and someone from the corporation had taken pictures and shot video, months ago. He thought that was the end of it. Then came the letter requesting that he come to D.C. for the announcement of the award, all expenses paid. He had misplaced the details of the contest, but Ross insisted that he go—it might be good PR, even if they did not win anything. The corporation had supplied a first-class ticket, which Scott had traded for coach-class fare, pocketing the difference for his company. *And here he was in first class anyway. Things were off to a good start.*

He closed his eyes, and the hum of the jet engines soon put him to sleep again.

~

He was standing in the river, the large hen steelhead trout pressed against his lower leg as he tried to ease the fly out of the mouth of the struggling fish. He wanted to avoid handling the wild fish, and he especially did not want to take her out of the water. He felt the strong pressure of the fish moving hard against his leg ... and Scott awoke with a start. The passenger in 1A was a woman, and she was straddling his outstretched legs, pressing against his inside leg as she attempted to step over him to the aisle. In the darkened cabin, he had trouble seeing her features, her sleep mask had fallen, obscuring everything beneath her nose. He realized his legs were apart and that she was unable to stretch over them. Just as he decided he had to make room for her to pass, the airplane rocked, a slight bounce, enough to cause her to lose the precarious balance she had with one hand on the overhead. She pitched forward toward him. At the last second, he put up one arm, and she caught it with both hands. As she steadied herself, she was able to step into the aisle without a word, and disappeared. Fully awake, he realized they were going to replay this little drama on her way back, so he released the leg rest and felt it retract. Scott closed his eyes and waited. The fish had been a dream.

"Excuse me." She was back. Eyes closed, he straightened, drawing his legs under, and he felt her pass through and resume her seat.

"That seat was vacant when we took off. Are you sure you are in the right seat?" she challenged. Without turning his head, he answered, "They moved me here."

A pause, then, "Oh ..." And silence. Scott pushed the leg-rest button and helped the mechanism unfold with his foot. He stretched out, relaxed, and stepped back into his dream and was soon fast asleep.

~

A blend of sounds and scents teased him awake. The rehearsed movements of the attendants assisting passengers, the unmistakable clink of a spoon releasing the aroma of stirred coffee. The signs of morning. He opened his eyes to a single beam of sunlight on his cheek from the window opposite, and through the partly opened shade he glimpsed the dawn chasing the darkness off to the west. He stretched, mindful of his seatmate, still asleep. He unbuckled and, shoeless, walked back to the beverage station. The flight attendant handed him his coffee, correctly guessing, *black.*

"Almost there," she said. "Seems as if the seat change was not too inconvenient, was it?"

"It was great, if you only knew," he replied, thinking of his ticket downgrade. "Perfect."

"Good, I am glad we could help," she smiled. He took a croissant, passed on the butter and jam, and nibbled it with his coffee, standing, glad to be on his feet. She handed him a small black case.

"Compliments of the airline," she explained. "Razor, shaving cream, toothbrush, soap, aftershave, ya da da . . ."

"Oh, that's great, because I was just going to ask you about getting my stuff," he replied.

The plane banked. "We are starting our descent into Dulles, but you have at least one-half hour," the attendant said. "Time to freshen up if you want and still have that breakfast. It goes with the seat."

"Actually, this is good for me. I'll pass, though it looks tempting. Next time," he laughed. "I'll settle for the fresh-up, since I have a meeting." The flight attendant raised her eyes, looking behind him as a young woman, almost his height, clad in a warm-up outfit passed him. He only caught a glimpse of her back as she entered the restroom. The "occupied" light came on. He looked back at his row. Seat 1A was empty.

He picked a restroom and removed his shirt, washed his face, and lathered up. As he shaved, he reviewed his schedule for the coming day: To be met at the airport, then to the company for a tour, followed by lunch with executives. The afternoon was reserved for meetings with those interested in his work. The evening at his hotel was free time. The next day he was free until the awards dinner. He had never been to D.C., and he hoped to see some of the famous landmarks before his flight out on Monday. A cold-water rinse and the aftershave revived him. He toweled off, put on his shirt. In the mirror he considered his tanned face and toned body from all those days on, and in, the river. He felt good, pleased with his life and excited a bit at what the weekend might bring. He had no expectations, and in fact he had not studied the grant conditions, content to have even been considered and in the running for any help he might get, whatever the amount. He released the lock, pulled open the door, and stepped out right into the young woman, forcing her up against the bulkhead.

"Oh, excuse me! I am sorry," he said. She recoiled, gaining her balance, and without meeting his eyes, moved up the aisle, and took her seat. The attendant, standing in the galley, had seen the encounter.

"Oops," she giggled.

Chagrined, he returned to his seat. As he bent down for his seat belt, he looked at her, "We have to stop meeting like this."

She raised her head.

Wow, she is beautiful, he thought. *Boy, have I screwed this up.*

"Well, that is what ... two?" she said. "I was beginning to wonder if I had done something wrong," her voice was strong, but her tone playful. He smiled at her and resumed his seat, leaning toward her as he reached for and snapped his belt. She edged slightly away, exaggerating her movement. He straightened in his seat, and facing her, extended his hand.

"Scott. Scott Ames," he offered.

She did not immediately take his hand, and he realized that he was stuck with it in midair. She seemed to be enjoying the moment, and just as he decided to drop it, she took his hand.

"Ja—" she began when the in-flight announcement interrupted her.

"We are on final approach to Dulles. Please take your seats. Fasten your seat belts. Raise ...."

"Visiting or coming home?" Scott asked.

"Sort of both," she replied. "My dad lives here, I grew up here, but I work on the coast."

God, she is something, he thought. *Soft brown hair, piled on her head, rumpled from sleeping. No makeup. Her skin glows.*

"You?" she asked politely.

"Business, for the weekend. I go back on Monday," he replied. He fastened his eyes on hers, green, gleaming. *I am staring at her!*

The plane banked on a final turn and leveled. He heard the flaps working and the gear come down and lock. *If I don't start talking, I am going to blow this,* he thought. However, she had turned away, and over her head he saw the Washington monument slide by and then the Capitol. The tires screeched and the engines reversed, and in a few moments they taxied up to the jetway. Before he could decide how to continue the conversation, he felt a tap on his arm, and the attendant leaned over to him.

"We can get your things now, Mr. Ames," she said. "Come with me, and you can exit with the first-class passengers. Beat the rush."

He looked up at the attendant. At this moment he could not have cared less about retrieving his belongings or beating the rush. He wanted to continue talking to this woman. She continued to look out the window.

"Mr. Ames?" the attendant asked. Reluctantly he undid his belt and stood.

As he turned to follow the flight attendant, he leaned back over his empty seat and said to the young woman's back, "It was my pleasure to have bumped into you, twice," he smiled. "Maybe there will be a third time?"

She turned to face him and met his gaze.

"Enjoy your stay in Washington," she said. "It is an exciting city, full of surprises." And she bent down to pick up her things.

By the time he retrieved his backpack from the coach section and returned to the first class exit, she was gone. He moved quickly up the ramp, but he was unable to spot her in the crowded terminal. Uncertain of his whereabouts, he had to stop and check for baggage claim and knew that he had lost her. *Gone. One of those "might have beens" that life is full of,* he mused as he headed to the baggage carousel.

~

While he waited for his bag, Scott glanced around the terminal area, but she was nowhere in view. He began to process a list of reasons why nothing would have come of it anyway. *But, you never know*, he thought. *Give it up, Scott*, he said to himself as his bag hove into view, and by the time he had elbowed his way to it and yanked it off the moving carousel, he had 'given it up." Outside at the curb, limos, vans, and taxis stood three deep, overseen by a whistle-blowing uniformed officer, whose constant command was, "Move it! Now!"

"Mr. Ames?" a tall, gray-haired man held a clipboard slate on which was lettered "AMES."

"I'm Ames," Scott answered, stepping forward.

The man extended his hand. "Welcome to Washington, D.C., our nation's Capital," he said, reaching for Scott's bag.

"I can handle it," Scott said maintaining his grip.

"O.K. Right here," he stepped off the curb and pointed to a black Lincoln Town Car. He popped the trunk with a remote, and Scott lifted the suitcase into it, followed by his carry-on backpack.

"That's it. Nothing else?" the man asked.

"Just the one and my pack," he replied. The trunk eased shut and locked.

"O.K. Good." The man opened the rear door for him.

"Is the front O.K.?" Scott asked.

"Sure is." He slammed the rear door and opened the passenger-side front door, and Scott slid in. The door closed behind him. The driver got in and looked to see that Scott was belted in, and offered his hand again.

"Fred James," he said. "I work for Mr. Williams at NEFCO." He pronounced it as one word.

"Pleased to meet you, Fred," Scott replied.

There was a metallic rap on Scott's window, and as it slid down, a worn face topped with a visored cap filled the opening. "Move it! Now!" the face said. "You know better, Fred!" The face disappeared. The whistle shrilled.

Fred leaned over toward the window, "Yes, ma'am. We are gone," he smiled at Scott, leaned back, and started the engine. He eased the car slowly into the line of traffic.

Fred looked over at Scott, "I am to tell you that I'm available to take you wherever you want to go, throughout your stay, within reason," he grinned.

"You're serious? I have you and this car at my disposal?"

"Absolutely. And I won't leave unless and until you are through for the day. That's what Miss Cecily said."

"O.K, Fred. O.K.," Scott replied. He looked over at the waiting cars as Fred circled the terminal, pausing and stopping for traffic. As they merged into a lane they passed a black stretch limo, its rear window down, and for an instant he looked straight into her face. *What? I never got her name!* Then the car accelerated and was gone. He sighed and laughed to himself.

"Everything all right?" Fred asked, glancing over at him.

"Fine, Fred."

"How was your flight?"

"The flight was great," Scott answered, settling back. "In fact it was perfect, *almost* perfect." They were moving quickly now over the busy freeway, the tall buildings of the capital city rising ahead.

~

The receptionist ushered him into a large corner office, overlooking what must be the plant buildings below and beyond, he thought. A large glass desk, cut into an elliptical shape, was centered in front of floor-to-ceiling windows. Suspended on two stainless-steel bases, the desk was matched by a glass-topped credenza, supported by two-wide sets of polished mahogany drawers, trimmed in stainless steel. The desk was bare. A black executive chair made of a web material, trimmed in leather, served the desk.

"Make yourself comfortable," she said, indicating the pair of black leather chairs in front of the desk, then pointing to a couch set to the side, near a round, small conference table with equally matching leather chairs.

"Mr. Williams's secretary, Cecily, will be with you in a moment," she explained. "May I offer you anything to drink? Flying makes me so dehydrated."

"Oh, no thank you," Scott replied. "I'm fine."

"There's coffee on the sidebar," she continued, pointing to the other side of the room. "The minibar has juice, soft drinks, if you change your mind. Just help yourself." With that she smiled, turned, and closed the door behind her.

He sat down, leaned back, his hand running over the soft leather arm of the chair. The entire office had a high-tech feel to it, which was softened by the polished hardwood floor. The desk was floating on an island of Persian carpet that reached almost to his chair. On the wall behind the conference table was a chair grouping and, behind a large picture, an aerial view of the office building and this plant, he surmised. The wall opposite was mirrored, and shelves cut of the same glass as the desk lined the wall above the matching credenza. He stood, stretched, and curious about the items on the shelves, he stepped closer. Out of place among the expensive tasteful mementos, made of small stones, each carefully fit together, was a tapered tower of rocks, which Scott recognized as a miniature cairn, similar to those made centuries ago by Indians, explorers, and trappers to mark a trail. He felt the weight and wondered what it represented in his host's life. On either side of the cairn were identically framed pictures: one of a young girl, the other of a boy who looked to be three years of age. As he mused about the arrangement, he heard and then saw in the reflection of the mirror the door open behind him.

A tall woman, hair showing some gray, impeccably dressed, approached him, a wide smile on her classically proportioned face. "Mr. Ames, how nice to meet you," she took his hand. "I am Cecily, assistant to Mr. Williams. Won't you be seated?"

"Thank you," he replied. He moved back to his chair.

"I see you spotted some of Mr. Williams's toys," she laughed. "This is *his* office, of course."

"Yes, frankly, I was admiring them and wondering about the owner," he said. He followed her to the couch and the chairs next to the table. She sat at one of the chairs; he took the other.

"First, Brad, Mr. Williams, sends his apologies. He had hoped to be here when you arrived, but he has been delayed at a meeting," she explained. "He will try to catch up with you later." She handed him a file from several she had placed in front of her on the table. The file bore the logo and name NEFCO over his typed name, and the words "Annual A.W.E. Awards."

"This includes the schedule of events for today and the weekend, with a brief description of our company, its history, mission statement, and some material bearing on the awards for tomorrow evening. You should find it helpful, and you can read it later." She paused. "Your hotel confirmation and voucher are included, though you can stay anywhere you like, if you prefer."

"No, whatever you have arranged is fine with me," he replied.

"Fine. Now here is what happens next. Your day is going to be quite full, I believe. I hope you were able to sleep on the plane? You took the red-eye, is that correct?" she inquired.

"I did, and I will be just fine," he said.

"Good. That's why we had you come in on Friday, so that you would be rested and able to enjoy the festivities on Saturday evening," she continued. "They are a lot of fun. I am sure that you will enjoy them." She consulted her file. "You are alone . . . you came alone?"

"Yes," he smiled. "I am single."

"All right. Let's go over the schedule and what you need to know in order to . . ."

Over the next half hour she reviewed the planned activities. When she had answered all his questions, she stood, moved to the desk, and pressed a button that Scott had not noticed.

"Send in Mr. Jeffrey, please," she said.

Immediately, a young man, dressed in dark suit, tie, entered. "Ed Jeffrey, Mr. Ames, my pleasure. I have read about you, and I will be your escort here today."

What could he have read about me? Scott wondered.

For the next two hours, the man gave Scott a tour of the office facility, followed by a trip to the surrounding manufacturing plant buildings. At each stop, technical people, some introduced as engineers, presented a detailed discussion of the particular part of the plant or operation in which they were involved. He was fascinated by their obvious depth of knowledge and their commitment that he understand their duties and operations. The two were joined at lunch by the other grant candidates. The meal was served in a small theater-like conference room and featured a multimedia presentation of the founding, background, and growth of their host corporation, and the history and procedures regarding the three grants to be awarded: one each for Air, Water, and Earth (the A.W.E. on his file folder). From their conversation, the others, one an earth scientist on the faculty of a large university; the other an expert on depletion of the ozone layer, who was employed by a nationwide firm of whom Scott had heard, seemed to know all about the grant and the award procedures. Scott knew nothing except what he had been told today. From a process of elimination he assumed he was the "W," for water. But he felt out of place in this corporate environment and wondered if maybe the invitation extended to his two-man company was some kind of mistake or misunderstanding. Uncertain, he resolved to let it play out. At least so far he had lunch, and his return ticket was in his pocket.

After lunch, Ed Jeffrey led Scott to a meeting room where he spent the rest of the afternoon explaining in excruciating detail his small company's operations, projects completed (there were three), current projects and plans for future work, the possible expansion of his company and his dire need for financial support. He was surprised that his interviewers were so well versed in stream biology, hydrology, threats to species, particularly salmon and steelhead, his passion; and the economics of his projects and his company. They questioned him extensively on his experience and knowledge regarding river and stream degradation due to farming, bank erosion, introduction of fertilizers and pesticides into the aquifer. He felt like he was sitting for an examination; at some point he determined that he was being tested. However, the subject matter was his forte, and he felt up to the challenge. He found himself describing his passion for taking action to protect the spawning grounds of the fish before it was too late. They seemed to not only understand, but also to agree with him on the importance of his work.

It was after 6:00 P.M. when they finished. One of the "examiners" showed him to the front of the building. The others were already gone, and Scott realized that he was on his own. The Lincoln Town Car was parked in front of the building.

"You O.K. from here?" his escort asked. "Need a lift to your hotel?"

He saw Fred get out of the car and lean on the top, watching him.

"I'm covered, thanks," Scott said, shaking the man's hand.

In the car, Fred looked over at Scott.

"Told you. Where to, young man?"

"My hotel, I guess, and I haven't eaten since lunch," Scott replied. "How about you, you eat yet?"

"No, but don't worry about me," Fred replied. "Here, you better read this first. Cecily said to be sure to give it to you." He handed Scott an envelope, addressed to "Scott Ames: A.W.E. Candidate."

The note inside read:

Mr. Ames,

I am sorry that I was unable to greet you on your arrival here today.

I did meet briefly with the two other gentlemen, who like you, are to be a part of this weekend's events.

I would like to extend a personal invitation for you to spend tonight and tomorrow, of course, at my beach house in lieu of your hotel. But it is to be your decision, and I fully understand if you prefer to stay in the city and enjoy what D.C. has to offer. Just tell Fred what you decide. Please understand there is no obligation on your part. I was thinking only of making up for the fact that we did not have a chance to meet.

Cordially,
Brad Williams

"Know what it says, Fred?" he asked the driver.

"Sure, the driver *always* knows," Fred smiled.

"What would you do?"

"Head for the beach, no question. Fabulous place, and *out* of this city."

"But how long and how far? You must be tired." Scott asked.

"This time of night, one hour tops; maybe fifty miles. Beautiful drive across the Chesapeake," he said. "I'm O.K. You go for it! Mr. Williams does not invite everybody out there."

"O.K., on one condition. I'm in charge, right?" Scott challenged him.

"Yes sir, you are," Fred answered.

"Ok, we stop someplace for (a) a drink and (b) something to eat. Doesn't have to be a big dinner, but you and I need to eat something. That's the deal!" Scott extended his hand to the driver. "Deal!? And I pay!" he added.

"Deal," Fred responded. He shook Scott's hand. "Except for the drink part. I am still working."

"What's that? I didn't hear you. Can't hear what you are saying," Scott winked as he buckled up and sat back.

Fred grinned, started the engine, and eased the Lincoln away from the parking area.

~

Though the sun was gone and the new moon had not yet risen, it was still light when they arrived at what Fred had called the beach house. The shingle and gabled two-story home was reached by a long gravel drive, common to this east shore area. Each side of the driveway was forested and trees provided treasured privacy. Fred grabbed Scott's bags and led him into the house.

"Vera? We're here," Fred announced to the empty room.

Through the living room, which resembled a library, Scott could see the sand dune hills behind. He could almost taste the saltwater in the air. *Perfect,* he thought. An older, short stature, dark woman entered from a swinging door, a lighted kitchen behind her.

"Well, lookie here. Fred come to eat, yet!" She hugged the embarrassed driver.

"Hey, Vera, good to see you," Fred replied, stepping back. "I've got a guest for you. Mr. Scott Ames, from California."

"I know who he is. We got phones out here, you know," hands on her hips. "My, he is a pretty one, too. Good evening *Mr.* Ames," she took Scott's hand. Her hand was rough, wet. "Been doing the dishes," she explained, wiping her apron. "Well, you boys want to eat, or what? Can't keep the kitchen open all night 'til you decide!"

Scott liked her immediately. *Who wouldn't,* he thought.

"No, thank you, ma'am . . ."

"Don't' you 'ma'am' me, sonny. I have a name, and it is Vera. Can't you say that?"

"Yes, ma—, Vera," he corrected himself.

"Good. So what will it be?"

Scott glanced at Fred and said, "Well, we stopped on the way and had a snack, so I am good, I don't need anything. But thank you." he said. Fred was shifting his feet, ready to go.

"Me neither, Vera. We ate, and Mr. Ames—Scott—he bought," he said. "Well, I want to drive back tonight, and you are good to stay here, Scott?" he asked. "But if you need me, just call. Vera has my number."

"We got cars here, and I 'spec he can drive, Fred," Vera said. "You get on home to your wife; it will be late enough as it is," she followed him to the door, her hand on his shoulder.

She showed Scott to his first-floor bedroom off the living room.

"This is the single man's guest room," she explained, "and Mr. W. said to put you in it." She watched him unpack, showed him the bath in his room, how to get to the kitchen, and led him out the living room door to the porch, where a wooded walkway stretched over the dunes to the beach.

"Goin' to be a beautiful moon tonight, if it don't cloud up," she gazed overhead. "Well, I think that does it for me." She turned and went inside. The screen door closed; the other door open to the warm night air. "Oh. Mr. W. called jus' for you got here. He's 'stuck,' he says, in D.C., but he will be out in the morning, for breakfast," she explained. "He don't miss breakfast if he says he is comin', so he will be here." Vera showed him the lights in living room and hall, and she explained that she lived in a cottage to the side of the main house. Scott begged off on her final sandwich offering. *He was fine. Good night.*

Scott changed into shorts and a tank top. The air was balmy, windless. He walked back out into the living room and picked a comfortable chair that faced the open door and the water beyond the dunes. He opened the file and for the first time began to read the materials Cecily had provided.

Over twenty years ago, Brad Williams joined the company then known as Filter Manufacturing as a salesman. The company designed, manufactured, and distributed a line of common household filters for furnaces and cooling systems for residential and commercial customers, and a few specialty items for filtration of swimming pools and spas and a few simple industrial uses. Williams and original owner Foster "Bud" Manning were the only employees together with a few production workers, whose numbers varied depending on the job, demand, or the season. The company had no business plan and no ideas for growth or expansion. One day Brad was asked if he could provide filters for a computer company that needed a "clean air" environment for its operations. He and Bud designed a simple system, which they built over a weekend, and to everyone's surprise it tested so well that the company placed an order for their entire building. The rest was history. Now known as NEFCO, the corporation was the largest of its type in the nation, providing state of the art technology to the design and manufacture of filter systems for air, water, and other materials—whatever needed filtration.

Several years ago, the board of directors adopted a policy of encouraging creativity and research in related fields, including environmental issues relating to air quality; the earth—soils, mining, agricultural, chemical, industrial waste; and water—river and stream degradation, pollution, and habitat. *(The "A.W.E." on the file I was given.)* A volunteer committee of company engineers *(the "examiners")* chose organizations or individuals from grant applications made to various governmental agencies, which had gone unfunded. Drawing on that grant information, the committee narrowed it down to three candidates, and the interview process *(today)* determined which of the three would receive *(they avoided the word "win"; each candidate got something)* the largest grant: $1,000,000. *(One million dollars!)* His jaw dropped.

Scott felt an immediate chill. The hair rose on the back of his neck, and he rubbed the hair standing on his arm. *That's what we're playing for?* The other two grants were $500,000 and $250,000. *My God, I'm getting at least $250,000,* he realized. *What that would mean to my company! The things we could do! That was like ten years of fundraising. It must be a mistake. But those guys today, they knew everything about me and my company, and they had asked about things that were definitely not mentioned in that grant request. Someone had done their homework on me,* he thought, *and I didn't even know. I have to call Ross!*

He reread the materials. Because his grant application had been prepared and submitted by an organization staffed by volunteers who searched for funding for environmental causes, and whose requests usually went unanswered, he had paid little attention to this process until now. *Well, look where mine ended up,* he smiled to himself. If he "won," that was the only way he could think of it, he would have to make an acceptance speech. He could handle that, but there was no way he was going to be the big "winner" against those other professionals. *But $250,000! Jeez!*

He set the file down. Looking out at the rising moon, he sensed how energized he was, though the only sleep he had was on the plane. He walked across the room, stepped outside. After a moment, he reached back and switched off all the lights except a small table lamp. Now he could see the stars and the rising moon. He wandered down the boardwalk and found himself on the beach. *Absolutely beautiful, What a special place,* he thought. Quiet, private, magical. *I could use a shower* he thought, *all I had today was that sponge bath on the plane.* The water was so placid, so inviting.

He walked to the water's edge. The waves lapped at his feet, belying the depth and the force that urged them ashore. He kicked off his sandals, shrugged off his tank top, and slipped out of his shorts. He left them in a pile near a chair that was almost buried in the sand, near the end of the walkway. He walked to the waterline. The moon, almost full now, painted a path only for him, an exclamation point out of a clear cloudless sky, and he stepped slowly into it. The bottom sloped gently, and he stroked slowly, wrapped in the warm water and the moonlight merging into one; water and air the same temperature.

Fifty yards out, he rolled over, the moonlight washing his exposed feet as he rocked on the gentle tide. He leaned back until the water covered his ears. He felt the pressure in his ears, the hum in his head, and the sound of his gentle sculling translate into subtle vibrations. He was always surprised when he did this that sound disappeared, or was it just changed somehow? The dark sky was crammed with stars, those on the rim of the areola multiplying toward the darkness. He floated motionless for a time, and then he raised his head and backstroked gently, pausing every few moments to look at the stars, to track the occasional shooting star. Time slowed and so did his mind, as if his thought process was on hold.

A small swell hit the back of his head, startling him and washing saltwater into his mouth. He coughed and spit it out, then rolled over and looked towards shore. He was much farther out than he had thought, and the dark cloud that now defaced the moon made him remember that things change quickly in the sea. Time to go. He took a bead on the beach, still visible in the moonlight, and began to swim in.

When he checked his bearings, he realized that the tide had carried him well down the shore; how far he was uncertain. He was not sure either if the house he was guiding on was the right one; they all looked the same. He continued swimming and was relieved, he admitted, to feel the swells at his back pushing him toward the shore. By the time his feet touched the sand, he knew he was damn stupid to have gone out so far at night in strange water. He stood up when he felt the bottom and waded ashore. Still in the water, he sat down in the sand and then realized just how tired and out of breath he was.

Imagine the headlines, he mused: "Award recipient disappears from Cape home . . . feared drowned. The ceremonies scheduled for . . . were suddenly cancelled yesterday . . ."

"Damn," he said to himself, "how would I explain that?" He laughed softly. "*You* won't have to, stupid. You'll be drowned!"

It was darker now, the moon was almost covered by the scudding clouds, and he shivered, sitting in the water. Then it hit him, as he looked over his shoulder at the sandy bluff and up at the houses faintly visible. "Where the hell are my clothes?"

He stood, and he knew that he had to walk up the beach, keeping the water on his left. He found that the wet sand marking the waterline on the beach was much wider now than when he had entered the water. The tide that had pulled him down the beach had also gone out. He could not distinguish the houses in the darkening sky, the moonlight was all but gone.

As he walked, he tried to calculate how far he might have drifted on the tide, how far back he would have to go to find the path to the house. He supposed that he would walk until he found his shorts and sandals, that would be easy. But the beach was so much wider, and what had been the water's edge when he went in, was now twenty yards or more to his left.

"Where in the . . .?" he muttered, stopping to get his bearings He ran his hand through his hair. "If I don't find those shorts, I am going to have to walk bare ass naked up that path, into the house. But which house?" More headlines: "Award recipient found wandering naked, arrested last evening at the Cape, while attempting to enter the home of . . .!"

"Which house is it?" he said aloud. *O.K., stupid, don't* panic, he thought, *just figure out what the path looked like. Was there anything near the end of the board-walk section?* His mouth was dry, his chest tight. *The fear invasion has landed,* he thought.

He looked back up the beach and noticed that his footprints had already disappeared in the wet sand. *I'm too far out,* he thought, and he turned inland and began to walk toward the houses, still unable to find his earlier footprints.

He looked ahead, right and left, looking for a sign, or his clothes on the dry sand. As his feet touched the dry sand, he thought he saw an object and turned toward it. An Adirondack chair materialized out of the darkness, so sunk in the sand that it resembled a backrest.

"That's it," he smiled. "Yes! This is where I started. This is the chair, I hope," and he rested one hand on the back of the chair. "I stopped here, looked at the water, walked a bit . . . it's got to be here. Or at least I should be able to see it. But . . .?"

That is *their* chair. This is *their* boardwalk path. He recognized the life ring and coiled rope hanging from the end of the railing, part of the path. "So I have the right damn house. But where is my stuff?" If he was in the right place, it was gone. But if this was the wrong house . . . It's going to be a long, and interesting night, he thought. He walked several yards up and down the beach looking for his shorts and sandals, now very aware of his nakedness.

Giving up, he started up the path, reconciled but dreading the walk up and into the house—unclothed. His bare feet felt the sand on the wooded boardwalk; the house should be close, maybe one hundred feet or so. As soon as he topped the first rise, he could see the dim light he had left on in the den.

"Ok that's doable; no one is up, the place is dark . . . who is going to see me? No one."

Confident, he slowly walked closer until he paused at the porch, covering himself, and listened. Nothing. The screen door was closed, but the door open, as he had left it. *God, if it was closed, locked. I'd be screwed,* he thought.

Inside, the table lamp so dim from the walkway was a glaring searchlight. "And I have to walk right through it to get to my room," he said to himself. He glanced up at the unseen balcony that led to the upper bedrooms. Not a sound. He carefully closed the screen and door behind him.

"Almost . . . no sweat," he muttered aloud, and he stepped forward into the light, his hands wide in case he bumped something he could not see. There was no avoiding the circle of light and for a second, maybe five steps, he was fully exposed, washed by the glow, in all his glory, and then he would be in the safety of the dark hall. He hesitated, if only to listen and bask in the thought that he had made it, when from upstairs, from the dark, he heard a soft giggle, the kind that comes from the back of your throat. A knowing self-satisfied chuckle. As he opened the door to his room, he heard footsteps above him, and the sound of a door closing softly.

~

He lay there uncertain whether he was dreaming or awake, unwilling to open his eyes to admit that the dream—*was it a dream?*—was gone, but unable to hang onto it, to get the images back. He often had this experience. He was jealous of those who clearly recalled their dreams, seemingly at will, in full detail. He imagined that he heard the bang of a car door, the catch of a tuned engine, and bite of tires on gravel? When he was on the cusp of waking he was never sure if he had been dreaming. Something was missing, some part of his consciousness faded like a spent sprinter without enough kick. The aroma of brewing coffee did not help. He heard voices, too soft to make out, coming from the veranda. Reluctantly he admitted dream defeat, opened his eyes, and reached for his watch. It was after 10:00 A.M.

He thought that he heard his name in a snatch of conversation. He got up. Foregoing a shower, he checked the mirror and ran a hand through his hair. He pulled on a pair of shorts, and then he remembered. *Dream? Last night happened!* Where were his other shorts and his sandals? He added a T-shirt and remembering Vera's instructions of informality, he stepped barefoot into the hallway. As he turned to close the bedroom door behind him, there, on the floor next to his bedroom door, were his shorts and tank top, stacked, neatly folded on top of his sandals. He glanced up to see if anyone was watching. He reached down, scooped them up, and with one quick motion opened the bedroom door and tossed them onto his bed. He closed the door and turned and walked through the den and out onto the veranda.

The sky was clear, the bay gleaming in the distance. Following the sound of voices, he walked around the porch to find a breakfast table set and, he assumed, his host chatting with Vera, who looked up and said, "Well look'a here what we got. One sleepy-eyed, young California man! They must sure get a late start on the day in California. Everyone sleep like that boy." She made California sound like a foreign country.

"Now, Vera, give him a break," the man seated at the table chided, as he stood and held out his hand. "He's had a long day yesterday, and he has come a long way. I'm Brad," he said as they shook hands. "You must be Scott, Scott Ames."

"Yes, sir. I am pleased to meet you." Scott shook his hand, smiled, and sat down at the table as Vera poured coffee for him and refilled the other man's cup.

"Thank you, ma'am," Scott replied.

"Don't you ma'am me, young man. My name's Vera, and that's what you call me if you want me to hear you," she cautioned warmly. "I told you that last night. Memory taken leave with all that sleep?" she teased.

"Yes, ma'am," Scott replied, smiling at both of them.

"Well, I guess you don't want to eat, 'cause ma'am ain't making no breakfast. Only Vera, and Vera's got eggs to order, sausage, toast, fresh-baked pecan buns. Guess you don't want none of that," she said.

Scott smiled at Brad and shrugged. He looked up at the woman, who stood coffeepot poised like a conductor's baton. "Vera, may I please have a couple of eggs scrambled, easy on the butter, and one of those famous pecan buns would be great, if you please," he said.

"Two *pleases* will get you all of that. Some folks got manners, even those from California!" She spun on her heel, headed toward the kitchen.

"Well, that's a great start," Brad said. "So, how was your evening? I'm sorry that I didn't get to spend some time with you, but I got stuck at the office, and then there were some details regarding tonight that held me up. By the time we wrapped that up it was too late, so I stayed in the city and drove out early this morning," he explained.

"It was fine, sir," he said. "The drive out here was great; the countryside is beautiful. Vera set me up with my room and wanted to do a big meal, but I talked her out it. Fred and I stopped for a bite on the way out, so I was not hungry. I think she was disappointed."

"That's Vera, and she is used to getting her way," he replied. "And please drop the *'sir'* stuff. It's Brad, O.K.?"

"Yes, sir. Brad. I really appreciate all the trouble you have gone to, inviting me into your home and everything," Scott said.

Brad leaned back, nursing his coffee, and studied the young man seated opposite him. He liked what he saw. Polite, comfortable with strangers, sense of humor. And, recalling the report that recommended the award he was to receive tonight, very bright and motivated. The committee has done it again, he thought, selecting this young man; another excellent choice. Everything he had read, and he had read it only yesterday at the insistence of his secretary, confirmed their choice—an outstanding young man, involved in his work, self-directed, serious work aimed at improving and preserving the environment. *Yes,* he thought, *this was a young man any father would be proud to call his son.*

He set his cup down and said, "Look, I am the one who is honored to have you here as our guest. Your room is O.K.? I thought the downstairs would be more convenient and private. We usually use that room for single guests. Depending on who is here, the upstairs can be a little noisy. I hope you weren't bored last night, I really wanted to get out here, I am sorry," he said.

"No, actually it was great, sir. Brad. I just hung out and was glad for the quiet and rest. That flight and the drive with the time change, I was beat," Scott offered.

"Breakfast!" Vera interrupted. "Eggs to order, easy on the butter, and *two* of those pecan buns. Save me a trip because Mr. W. will eat one of yours if you don't watch out!" Vera warned.

The plate in front of him, Scott surveyed the steaming eggs, surrounded by sausage and two pieces of French toast and two of the promised buns. Looking up at Vera, he knew she had set him up for a protest and he made none.

"Thank you, Vera," he said, "this looks great, especially the sausage."

"Well, we ain't got none of that funny cereal, oats, grains, and all that California stuff, what'cha call it?" she asked.

"You mean granola," he replied.

"Ain't real food that gran-o-la! Whoever heard of that?" she challenged. "Can't even cook it. Grind down your teeth is what I heard," she argued.

"Thanks, Vera," Brad interrupted.

Undaunted she continued, "That's real food, what you got there," she said, refilling Brad's cup with a nod before she turned away.

After a moment, Brad said over his cup, "She came, she saw, she conquered."

Scott turned to his food and, without really thinking, found he had eaten most of the sausage, and he had started in on the second bun, when he paused, embarrassed looking up.

"No," the man laughed, "I have had enough, really. Vera is always worried. No one eats enough for her."

The late morning was warm, and Scott finished his breakfast, not wanting to have to duel Vera if he left something on his plate. He was conscious of the man looking at him, studying him, but he felt comfortable, here with this man he had only just met.

"So, tell me a little about yourself, Scott," Brad asked, settling back in his chair. "I read your bio, quite impressive for someone your age, but I'd like to hear it from you," he said.

"Not, very exciting," Scott replied. "I grew up in Austin, Texas; went to local schools through high school. While I was in Boy Scouts, for my Eagle project, I got interested in streams, fish, stream ecology, although I didn't call it that then. I just set out to clean up a local creek. It got a lot of press because while we were doing the work, we discovered old car batteries, even an old refrigerator, acid had leaked out, leaching into the streambed. A local junk yard had been dumping toxic stuff near the bank and had pretty much messed up the stream. I got my picture in the newspaper, thanks to a reporter who happened to hear we had found these batteries and couldn't get anyone to take them."

He finished his coffee, set his cup down. As he continued, he ran his finger around the handle of the cup occasionally. "One thing led to another, and the mayor got involved, then the city council, and the next thing I knew people were asking if they could help. When it was over, this is now almost six months later, we had two miles of creek cleaned up and a permanent task force set up to plan and restore the remainder of the stream, with the goal of reintroducing fish—trout—into the stream, which was the outlet for a nearby lake. In fact, as of today the locals are fishing that creek, really a small river, and it is a thriving fishery."

"Well, I'll be. That is some story." Brad said. "The report just said something like 'showed interest in stream biology at an early age' . . ."

"Well, maybe I got lucky. It might have been a slow news day," Scott replied. "My mom sure did not like the newspaper stuff, my picture and all. She is a very private person. She said that it would interfere with her work."

Brad nodded. "I understand people who like their privacy. I'm one of them. Besides, *you* were the story, right? What about your dad?" he asked.

Scott looked at Brad and paused before he said, "My father died when I was only a year or so. A drilling accident. He worked on one of those offshore rigs."

"Scott, I am sorry. That must have been difficult for you," he said. "No brothers or sisters? Just you?"

"Just me."

"So then what, a scholarship? How did that happen?"

Scott noticed that his plate was gone, and he vaguely recalled that a satisfied Vera had taken it while he talked. Brad sipped his coffee while Scott continued.

"When I finished the project, I was a senior in high school. I had good grades in science, but I didn't have a clue what I wanted to do. A Texas company had a foundation with grants for college students interested in the environment. They contacted me, actually, and it was pretty much a free ride, so long as I kept up the grades and focused on something relating to the environment. I met with a committee, in Dallas, and that was it. My Eagle badge didn't hurt, and I had good references from part-time and summer jobs, that all helped. It sort of fell into place," he said.

"Could you have gone to college without it?"

"Not where I ended up, no way."

"Indian name, right? In Pennsylvania someplace."

"Oneka College," Scott replied. "It is from the Iroquois, Mohawk actually. Means 'water' in Native American Indian. They have one of the best stream biology departments in the country, and it got me out of Austin," he laughed.

"And then? What happened next?"

Scott felt comfortable and found it easy talking to Brad as if he had known him for years. For a moment he forgot that Brad was the president of a major corporation, whom he had just met. He continued, "Well, Pennsylvania was actually a world away from Austin, and it took a little getting used to. But the four years seemed to fly by. The first year I went home for the holidays, but my mom's job is so demanding and time consuming we didn't see much of each other, and most of my friends had gone away to college, out of Austin. When summer came, I got a job offer and stayed in Pennsylvania."

"Not homesick?" Refilling his coffee, he gestured with the pot. Scott, a hand over his cup, declined.

"No, I actually liked being on my own," he said. "So, from then on I sort of settled into life at Oneka. I made a friend whose father had a fishing lodge in upstate New York, on the Beaverkill, which is a classic trout stream, one of the most famous streams in the country. His lodge accommodated five guests, plus my friend and his family were usually there on weekends. They needed someone to caretake the place, and I could cook, so my weekend guest trip turned into a job, and I spent the next three summers there," he said. "It paid a little, enough to cover my gas and beer money, and it was a free place to live, with meals."

"Sounds great, almost like you should have paid them." Brad grinned.

"Right, exactly," Scott replied, resting his arms on the table, toying with his coffee cup. "But the best part was the fishing. I had never done fly-fishing, and here I was a stream biology major. All about the fish, right? It was pretty funny," he said. "Well, my friend Rick's grandfather spent lots of time there, and he taught me how to cast and read the water—knots, fly patterns, entomology, the whole works. It was an education." He continued, "I loved it, the whole catch and release thing; the idea of a sustainable sport; putting these beautiful fish back after enjoying them. I got hooked," he shrugged, smiling.

Brad found himself drawn to this pleasant young man and his story. *I might have had a son like this,* he mused. *A son to share these experiences with, the progress of his young life, the excitement of a promising future, doing something important, if only* . . . But long ago he had locked away those painful memories, the guessing of what might have been. His life was fulfilling, he had a beautiful daughter, whose independence delighted him. That was enough. But still, this young man, whose life was about to change more than he could imagine, he was glad that he could help him. Yet he felt something more. What was about him?

"But how did you get from that to what you do now? "Brad asked. "It sounds like too perfect a fit. Just luck?"

"Yes, a little luck helped," Scott replied. "I was studying stream biology."

For the next hour, Scott related his college and postgraduate experience. "Field" trips to the waters of Montana, Wyoming, Arkansas, Utah, and a summer spent guiding for a fly-out lodge on the Naknek River, in Alaska. Next came a job and teaching opportunities in California and out of that a river project restoring some of the western Sierra slope rivers: the Tuolumne, Merced, and parts of the Stanislaus. Then a chance to attempt to rehab a small stream in Northern California, home to spawning salmon and steelhead. That success let to the formation of his own company, several other small jobs, and their current project: the most ambitious he had ever undertaken. Scott saw Brad check his watch, and said, "That's about it."

Brad stood. "Well, my people checked you out, and they know what they are doing. It seems to me that they made the right choice," he said. "Look, I have a couple of things to do, errands to run, then we need to get ready for tonight. Want to ride along?" he asked.

"Sure, sounds like fun, and a chance to see more of this beautiful area."

"Ok," Brad answered. He slapped both his thighs hard and reminding himself added, "And we need to be back here to get dressed up. Tux tonight,"

Scott was standing, stretching, but stopped at the word, "Tux? You're kidding. I do not have a tux. I mean, no one . . ."

Brad put a hand on the young man's shoulder, "Relax. Forty-two long, thirty-four waist, size eleven shoe, close?"

Scott frowned, puzzled, "How did you . . .?"

Brad slapped him on the back, "It is in your closet, young man. *We* got you covered, at least Vera does. She can do anything," he laughed as Scott followed him into the kitchen, while Brad recited, over his shoulder, "Leave here at 6:00 P.M. or so, cocktails at 7:00, dinner at 8:00, awards over dessert, and then the music starts," this last part was delivered in musical format of some unintelligible melody.

~

As he crossed over the Chesapeake Bay Bridge for the second time, Scott marveled at the beauty of the magnificent bay, its placid surface hatch-marked with the wakes of power boats and dotted with the billowing canvas of sailboats reaching for the warm evening breeze. The serenity seemed out of place in proximity to the tumult of the nearby capital. Fred delivered them to the downtown Presidential Hotel, just off Independence Avenue, at 14th Street. The Adams Room was the grand ballroom, and it was set for at least two hundred people, Scott guessed.

Brad had explained that he would need to mix with the guests, his employees, some clients, and others who were personal friends, but that Scott should feel free to mingle as he saw fit. Scott assured him that he could "get by," resplendent in his tux. They laughed, and Brad mentioned that several single women should be present, after all this was Washington, D.C.

The room was almost full when they entered, and Brad found himself surrounded by men who were in formal wear, women fashionably and expensively dressed. At first, Brad included Scott in his conversations, but Scott soon realized that his presence was limiting for Brad. At the first chance, he eased away and located his table and seat. He was pleased to be seated with the other grant recipients. The calligraphy placecard to his right read "Guest/NEFCO." The assembled wine glasses suggested several courses. Scott was relieved that he had skipped lunch, after Vera's mammoth breakfast. The ballroom was decorated tastefully, flowers in stanchions close to the walls, the floral table arrangements thoughtfully low so as not to block the views of the diners; the lighting subtle.

He wandered into an adjacent bar and ordered a Samuel Adams in a pilsner glass, mindful that he might have to participate, somehow, in the evening's events. He stood to the side, admiring his luck and the guests. He had never been to an event of this caliber. He was even comfortable in his tux, admiring as he looked in the reflective glass of a nearby door. *If they could only see me now,* he thought of Ross and his friends at home. *No one will believe this.*

He chatted briefly with the Air candidate, but found him corporate and the conversation forced. As he glanced around, he still had this gnawing sense that his presence here might be a mistake. A voice from a podium announced that dinner was served, and guests began to take their seats. He threaded his way to his table. The Air man introduced his wife; the Earth man, his date; and Scott waited for the women to be seated. The seat next to his remained unoccupied. As he pulled his chair back to sit down, he was bumped sharply from behind. Embarrassed and certain that it had been his fault, he turned to apologize.

"That's *four,*" the young woman said, holding up four fingers, her other hand resting on a hip. She was smiling broadly at him as she lowered her hand and extended it to him. And there she was. He remembered his last words to her on the airplane the day before. He realized that he had not moved, had not said a single word. He was just standing there, gaping. She was dressed simply but elegantly in an off-the-shoulder silk dress, soft, gold, tight at the waist, cut at the knee, high heels. The others at his table had stopped talking and were staring puzzled at the two of them. He felt helpless and stupid; he knew he looked it. Jeff, Scott's guide of yesterday, broke the silence.

"Scott, have you met Jamie? No? I guess not," he said. "Jamie, I have the pleasure of introducing you to one of our honorees. Scott Ames. Scott," he paused, "This is Jamie Williams."

He took her warm hand. Her smile said it all—she had him, and she knew it. She glanced down at her chair and up at Scott. He realized that he was supposed to seat her, and he pulled her chair out. As she sat, her eyes followed him, and she nodded when he pushed her chair in and sat down next to her.

"Thank you," she said softly.

Table conversation resumed, and Scott, unable to take his eyes off her, leaned to her and said, his voice a whisper, "Williams? *The* Williams, as in Brad Williams?"

"Yes, *the* Williams." She laughed softly as she put a hand on his arm. "I'll explain later," she smiled at him. "Your appetizer," she indicated, reaching for a fork. "Don't let it get cold."

He continued to stare at her. Then he took his seafood fork and extracted one steamed clam from its shell and paused, looking at her, the clam clinging precariously to the fork, in midair, "What did you mean 'four'? This is *three*. The seat, the aisle: three," he asked puzzled.

"No, this is four." She paused, her eyes glistening. "*Three* was last night. Well, maybe three for you, but four for me—definitely four," her eyes flashed. She glanced up from her food and smiled, and then she laughed, a soft, knowing—familiar—laugh. He reached for his beer and drained it. He knew he was blushing.

~

The dinner over, service cleared, a distinguished looking Vice President introduced executives, department heads, international officers, everyone important, it seemed. Scott felt both lost and overwhelmed. It was as if one dream had invaded another, piling on his emotions, overloading them, and him. He had maintained his composure throughout the dinner, at times adding to the polite but casual conversation. But somehow, as he had earlier, he felt removed from it all. And, he wanted to get away, with her, just to be able to get to know this beautiful creature who had inserted herself somehow back into his life. He felt as if their meeting had been scripted.

The speeches dragged on, and finally the emcee announced the award presentations by introducing Brad, who, in turn, after a few brief remarks thanking the committee for its hard work, introduced the chairman of the A.W.E. committee, who gave a brief synopsis of the history of the awards. The chairman then opened an envelope and announced that "Air" had won $250,000. Scott heard the words, but he was too slow to absorb the consequences applicable to him. Scott reached over to the Earth candidate and extended his hand, so certain was he that the man's far more prestigious enterprise would be the ultimate beneficiary.

"Congratulations," Scott offered. "You have done some great work and this means … You deserve it," he said. The man stared blankly at Scott and did not accept his hand. He felt Jamie's cautionary hand on his other arm. In the recesses of his mind, almost inaudible to him he heard the presenter awarding the next grant to Earth, and he still did not understand, until again, her hand squeezed his arm tight enough to hurt, and through a mental fog, he saw that the people at his table, including Air and Earth, were all standing, looking at him—and applauding.

And in the next moment, the room darkened and behind the podium a huge screen dropped down on which appeared a roaring, plunging cataract of water, foam and spray rising, and out of that surging flume rose one, and then two, and then another, and another, great arching salmon, bodies bowed with the energy of their leap: out, up, suspended in midair, brilliant silver sides and spray shimmering in the sunlight, spawning colors glowing, each seemingly impossibly propelled up, always up, farther up the river that was their ancestral home. The music rose and the video continued. Scott was transfixed. And there he was, in living color, emerging from the river in scuba gear; then waist deep in water struggling with a cable to place a log barrier into the river; and on the bank, arm around Ross, raising their beers to the camera; their beat-up truck and Ross's jeep; and on the video continued. He could not remember them taking these pictures. Now headlines in the Austin paper: "Eagle Scout saves local stream …" and his picture, and more. Then a pause, darkness and alone on the screen the letters and the words:

Ames Environmental: Saving the Future
A.W.E. Winner—$1,000,000.00
Congratulations, National Filter and Environmental Corporation

Two hundred people rose as one, applauding, cheering. Scott sat there stunned, and then the tears came. All the years, the work, the seemingly thankless backbreaking work, fighting landowners, the government, and nature itself, everyone and everything, it seemed, all for those amazing animals, for those beautiful, magical, magnificent fish and their way of life, and what they represented to the earth, the planet, the video voice-over had said. He knew through the din of the applause—Jamie tugged at his sleeve—that he had to stand, that he was supposed to say something. He stood and walked slowly to the podium.

~

Later, after a speech that he would never remember giving, the toasts, the backslapping congratulations, the warm regards from, it seemed, everyone, the crowd gave itself over to the music and dancing. On his way back from the restroom, he ducked into the lobby bar. He called Ross in California, whose immediate response had been, "Don't bullshit me, I'm stuck here in this dump while you . . ." No amount of arguing could convince him, so Scott hung up. He ordered a vodka over with a twist, and he sat on a stool facing the bar, his back to the lobby, and tried to put it into perspective. This was real; his company was going to have one million dollars over the next year; no more service club lunches, dinners, fundraisers, begging for equipment and volunteers. He would have the money for environmental easements, everything they needed, and at last his time could be put to doing the real work that waited. He saw her in the mirror as she walked up behind him. He smiled and turned. She put one hand on his cheek; a finger traced where the tears had dried, and then she stepped back, looking at him.

"So, Mr. Ames, now that you have a million dollars of my daddy's money, what happens next?"

"Vegas. Put it on eleven. A one-roll bet. Fifteen to one odds, bet it all and get some serious money," he deadpanned as he sipped on his drink.

"I'm going to get my father," she pouted, starting to turn away. They both laughed. Scott, hearing the orchestras, slid off the stool and he held out his arm.

"May I have this dance, Miss Williams?"

"Well, Mr. Ames, since we, the company, have such a significant investment in you, I suppose it is my obligation not to offend one of our *partners,*" she said, placing her arm in his. They walked together and back into the ballroom. She turned into him, and Scott put his arm around her waist and held her, his other hand at shoulder height. She looked up at his hand and smiled as he took hers. *When certain events occur, you always remember where you were and what you were doing,* Scott thought, *and he knew that whatever happened, he would always remember this moment.*

Across the ballroom, Brad glanced up and saw Scott and Jamie. His smile drew into a frown as he considered the possibilities. The daughter of whom he was so proud, and this bright young man whom he only met yesterday and now in whom he had a substantial investment. They looked so perfect together. His thoughts melded into the picture of the small boy in his office. He shook his head and turned back to the conversation.

~

They were in the car. Fred was driving. As they crossed over the darkened bay, Scott asked, "When did you know?"

"That it was you, from the plane?" she had one leg tucked under her, a take-out coffee in her hand. "When I saw Fred at the airport," she said. "I was surprised that he was not picking *me* up. Fred!" she laughed and scowled. "But I didn't put it together until I got to the office. I checked with daddy's secretary, and she filled me in—on you." She took a sip. "I actually got a look at your resume. Much better impression than on the plane," she smiled.

"Yes, but—"

"Let me finish," she said. "I had plans to meet some friends in George-town. You have heard of Georgetown?" she paused.

He shrugged and then nodded.

"I asked for Fred because I knew I would be late and I do not like to stay in the city. Well, he was 'taken,' I was told and that is how I learned that you went to the shore." She stopped.

He knew he would have to ask if he wanted more. *Let him ask me,* she thought.

"And?" Scott said.

"And, I thought, well, maybe I will see what this smart 'fish' guy is about. So, later I caught a ride to the house, 'Caught' not bad, huh?"

Scott grimaced.

"But, no Mr. Ames. Vera was already gone, and I checked the rooms. I figured you for the single room, and there were your things. But no one. Gone. Now where could he go? The beach? It *was* a beautiful night. Huge moon. For a walk. Yes, that's it, a walk. So, I went down to the beach. No you. I gave up and went back."

"And?"

"And nothing. I had a date to go sailing early the next morning, so I took the Healey and left. You were, they told me, sleeping in."

"That's it?"

"Why, yes. that's it," she said. "Oh, tonight? We were late getting off the bay, so I caught a ride back to D.C., and here we are. I knew, of course, that you might still be here, unless . . ."

"Unless what?"

She looked at the back of Fred's head, and her eyes met Fred's in the mirror. *He knows* she thought: *Vera.*

"That's it," she concentrated on her drink, breathing into it, making the steam rise in her face. He continued to look at her.

"You stole my stuff," he glanced at Fred. *He knows,* Scott thought.

"Excuse me! What are you accusing me of? Did you hear him, Fred?" She looked for help from Fred. Fred was concentrating on the road.

"You know," Scott replied, "I could have been in a real mess," his voice strained.

"Really. Why is that?" she mocked his tone, her head tilted.

Scott sat back and looked out at the passing houses, a church steeple silhouetted against the darker sky. He turned back to her and smiled.

"Are we even?" he said softly.

"For . . .?"

"Everything," he extended his hand.

"Even," she said firmly. *He does not mean it. Not for a minute.* She could see it in his eyes. *I have not heard the end of this,* she thought. *And that is just fine.*

"O.K.," Scott continued. "Tell me about tomorrow. What you are so excited about that you conned, talked, me into leaving the delights of D.C. and coming back here?"

"Fred! Turn the car around," she snapped.

Fred's neck stiffened, and he watched them in the rearview mirror. He slowed the car.

Scott was puzzled. "What! O.K., not conned," he said.

"If you do not want to go," the pout again.

"No, it's great," he replied, the car still slowing. He was surprised.

"Just kidding," she laughed. "Home, Fred," and she saw that she had startled him. *Good,* she thought. *This may be fun.* "You just be ready by 7:00 A.M., or I will have Vera wake you and *that* is an experience," she warned. "I'll explain it all on the way. We have about a two-hour drive in the morning."

CHAPTER 9

HE FOLLOWED THE AROMA OF THE COFFEE into the kitchen. He was dressed in shorts, a polo shirt, and a pair of Pumas. He set his windbreaker on the counter and poured a cup of coffee. He heard her behind him.

"Ready?" she asked. "I've got coffee in the car. Let's go," she said.

He turned. She gestured for him to follow. Outside, the Austin-Healey idled in the drive. She slid behind the wheel.

"Better put this on. It will be cool for a while," she pointed to a cable-knit sweater on the passenger seat. He pulled the sweater over his head and settled into the open red roadster.

He noticed her hand flexing on the shift knob.

"O.K.," he said.

She revved the engine once and eased out the clutch. The car moved forward cleanly down the tree-lined drive. He admired the ease with which she took the sports car through the gears. At the end of the gravel drive, she downshifted, slowed, and checked the roadway for oncoming cars. Nodding to herself, she turned onto the main road, and the tires spit gravel as she accelerated on the pavement. The taut whine of the engine was the only sound on this still, early, morning. He felt the cool air washing around him.

"Pull up that windscreen," she said. The wind noise abated almost entirely.

"Much better," she said, smiling at him for the first time, now relaxed.

"Great car," Scott said. "Brad's?"

"Actually, it's mine," she answered. "A graduation present. Dad had it fully restored, but I picked the color."

"Perfect choice," he replied. "This car has to be red." Her right hand was poised on the shift knob, the other comfortably on the wheel. *She knows what she is doing.*

St. Michael's was still shuttered at this early hour, the normally busy streets deserted except for a café whose lights came on as they drove past. Soon the roadside businesses and homes gave way to small farms and fields. In patches, the overhanging trees created an arbor-like tunnel, and he was glad for the sweater. He looked at her. She wore her hair up, the ponytail protruding from her baseball cap. She had on khaki shorts and running shoes, a dark green windbreaker, her shirt collar turned up inside the jacket collar. He noticed the soft leather, vented, driving gloves. Her sunglasses looked expensive, the logo concealed by her hair and hat. If she had on any makeup, he could not see it. *She looks perfect,* he thought, as if the car had picked *her* out.

They had both been quiet until he asked,

"So where is this horse show, or whatever? Where we are going? *Chin*—something?"

She laughed. "It's *shin,* like your leg, not *chin.* Chincoteague. It is an Indian name, I think. And it is not a horse show. It is a pony swim," she said.

"A what?"

"They, the local fire department, swim the ponies across the channel from Assateague to Chincoteague, from one island to the other."

"I passed up the Lincoln Memorial, the Washington Monument, the National Gallery, for swimming ponies from, what is it, Ass-something to Chin . . . ?" he groaned.

She slowed as they negotiated a small village, and soon was back up to speed. She laughed and shook her head, her ponytail swinging. "Stop it, Scott," she scolded. "If you will stop, I will tell you the story."

"It better be good to beat out the White House and the Space Museum," he countered.

"Well, it is, and no one you know will have ever heard of it, or seen it. Not unless they read the book about it."

"There is a book? What, a coloring book?" he chided.

"No, Scott. Not a coloring book, though there is probably one we can get you! No, actually a best-seller."

"Right, and a movie too!"

"Yes, actually, a movie. It was called *Misty*. *Misty of Chincoteague*, the book and the movie. Actually the movie was very good, it had only four real actors in it, one of them nominated for an Academy Award, twice I think, and the other one was Alan Ladd's son," she said. "And the others in the movie were all real people, townspeople."

"You know all this?" he leaned toward her, watching her expression.

"Of course," she nodded.

"O.K., shoot. Let's hear about, what's her name, Misty." He leaned back against his door facing her.

"Once upon a time . . ."

"Oh, my God . . ."

She laughed and continued.

"It all started in 1750, when a Spanish galleon left Havana for Spain and was blown off course, way off course. It was wrecked in the ocean off what is today Assateague Island, which is a mile or so across the sound from Chincoteague. That's where we are headed. They are both located in Virginia, near the Maryland state line. There were no survivors from the shipwreck, except several Spanish horses, small horses, more like ponies today. The horses swam ashore on Assateague and their descendants survive to this day. Penning is like a roundup for branding and sorting the ponies, and dates back to the 1800s. But, starting in 1920 or so, the locals began to swim the ponies across the channel from Assateague, their home, to Chincoteague, and they penned them up in the town. At some point the local fire department took over and began sponsoring the swim and the penning, and they auctioned some of the ponies to support the fire department. They limit the herd on Assateague to not more than 150 now. The swim and pony penning and the auction have continued to this day."

"Wow! You are right, I never heard of it," Scott said. "How many people show up?" he asked.

She smiled over at him. "Thirty" she said, pausing. "Thirty *thousand*, plus."

"You're kidding!" Scott straightened up.

"That was last year. Maybe more; never less," she said. "And, the two most important things? A place to park and a seat for the show."

"How many seats?" Scott asked.

She continued looking ahead, and then tilted her head his way. "Two, Mr. Ames."

She downshifted as the road merged with the southbound highway, and soon they crossed into the state of Virginia.

~

When they entered the village of Chincoteague, the traffic began to slow; the streets were packed with people and cars. Jamie followed the signs reading "To Parking/Shuttle." When they had slowed to a crawl, she said, "There's a pass in the glove box. Would you put it on the dash?"

At the next intersection, seeing the pass, the traffic officer waved them ahead, and he pulled a barricade open for them to pass through and away from the lines of cars. Jamie smiled a thank you at the officer who, smiling, nodded, admiring the car, or its driver, Scott was not sure which.

"Neat, huh?" she said as she moved quickly down the street, slowed only occasionally by pedestrians, all headed the same way. After a few blocks, she turned into a driveway and parked. She tooted the horn. A middle-aged, woman came to the screened door and waved, disappeared, and then appeared again as the garage door rolled up.

Jamie got out of the car and was enveloped in a hug, and the woman kissed her head.

Jamie said, turning, "This is my friend, Scott Ames."

"Oh, I heard all about this Scott Ames," the woman smiled, approaching Scott as he stepped from the car. "He is the rich one now, I hear." She ignored Scott's extended hand and folded him into her arms. Jamie winked. Released, he stepped back.

"I am pleased to meet you, Mr. Ames," as she shook his hand.

"Scott, this is Iris, Vera's sister. She lives here in Chincoteague, and she is going to let us park here. Vera gave us her resident's pass. That's how we were able to drive through the control point. Without it, we would have had to park on the far side of town and take the shuttle in and back," Jamie explained.

"Thank you, Iris. We appreciate it," Scott offered.

Reaching into her pocket, Scott saw Jamie take out a few bills and hand them to the woman. "This is for your church project, Iris," she said. "I should have mailed it earlier. I hope it is not too late," she said.

"You sure this is for the church and not for the parking?" Iris said, hesitating to accept the money. "'Cuz I ain't taking no money from you for the parking!"

Gently Jamie pressed the folded bills into her hand. "Iris, you know that I would not offend you by trying to pay for parking in your driveway. It *is* for the church, and I would have mailed it if I had not been coming today."

"O.K., you sure? O.K., then. We are happy to accept your kind offering. Knows we need it," she gave Jamie another hug and kiss. "You two better get along, or you will miss the swim, I think."

Jamie handed Iris the car keys. "Scott, give me a hand with this." She opened the rear boot and removed a small backpack, which she set down on the grass. Then she lifted out a tonneau cover, and with Scott's help, in a minute they had the sports car buttoned up. Iris watched them and nodded at Jamie's efficiency.

"Ok, Iris, that's it," Jamie said as she snapped the cover over the dash. "We will see you later."

"Be sure you leave time for a visit."

"We will," Jamie replied. She picked up the pack and, before Scott could offer, she slipped it over her shoulders. As she took Scott's hand and led him down the driveway, she saw Iris's eyes widen and then smile approvingly. She winked back.

Scott noticed that the street and sidewalk were now packed with people. Between the buildings, Scott could see the glistening bay.

"Church project?" he asked.

"Yes, it's our game. She could have charged at least $100 for that parking place today. All the houses had cars in their driveways. People who come every year have 'reserved' spots to park for years. It sort of runs in the family for many of them, handed down, like football tickets," she explained.

"Here," she said, handing Scott a lanyard with a plastic badge clipped on the end. "Put this on."

Ahead Scott could see that the buildings opened up to give way to the shore, a park on one side and on the other a launch ramp and a pier, which extended out into the bay.

"This is where ponies come ashore, and they run, or herd, them through the town to the park where the pens are set up," she explained.

At a break in the barricade in front of the pier, their badges allowed them to pass quickly through the checkpoint, and they walked out onto a pier that was an extension of the ramp. At the end there were rows of seats facing the water, some elevated, stadium style. Jamie checked her pass.

"Here, this is it." Their seats were at the very edge of the pier facing the ramp, the water only a few feet below.

"They will swim them right by here," Jamie said indicating the area in front. "We can almost touch them with our feet. They will go past us, and up alongside the pier, and then up the ramp. We will be practically on top of them," she said. "And, from here we can also see them as soon as they round the point, over there," she pointed out into bay.

"Wow," Scott said. "How did you swing this?"

"Pull, Mr. Ames. And money," she laughed.

"Well, let me at least pay for the tickets," he said, reaching back for his wallet.

"I'm kidding." Her hand was warm. "We get these every year because dad supports the Fire Department. He did a project for them years ago, and since then every year they send us two tickets, and, if we don't use them, he gives them to someone at the office. I asked for them this year because I had not been here for a while." She opened her backpack and pulled out a thermos and cups. She poured their coffee and handed one to Scott. With a grin, she gave him a round object wrapped in its own napkin. He carefully opened it as she watched.

"Oh, no," Scott groaned. "Not again!" He admired Vera's handiwork; the sugared bun gleamed in the sunlight. "You only live once," he mumbled as he bit into it.

Jamie smiled at him over the roll in her hand. While they ate and drank their coffee, the pier filled up quickly. Scott looked in at the shore and every conceivable spot was occupied. *There must be thousands of people,* he thought, *and we are on the fifty-yard line.* He heard a hum from the crowd; it seemed to be several blocks away; then a rising crescendo of noise.

"They are coming," Jamie said. "That's the noise from the other end of park. They see them first, before they round the point. It will be a few minutes, yet," she said. "You might finish your coffee, because it is going to get a little crazy here." She took a last sip of her coffee and tossed the remainder into the water in front of them. Out on the bay, Scott could see a few small motorboats rounding the point, and then more.

"Here they come," Jamie pointed, and as one the people on their pier stood up. Out in the bay, Scott could see heads in the water, first a few and soon many more, and as they drew closer, he could make out the swimming horses, flanked by a cordon of boats on each side. He started to count them but soon gave up.

"There must be what? Fifty?"

"More. Usually a hundred or so."

They were closer now, and he was able to pick out individual animals. The excitement of the crowd was palpable as onlookers commented on individual horses, picking favorites.

"Look at that one, mommy! I want the black one with the blaze! Can we touch them, daddy?"

Children and parents shared the spectacle. *She was right; this is really something,* Scott thought. *I would have never seen this.* The first of the horses were now in the area between their pier and the shoreline, and the leaders touched the bottom and lunged ashore. Behind them, others labored, some obviously tired, all anxious to finish their journey and gain the firm footing of the land.

"They look beat," Scott observed, raising his voice over the cheering crowd.

"Sure," Jamie replied, "they are. They have swum about a mile, and it is a little scary for them. All the noise. Look," she pointed. The horses were now bunched up right in front of them, almost touching the pier, as they waited to clamber ashore. Scott could see the boats pushing them in. He was almost on top of them, and he thought that he could read fright in their eyes. The horses surged, still in water too deep to touch bottom. Some bumped and jostled others. Scott wondered that some did not kick and injure others in their urgent push to the shore.

"Oh, oh," Jamie, said, alarmed. "Look! That filly, she's in trouble, Scott!"

He followed Jamie's outstretched arm to a horse almost directly in front of them. As he looked, a pony next to the one Jamie was watching, butted the other animal's head and the filly disappeared under the water. Later, he could not remember deciding to jump after Jamie, and he had no recollection of doing it. He did not even remember her jumping. But they were both in the water, and Jamie grabbed a handful of mane and yanked the filly's head up out of the water and he was alongside, helping her. Together they managed to pull the horse's head up so that she could breathe. Around them, horses surged, bumping them and passing them on either side. They struggled to hold the horse's head up and could feel her trying to regain her strength. She snorted once, twice, clearing her nostrils and moved forward, swimming slowly, not fighting them. They hung onto her, careful to stay clear of her hooves. She continued to struggle, and Scott felt something hit his arm and fall over his shoulder.

"Over her head. Slip it over her head!" he heard the shout from above.

He grabbed the noose with one hand, and it slipped on easily, on the first try—*lucky,* he thought—up her muzzle, over her ears, and onto her neck. He watched as it tightened and the rope held by someone on the pier deck above him provided just enough lift and pressure to keep the horse's head up. Whoever was holding the rope walked it toward the shore in time with the animal's progress. The pony was able to keep swimming, and they hung on, helping her. He could hear Jamie talking, soothing the frightened horse.

As they approached the ramp, Scott, now behind Jamie, let go of the filly's mane, and he kicked away from the swimming horse. All the other ponies, except a few stragglers, were out of the water, the last of them now moving up the ramp. They stopped to shake off the seawater, whinnying their excitement and relief, and then they loped to catch up with the leaders. Scott swam for the ramp. He could see Jamie standing now, gently easing the pony up the ramp. As the horse stopped to shake, Jamie, one hand still clutching her mane, stepped aside, and then slipped the now slack rope off her head. Out of the water, the filly seemed smaller than Scott imagined. Scott felt the bottom, and he started to walk up the ramp. He paused to watch as the pony danced once to the side, looked back at Jamie and with a loud neigh and a toss of her head, she trotted off after the others and quickly disappeared among the moving herd.

Jamie stood still, facing away from Scott watching the horses as they moved into the town. In profile, her hat gone, hair drenched, her silk blouse transparent, wet, clinging to her—*she is beautiful,* Scott thought. She turned toward him and smiled.

"Are you nuts!" she said. "Jumping into water to save a horse!"

"Horse? I thought I was saving you!" Scott laughed.

She smiled, but it was a different kind of smile—in her eyes. She stepped forward and without a word, she put both arms around his neck and held him pressed to her. He felt her shaking. Scott was surprised, until someone on the pier clapped: one person. And then several more, and finally suddenly a loud round of applause. He felt Jamie—wet, leaning on him—and then she lifted her head, looking up at him.

"That's for *you*, for saving *me*," she grinned and she stepped out of his arms.

"Right," Scott groaned. He waved at the people on the pier. When they reached the top of the ramp, someone handed Jamie her pack.

"Thank you."

"Nice job, you guys. You saved that filly. She would have never made it," the man said. At the head of the ramp, they looked at each other, both were dripping wet, shoes soaked, shirts and shorts drenched.

"You lost your hat," Scott said. "Got your car key?"

"I left them with Iris. Thank goodness."

Scott felt for his back pocket. "I got my wallet, but it is soaked," Scott replied. "So, now what?"

A uniformed fireman appeared with two towels. "Saw you two, here," he said. "From the aid station, over there. Nice work; quick thinking. Let me know if you need anything else. Hot coffee?"

"Thanks," Scott said as he dried off his head and then blotted his clothes.

Jamie did the same, shaking out her damp hair. "Unless we are going to walk around like this for the couple of hours it will take us to dry out, we probably ought to go back to Iris's and get cleaned up."

Looking at her, Scott said, "Probably all right with the onlookers if you walk around like that."

Jamie looked down at herself. Her wet blouse was clinging to her body.

"Men!" she snapped. "Let's go!"

Scott followed her through the park, away from the water. Ahead they could see the herd gathered, entering the park and the paddocks constructed especially for pony penning day.

～

They slogged back to Iris's house to wistful glances and outright stares. Iris was standing inside her open garage, a disapproving look on her face. She had heard about their exploit: a call from Vera, who had received a call from someone she knew who recognized Jamie. Ready for them, she supervised the washing and drying of their soggy clothes and shoes while Jamie took a shower. Scott accepted her light bathrobe, and he settled into a chair on the rear lawn, sensing that something tasted good and felt better in the tea Iris had given him. Jamie, her hair wet and shining, joined him. In the interim, they visited with Iris and recounted the details of what was being referred to as the "rescue."

Later, dry and dressed, they walked back into town and browsed the stands and shops. Scott had to have a "Misty" T-shirt, and he purchased an extra one for Ross. Jamie took him to the pens, and after a time they located the filly. Someone had put up a hastily crafted sign on the railing, "Saved" and the date, and they had also tied a yellow ribbon in the pony's mane to show her off. She was receiving a lot of attention, one of the pen attendants told them. The man was certain there would be heavy bidding on her at the auction tomorrow.

Having taken it all in, Scott and Jamie walked back to Iris's house and said their goodbyes. Jamie got them quickly out of town. On the way, she mentioned that they had not eaten since the pier, and it was late afternoon. She asked whether Scott had ever eaten Maryland crab cakes.

"Never heard of them," he replied.

"We're going to Oxford, then," she announced downshifting into a tight turn and revving the sports car out onto the straight highway.

An hour later, she pulled up at an imposing inn, which was set at the edge of a large bay. She stretched from the long ride, and said, "Get ready for the best crab cakes in the world. I mean it," she reacted to his raised eyes. "*The* best, and they have James Michener to attest to it. C'mon." She led the way up to a covered porch under the sign Robert Morris Inn: 1710.

"1710!" Scott said.

"Exactly," Jamie said proudly. "And check this out," she touched his arm and pointed out into the wide river in front of the Inn.

"What is that?" Scott asked.

"A ferry. You'll see later," she smiled. She led him into the restaurant dining room. Seated beneath the massive beamed ceiling, the mural-sized wall paintings offset the eighteenth-century period furnishings. Jamie smiled knowingly at the waitress and ordered an appetizer of Parrot Bay Oysters, garden fresh salads, and entrees of crab cakes, for two. Scott managed to slow her down long enough to scan the extensive wine list, and he was puzzled to see a Stone Fly Cab Franc, so far from its Napa origins. When the bottle he ordered was served, he pointed out the fly line circling from the front label to the rear where its fly was snagged in a grapevine.

"Fish! Always the fish," she smirked. During the meal, which Scott admitted was one the best he had ever eaten, they relived the events of their unusual day.

"You have about ten minutes," the waitress warned Jamie over their coffee.

"For what?" Scott asked Jamie as he settled the bill.

"You will see. My surprise, and I have saved the best for last."

"Haven't we had enough surprises for one day? I have."

"You can never have enough surprises, Ames. Not good ones," she took his arm when they left the dining room.

They stepped off the porch into a westerly sky of mottled blue with patches of rose and yellow pouring underneath. The brilliant setting sun was a golden path directed at them, across the dappled river in front. Its random glistening ripples gave movement to the dying light.

"Magnificent," Scott whispered.

"Good word, Ames," she replied. "Get in."

She backed the sports car out and headed toward the water. Without a pause, she drove down the nearby ramp and onto the ferry boat waiting at the end of the quay. Scott was so entranced with the changing sunset sky, he had not noticed the boat. They were the first car aboard and were soon joined by three others. Jamie pulled to the front and shut off the engine. The river was now a sheet of gold, gently spilling to either side by the moving vessel. They got out of the car, and Jamie walked to the front and leaned back against the hood. The liquid gold slid beneath their feet.

Scott stood for a moment beside her, and then he reached down, taking her hand and pulled her up. He leaned back against her car and folded her into his arms, both facing the sunset. Neither said a word as the boat moved out into the river, and for most of the ten-minute ride to the St. Michael's side. As they neared the shore, the afterglow of the setting sun faded to early dark. Jamie straightened to get back in the car. Scott rose, and turning her toward him, he took her in his arms and, sensing that it was somehow all right, he leaned down and kissed her gently on the lips. She met his kiss, and they lingered until the whistle of the ferry sounded.

"More surprises," he said softly.

"The whistle? Or . . ." Jamie asked, looking up him.

"The whistle," he smiled.

The ferry had taken only a few minutes to cover the six miles from Oxford to the St. Michael's dock. During the short drive remaining, neither of them spoke. Jamie put the car in the open garage. They entered the darkened house through the kitchen. The house was quiet. Jamie paused in the living room and put her hand on Scott's arm. He took her hand, uncertain of his next move.

"Jamie, thank you for an absolutely great day. I do not know when I have had so much fun and experienced so many different places and things in one day. It was great. Just great."

She shook his hand, gently, and withdrawing hers, equally uncertain, said, "Scott it was my pleasure. All of it. I had a great time, too. See you in the morning, and we can talk about the flight home. Good night," she said, and she turned and mounted the stairs.

Scott watched her up the stairs and just as he turned toward his room, from the darkness above he heard her say, "Better not go for a swim tonight, Ames. We have had enough surprises for one day," and her door closed.

~

"I changed my flight," Jamie said, walking on the deck where Brad and Scott were lingering over coffee. "But then I am in first class and it was easier than trying to change yours. At least we are on the same flight and we arrive together," she said taking a chair across from them.

"That's good," Brad said leaning forward. "Maybe the two of you can work something out at check-in once you are at the airport, so you can sit together."

"I'm sure Jamie could swap her first-class seat with whomever I'm seated next to," Scott deadpanned.

"Nice of you to offer me up," she said. They all laughed. Scott and Jamie were scheduled to fly out of Washington Dulles at 4:00 P.M. and arrive in San Francisco in the early evening. He had called Ross to give him the arrival time, so he could pick him up at the airport.

"Well," Brad said, "It has been quite a weekend for you, hasn't it, Scott?"

"Yes, sir, Brad," Scott replied. Brad frowned at the "sir." "Frankly, it seems like a lot longer than, what, four days," Scott replied.

"After you get home, Jamie will contact you and fill you in on the funding for the grant. If you had more time now, I would have my people go over it with you, but since she is on the coast and near you, she will actually handle the details from her office," Brad explained. "That should be O.K.?"

"Well, I am not sure about having to deal with her," Scott quipped. "She has a tendency to jump in over her head."

"Stop it!" Jamie reached out and hit his arm.

"She does that," Brad laughed. "Fred will be here to take you two to the airport."

"I spoke to Fred," Jamie interrupted, "we are all set," nodding at Scott.

"Well, that does it then," Brad said rising. "Scott, I could not be more pleased and frankly excited with our selection of you and your company for the grant."

Scott accepted the other man's extended hand, a firm grasp.

"And it has been my pleasure to have you as my guest these past few days," Brad concluded.

"Thank you, *sir*. It has been my pleasure, and there is no way that I can express my gratitude for the grant. When I came here I really thought that even considering our small company must have been some sort of a mistake," he replied. "In fact, since Saturday night I have half expected someone to walk up and say that this is a terrible mistake, sorry."

"Well, it is not a mistake, and you have earned it. All of it. And I know that you will put it to good use. I do not normally get to the West Coast, I cannot remember the last time. Well, maybe I can . . . anyway, it was a long time ago. Maybe this will give me an excuse to get out there and see your operation," he finished.

"It would be an honor, sir, just let us know. There are some times of the year when it is more exciting than others, like the spawning run. That is when you want to come."

"I'll keep that in mind," Brad said warmly. "Until then," he shook Scott's hand and then without thinking, almost as a reflex, reached out and hugged the young man. He stepped back, surprised at himself, and then without another word he turned away and entered the house.

"Oh," Jamie said, her voice a whisper. "I have never seen him do that. Never."

She looked at Scott, puzzled, and thought she saw the beginning of a tear.

Inside, Brad glanced out at the two on the deck. *There is something about that young man. What is it? It is more than his apparent interest in Jamie, or her in him? But why do I feel so . . . connected to him?*

~

Their flight landed at 7:10 P.M., slowed by the eastward jet stream. It was dusk beyond the sidewalk outside the luggage carousel as Jamie awaited their bags. Scott had gone looking for Ross. She looked up as he walked back in.

"We can fit you, barely, if you want. It will be tight," he said.

"As long as I do not have to sit on your lap or the floor, it is O.K. with me," she replied.

"Lap, no. Seatbelt required. Floor? No, same," he smiled. "Here's mine," he said as he stepped around her and grabbed his soft duffel, emblazoned with Trout Unlimited, Cal Trout, Save Our Steelhead, Salmon, and other stickers.

"Can't miss that," Jamie smiled at him.

"It is who I am," he said.

They retrieved her bags and walked out into the warm summer evening. A jeep, unmistakable for its identical but more elaborate stickers and lettering, idled at the curb. A long-haired, unshaven young man, Scott's age, in T-shirt and shorts was behind the wheel. He turned toward them as Scott heaved their bags into the rear of the open vehicle.

"Wow, you were not kidding!" A low whistle preceded his remarks.

"Ross, this is Jamie," Scott introduced her. "Jamie, this *thing* is my right hand. Could not do it without him." Scott stepped over the passenger seat and settled into the rear jump seat, forced to lean forward due to the luggage behind him. Jamie accepted Ross's hand as she buckled into the passenger seat. And she returned his look.

"Meaning?" she asked Ross as he pulled away from the curb into the airport traffic.

"Meaning? Oh? That . . ." Ross faked a stammer. "Scott, he, well, he described you on the phone and when he came out just a minute ago."

"And?"

"Smart," Ross replied. "He said you were really smart. As in very intelligent." His entire face a broad grin. Instantly serious and anxious to change the subject, Ross said, "How was the flight?"

"Interesting for Jamie," Scott laughed, and he explained that they were unable to switch Scott to a first-class seat, so taking his dare Jamie traded her first-class aisle seat for a window in the very last row of the coach section. Three across, but no one in the center.

"Slumming," she kidded. "But," she added, "the attendants were so sympathetic they left the wine bottle and did not charge us for the movie."

"Which we never watched," Scott added.

On the long flight they had talked the entire time, exchanging histories, education, ideas, with never a break in the dialogue. They had not finished when the cabin announced their arrival in San Francisco. Scott knew that Ross was waiting with the jeep, and he offered Jamie a ride into the city. Without Scott knowing it, when they arrived she had called her car service and cancelled the pickup she had arranged when she had flown out the week before. Scott warned her that his ride was risky and open to the elements. She did not care.

Jamie directed them to her apartment in the city, off Broderick Street, the bridge glowing in the darkened sky. Scott took her bag and walked her to the door of her flat. As she did the key, they were silent. The door open, she said, "I can get it from here."

"Are you sure?"

"Yes. Ross is waiting."

"And if he was not?"

"I can get it," she smiled, one foot now over the threshold.

Scott stepped back haltingly, unsure, and it showed.

"I'll call you, Jamie," he said softly but firmly. "Tomorrow."

"You better, if you want your money," she smiled as she reached down for her bag.

Scott moved toward her, and with one hand on either side of her face, he kissed her gently on the lips. She started to straighten up, and Scott backed up, afraid that he had made a mistake. Jamie set her bag down slowly, her eyes on his, and moving into his arms, kissed him. And he knew it was no mistake as he returned her kiss and held her tightly against him.

~

Over the following weeks, Scott spoke almost daily with Jamie regarding implementation of his grant. Jamie worked in San Francisco for a boutique investment firm that specialized in high net worth individuals, including monitoring some of her father's personal and corporate portfolios. Brad had placed Jamie in charge of the funding and oversight of Scott's grant for a couple reasons: one, her proximity to Scott and his operations, and the other (not shared with Jamie), the thought of increasing that proximity, personally. Brad liked the idea of Scott and Jamie.

Now, Scott found himself buried under necessary paperwork: financial statements more complex than his check register; the need for defined projects, with budgets, cost projections, manpower and equipment analyses. Early on, Jamie had arranged for a CPA to help him with these matters for which he had little aptitude and less patience. But soon, Scott came to appreciate the details and the necessity of managing this large sum of capital, which would have such a dramatic effect on his operations. He found himself traveling often from his house several hours north of the city down to San Francisco for rounds of meetings with Jamie and the CPA.

During one of his early trips, Jamie convinced him that he needed a new truck, and she took to him to a dealership belonging to one her clients. The deal she struck for him impressed Scott. In the evenings, they usually dined together at restaurants selected by Jamie. Their discussions were often a continuation of the day's business, and little time was left for them to explore each other's personality. Jamie assumed responsibility for the investment and distribution of the funds, which Brad's company had forwarded in full to an account that Jamie opened at her firm, making Scott her client, as he was fond of reminding her. Scott found that she knew almost nothing about the science or practical applications of what he was doing; but, she was a quick study and before long she was speaking "fish" as Ross called it.

Because of a special-ordered front-mounted winch for his new truck, Scott had to stay over on a Friday. After they finished their business in the early afternoon, they drove to Muir Beach in Marin County and spent the late afternoon relaxing on the beach and cooling off in the surf. At dusk, they walked over to the nearby Pelican Inn and lingered over the inn's popular draft ale, before tackling the infamous bangers and mash recommended by Jamie. For the first time their conversation turned to the personal. Scott knew that Jamie had lost her mother, but he had not told her about the father he had never known.

Later, now dark, they walked hand in hand back to the beach parking lot. Drawn to the sound of guitar music, they joined a small group of young people seated around a fire, listening to the woman's soft ballads. Scott held Jamie as she rested against him until it grew chilly and they headed back to her car. When he opened her door, she smiled at him and he reached up, brushed her hair off her face, and he kissed her gently, for a long time. She returned his kiss, her body fitting into his. Neither spoke.

Back in the city, they sat in front of his hotel and discussed a few last items of business. Scott did not invite her in, and she had not suggested that they go to her apartment. He was, he thought, glad for that, for now. While they were clearly attracted to one another, the business aspect of their relationship and the opportunity that the grant represented for his fledgling company was an understood priority. Scott was mindful that she held the keys to the treasury, and he was not anxious to complicate their relationship. Neither seemed to be in a hurry, and both had made it clear that neither was seeing anyone special. Jamie said she had sometimes dated. Scott had Ross, he laughed, and the indigenous population in his area was way short on young women.

She suggested that they meet monthly in San Francisco to attend to the organizational and financial matters, which they agreed could not be done over the phone or by mail. Scott accepted that, even though it meant a long round-trip by car, so long as Jamie promised to come up to the river soon and see what they were doing firsthand. As he got out of the car, Scott leaned over and kissed her good night. He felt that they both wanted much more, but that this was not the right time.

After Scott returned to his house on the river, at first they spoke every few days, usually late in the evening. But soon, the calls were almost every day, and as Ross pointed out, they lasted longer and longer, and did not seem to be all that much about business, either. When she did not answer his telephone call, Scott found himself growing impatient, anxious to hear her voice. Each time the phone rang, Ross simply groaned "I know who that is! Here we go again!" Scott welcomed the intimacy of their talks. During one of their calls, he mentioned their next meeting, and for days uncertain how to bring it up, finally he simply asked her out on a date.

"You mean like a *date?*" she said. "Are you asking me out, Ames? I may have to check with daddy," she teased.

He did mean "like a date" and he was asking her out and she could check with her daddy, he replied, and then said, "Was that a 'yes'?"

"You mean mix business with pleasure, or at least mix it with *personal.* I do not know," she chided. "I may have to run this request by my supervisor; question of ethics, that sort of thing."

"You do that, whatever. I am taking you to dinner and I am making the arrangements this time, even though you keep telling me it is *your* city," he declared.

"Well, since you put it that way and you are the client, Mr. Ames, and even though you do not have a large, by our standards, account, I suppose I do *owe* it to the company. Friday may be open. See you then. Bye," and she hung up.

"Was that a 'yes'?" Ross asked from across the room.

"We need another phone in here," Scott snapped.

"Or at least another room," Ross answered, ducking a magazine.

~

One week later when he picked her up in the new truck, it was the first time he had been inside her apartment. It suited her perfectly: almost surgically clean, organized, efficient, and her taste and personality were evident in the wingback chair done in zebra and the hand-carved wood sculpture of a stork atop an owl. Framed photographs and a mixture of art set off the main attraction: beyond the rooftops was a 180-degree spectacular view of San Francisco Bay, from the Golden Gate Bridge on the left to a slice of Treasure Island on the right, framing Alcatraz Island.

"How did you luck out finding this place?"

From her bedroom, she replied, "A daughter of one of our clients. Her mother died, and she did not have the heart to sell the building. She grew up downstairs. She kept it and fixed it up, starting with the top floor; there is one above me. She mentioned it one day when we were going over her finances. I took one look at it even before she started the work and took it. She was delighted to have a tenant, and I just waited it out until she finished. She even let me pick the colors, and I designed some parts of the kitchen," she said. "I will have been here two years, next month."

Scott saw her reflection in the window as she walked into the room. He turned and caught his breath. All in black, smart linen pants topped by a silk blouse, set off by a small gold chain and bracelet, she was elegant. Jamie hesitated, awaiting his reaction.

"Wow!" he said after a moment, wetting the same dry lips he now remembered from D.C.

She was pleased. Never one to worry over clothes, as styling came naturally to her, she nevertheless had pondered all afternoon what she should wear.

She looked at Scott's sport coat, open shirt, and slacks and thought they would set him apart in any group. Even without socks.

"You like it?" she asked. "You were no help, since I do not know where we are going."

"Perfect," he replied. "Just right. You may want a light jacket or sweater," he added. Jamie held up the arm behind her back: a sweater.

~

Scott guessed correctly that, like many who lived in San Francisco, Jamie had never been on a bay cruise. The 183-foot Hornblower Yacht featured a full dining room, gourmet dinner, several bars, and a musical trio.

"You are kidding, Ames?" she asked when he gave the valet his truck at the boat dock. "This is for tourists."

"Just you wait, Ms. Williams," his hand on her back, pressing her forward up the lighted gangway. Only half full, the majestic vessel glided easily out of the pier and turned east up the bay while the waiter poured for them.

"Champagne?"

"Of course. They do not serve beer, so . . ."

"And who is paying for all this?" She gestured over the table and around the room, smiling behind her frown.

"Well, my CPA, who is also your CPA, said . . ."

"Oh, no," she interrupted. "Tom would never O.K. this as a business meeting! Not Tom!"

He held up one hand and replied deliberately, "I asked *your* CPA, and he said that it was definitely *not* a business meeting. I assumed that, experienced business woman that you are, *you* would say that we ought to write this off for tax purposes," he paused. "But no, I am paying. It is personal." He noticed her satisfied expression as he sipped his champagne. "Unless, and Tom said to remind you this, that since *I* am a client of *your* firm, if *you* wanted to pay, in which case *you* can write it off."

"No chance, Ames," she said. She held up her champagne flute for a refill. This Gloria Ferrer is pricey stuff. No chance."

"I would not accept your charity, anyway," he smiled, and then he flinched realizing what he had said. "Well, your father's maybe."

"Right. Uh huh!" she laughed as they clinked glasses.

The vessel swung in close to the Embarcadero waterfront, lighted office complexes towered in the background. "I have never seen the city from this side, on the water," Jamie said. "It is really quite different and very beautiful."

Their table was the only one with fresh red roses, and when she nodded at them, questioning, Scott simply shrugged. *Two can play this "perfection game,"* he thought, pleased. For the next two hours as they dined, they cruised the Oakland Estuary and the East Bay waterfront, up to the north end of the bay and then turned and headed south. Dinner cleared, Scott ordered brandy snifters and then led Jamie outside to the deserted rear deck. He held her as they approached, and then passed under, the magnificent Golden Gate Bridge, the roadway rising more than two hundred feet above them. Under the bridge, the yacht turned and paused. They could see the flash of cameras from the bow of the vessel as passengers took pictures of the lighted cables and the towers soaring far overhead.

"The towers are seven hundred feet plus," Scott said. "I looked it up, today. In case you asked."

"I didn't," she said softly. "But thank you anyway." She put her head on his shoulder.

Inside on the dance floor, Jamie looked up at him.

"You did this right, Ames. I have never been on the bay, except the ferry, and never outside the bridge."

"You are welcome, Jamie," he said into her ear, holding her close, feeling her against him, warm, firm.

~

It was after midnight when their boat docked. Scott gave the valet twenty dollars to keep his truck overnight, since they had both been drinking, and he hailed a cab as the attendant pulled the truck inside the covered pier. In a few minutes they arrived at Jamie's apartment. When he got out to open her door, Jamie heard Scott ask the driver to wait. She looked up at him thoughtfully as she accepted his hand out of the cab. He closed the cab door, took her hand in his, and walked her to the entrance of the apartment building. It was dimly lighted. Scott had mentally rehearsed several scenarios of this moment; he now knew what he would do. He stopped. He turned her and took her in his arms. He kissed her on the lips, slowly, tasting her. She was relaxed, and there was no reason to stop. He stopped and moving slightly away, and as he still held her, said, "This is the place, the moment, when I ask you if I can come up for that nightcap, or whatever. Or you ask me, presuming I am so lucky, 'would you like to come up,' or . . ."

She started to respond; he stopped her.

"No, don't," he said gently. "There is nothing I would rather do. Nothing. But," he paused, "I have never felt this away about anybody, anyone, and I do not know how you feel, but I do not want to mess this up. Oh, I am so messing this up," he froze.

"Scott, you *can't* come up, is that better?" she said softly, but with just an edge. She touched his cheek. "Is that what you wanted to hear?"

"No, I don't want you taking me off the hook, I guess. Jamie, I feel that something special is . . . has happened to me, with you. Since that first moment when I turned and found you at the dinner table in D.C. I have known it, and I did not want to do anything to be presumptuous. We hardly know each other, and this whole thing . . ."

"Thing?" she smiled.

"You know. God! I feel so stupid. But . . ."

"So, let me see," she said, taking one step back, still holding his hands, "You take me out. Wine, make that champagne, *then* the wine. Flowers on the table, the only ones on the boat. Dancing, kissing me under the most romantic bridge in the world . . ." She raised her head a bit, watching his response. "You ply me with cognac, more dancing. All on a romantic moonlight cruise. Then! Then you arrange to cab back so you would not have to worry about parking, *overnight*, I thought. And here we are." She met his gaze.

Scott was totally crushed. He had blown it, he knew it. She wanted, expected, him to stay. What must she be thinking? She continued, her voice soft, understanding.

"I suppose that is what anyone would have expected if they were me, and what any *guy* would want." She put both her hands around his neck and moved closer to him, their bodies touching, "But you, Ames, you are not just any guy. I know that; I knew it then in that hotel ballroom, in Chesapeake Bay surrounded by thrashing horses, and when we kissed on the ferry boat." She was smiling. Her eyes glowed and her face was radiant in the soft light. "With the possible exception of your bumbling on the flight out, you are someone special, Scott. I know that and I appreciate it."

"Jamie, I—" she put one fingertip on his lips.

"Good night, Scott. I had a lovely time. It was perfect, actually. It could not have been better, including this good night." She held him tight, and she let her finger trace the line of his lips, and then she kissed him. He met her kiss, and they stood for a long moment. She eased back and, as she turned away, she smiled back at him as the door closed behind her.

"The Argonaut Hotel," he told the cab driver. When they had stopped for a light, he met the cabbie's eyes in the mirror.

"No luck huh, buddy?" the cabbie said. "Tough when you spend all that dough on the Hornblower, huh?" He looked away.

Scott said nothing. He paid the driver at his hotel—no tip. He lingered outside and looked at the waning moon while he stood alone on the sidewalk. *Well?* he said to himself, pensive, *how was that?* After a moment, he smiled and he pushed through the revolving door. He knew how it was; he was it certain of it. *Perfect, it had been, it was, perfect.*

~

"Clare, it is so good to see you. Come on in," Jamie greeted her friend.

"You, too, it has been too long, Jamie," the young woman replied, giving her a hug. "Wow, you have done wonders with this place. You just moved in, what, two years ago?"

"Not quite, it will be two years next month." She followed Clare into the living room.

"My God, the view, this is fabulous. Enough to make me want to move from Manhattan."

"I doubt that, Clare," she laughed. "I thought you loved New York and your job."

In front of them, the afternoon sun sparkled off the bay. "I do," Clare said, "and it gives me the chance to travel, like this trip."

"Well, have a seat for minute while I finish up," Jamie gestured to a couch, "… and enjoy the view."

Clare wore her dark hair short, was dressed in designer jeans, a loose linen blouse, and flats. From the other room Jamie continued, "I saw you on your last trip, but that was just for coffee, right?"

"Right," Clare replied, "but I have never been here to your apartment. This time I had an extra day, so here I am."

"I am glad you called, Clare," Jamie replied. Clare was looking at a stack of videos and CDs, with a curious look on her face.

"And who, or what, is Fanny Krieger? *Fly-Fishing for Women?*" she asked.

"I'll fill you in at lunch," she said. "A couple of interesting things have happened to me in the past year or so since I have seen you," she smiled as she took the woman's arm. "Come on, we can walk. It is a beautiful day."

"Not fishing, Jamie. You? I can't wait to hear this!"

~

At a corner table, under the pleasant shade of an awning, lunch cleared, Jamie and Clare lingered over their cappuccinos. Locals and tourists strolled by on the other side of the boxed hedge that set the outside dining area apart from the sidewalk traffic. Clare caught Jamie up on the happenings of several of their college dorm- and classmates from Maryland, where they had roomed together.

They had shared an off-campus apartment during their senior year, before Clare left for her advertising career in New York. Jamie stayed behind to join her father's company. They kept in touch, not as often now that both were so busy, and particularly since Jamie had moved to the West Coast. Jamie kept Clare busy answering questions about her life, loves, labors, the ups and downs, and she was not aware that she had avoided what was going on in her own life until Clare, realizing she had been dominating the conversation, put her cup down slowly and said to Jamie, "Ok, I get it. All about me, huh? Well, now it is *my* turn. And let's start with this fishing stuff. I remember you mentioned in a phone call or email that you had met someone. What is he, a fisherman?" she paused, smiling over her large cup.

"Not exactly, Clare. Not a fisherman, though this North Beach neighborhood is full of them. He works *with* fish, I guess you could say."

Jamie told Clare of her flight to D.C., the irony of meeting Scott at her father's event, the award of the grant, the pony swim. (*"The two of you dove in the water with your clothes on to rescue . . . a horse!"*) Prompted, Jamie found herself discussing Scott in a context that she had not previously addressed, even to herself. Clare stared at Jamie until there was a pause, and then she leaned in, took one of Jamie's hands in hers, and said softly, "Jamie, you should listen to your own voice and see your eyes when you talk about him. You know, don't you, you are in love with him?"

"Well, what?"

"Come on, girl. You *are* in love with him, aren't you?"

Jamie was stunned, trying to recall what she might have said to produce such a reaction from this friend whom she had known for many years and who knew her so well.

"You don't know it, do you?" Clare continued. "My God, Jamie, this is it, and you don't get it. Are you sleeping with him? Jesus, I hope so!"

Off balance, as if she had not herself considered it, and uncertain of voicing her feelings even to her friend, she replied, "No. No, he is not that kind of guy. I mean . . ." She knew that she was blushing, and Clare's look confirmed it. "No, we haven't," Jamie conceded.

"Still a little of the ice princess, huh?" Clare sat back, nodded, and grinned at her.

"Oh, God, Clare, is it that obvious?" she moaned.

"On your sleeve. Hell, your face!" she laughed. "At least to me."

Jamie relaxed and sighed, "Clare, until now I never asked myself, not until you asked me."

"Have you told him? Oh, God. I know the answer to that one," she said. "And has he told you? No! Same answer? God, how people waste time. So much for communication skills," Clare laughed. "Well, someone ought to tell someone, because Jamie, what I see in your eyes and hear in your voice, when you talk about him, just saying his name, is about as secret as this empty cup," as she signaled the waiter for a refill. Clare slid her chair back, stood up, and looked down at her friend, "Restroom break. Don't you move!"

Jamie sat lost in her thoughts, some of which she knew she had denied until Clare confronted her. Back in her seat, Clare continued: "You and I are not getting any younger, Jamie, as attractive as we are, well, you anyway, we are being overrun by twenty-somethings.'"

"Clare, Scott is something very different. I have never met anyone like him."

"Jamie, he is a man. M-A-N, man. Whatever it is you have, the two of you, you better figure it out, and you better find some way to tell him how you feel. Someone has to make the first move," she said. "I found that out the hard way, more than once!"

"Clare, he loves me; he has told me that. I know he does. But we are both taking it slow. He is a lot like me. His family and stuff. I think we are both afraid," she pleaded.

"So, get over it, Jamie, and get on with it. Life is too short," she warned. "There is not enough time to wait for happiness, and for sure, no time to be unhappy. Where is he? I'll tell him for you!" she chided.

"Right, you would, too," Jamie laughed. "Sorry, he lives up the coast, two hours away."

"No problem, I'll change my flight," she laughed.

"There is no need to, Clare. You have opened my eyes. Anyway, he is taking me fishing next week, and maybe, no, not maybe, it is time we had a little 'chat,'" she grinned.

"A little something. But a 'chat'? I don't think so!" she replied. "Let's go back to your place. I still have a few hours before my flight," Clare said, standing. "You must have some pictures?"

"Oh, God!" Jamie mimed.

~

Scott stopped his jeep against a log in front of the cabin, which he had rented for the weekend. He switched off the engine and put a finger to his lips.

"Shh," he whispered.

Jamie looked over at him, curious.

After a few seconds, he said softly, "What do you hear?"

Listening intently, she replied, "Nothing."

"Exactly!" He slid out of the vehicle.

"Oh, I get it, nature boy," she laughed and reached for her bag behind the seat.

"C'mon in first, you have to see this. This is so much better than where Ross and I live."

"Which I have yet to see . . ."

A small living room was separated from the kitchen by a fireplace. The early afternoon light flooded the rooms. A dining deck offered a view of the stream that could be heard and seen through the surrounding redwood trees. Scott took Jamie's hand and led her across the lawn and down to the stream. Continuing around the house, he pointed to a path off the bedroom that led into the forest. Inside, floor-to-ceiling vaulted windows dominated the one bedroom. Jamie glanced into the bathroom; tub but no shower, she noted.

"Check this out, city girl." He opened a door in the bedroom. "Mademoiselle, your 'private' shower." He bowed and stepped outside. Set against the wall of the cabin, paved with flat stones, a rain showerhead and hardware protruded from the wall, and a stone birdbath doubled as a washstand and soap dish. The outside shower was screened from the front parking area by vegetation, but it was otherwise open to the forest and the sky.

"Right. Dream on, Ames," she snuffed.

Jamie carried in their gear while Scott attended to the food and supplies for the long weekend. When Jamie had finished in the bedroom, she found Scott on the deck off the kitchen.

"Need any help?" she asked, settling onto the cushion of one of several reed-backed chairs.

"No, it's all put away. I left the steaks in the fridge for tonight; the other stuff I put in the freezer," he replied as he rigged the fly rods. "You have enough room for your stuff?" he asked looking up.

"Enough for mine," she sighed. "I piled yours in the corner," she kidded.

"Figures, but then we're roughing it, so that's O.K.," he smiled.

His smile covers his entire face, she thought. *Where does that come from?* She could not recall ever seeing him sad. Angry, but not sad.

Scott put the fly rods into holders that were built into the deck railing. He held out his hand. "Come on. Now for the grand tour." She took his hand, and they headed into the woods. They walked to the water's edge and turned upstream. The stream wandered through the trees and clearings, tumbling over rocks and sliding into flat pools, "slicks," he called them. She noticed that he paused from time to time, cautioning her to be still while he looked for and then pointed out fish, which he said that he could see, though she could not. What looked like a fish to her turned out to be a stick or rock underwater. She had to take his word for it each time. They stopped, waded, sat, talked, and explored until the slanting sun began its fade.

Back at the cabin, she opened a bottle of Pinot Noir while Scott grilled the steaks. Jamie made a salad. They dined to the hum of the cicadas, the bubbling of the stream, and a tender whisper of the breeze in the trees. Scott insisted he clean up, while Jamie sipped a late-harvest Riesling Scott had brought. He watched her from the kitchen window and smiled to himself as her head slowly sank to her chest. The four-hour drive, the excitement, or the wine, whatever, he was not surprised. Finished, he went outside. She stirred as he started to pick her up.

"C'mon, lady, you are done," he whispered as he lifted her into his arms. She looked up and smiled and was asleep. He pulled the covers back as he set her down on the bed. He gently pulled off her shoes. In her T-shirt and shorts, she would be comfortable, he thought. He walked back into the kitchen, closed things up, and turned out the lights. In the living room, moonlight painted the furniture and framed the windows. He looked in on Jamie. She had not moved. Stepping out of his top siders, he slipped off his shirt and, rearranging the cushions, he lay down on the spacious couch in the living room and was soon asleep in the warm night air.

~

Jamie woke to the sounds of rattling pans and silverware, and the tantalizing aroma of fresh coffee. Rolling over, she eyed the steaming cup on the nightstand. She freshened up quickly. She noticed the rumpled cushions on the living room couch and Scott's shirt and shoes on the floor as she walked to the kitchen. Scott wore only his cargo shorts and a chef's apron.

"Hey, good morning, sleepy head," he smiled. "No shower? Let me know," he laughed.

Jamie took one of the two stools at the counter fronting the range.

"Wow, what happened?" she asked.

"Nothing, I slept on the couch," Scott deadpanned.

"I saw that. Your choice," she shrugged; her flippant response surprised her.

"Over easy, two chicken apple links, toast up in a minute," he announced plating the food he had removed from the propane gas burners. "Outside. Set up, please, I cannot do everything." The toast popped up.

They relaxed into the late afternoon. The weather had warmed dramatically, and the stream shimmered in the heat. Scott explained that the "bite would not turn on," as he called it, until it cooled down toward evening. He gave her a lesson in fly casting on the lawn, but the sun was too hot, and she became impatient. They read, napped, and sipped iced tea and nibbled on watermelon.

The shadows lengthened as evening approached. Scott helped Jamie with her booties and boots; they would "wet wade," he said. Wearing shorts, longsleeve shirts, and wide hats, they set out upstream where Scott liked a riffle he had seen on their walk. He carried the two rods and a small chest pack for his leaders and flies. Jamie followed.

She was content to watch as Scott cast to what he referred to as rising fish, and he quickly landed and released several out of one pool. She admired his skill and the ease with which he handled the long rod, and the even longer thin leader with its tiny fly, as he played, landed, and released the fish. She loved the feel and coolness of the water as it washed over her feet and legs.

Moving back from the edge of the stream, he set his rod down against a bush and motioned for Jamie to stand with him in the water. She held her rod. He positioned her in front, and moved his chest pack to one side, over his hip. She leaned against him, bracing herself in the gentle current. He held her rod hand with his on the cork grip, the fly line in his other hand.

"We're both left-handed, right? She nodded. "That's good. Don't grip it. Just follow my motion. Let me do the work. Easy. Keep your wrist stiff. Don't bend it, if you can help it. I just want you to get the feel of it." He positioned her left elbow against her side, and reaching around her waist he locked her arm against her side with his. With his right hand he reached completely around her and placed the loop of loose line in her right hand, his hand over hers. Then, he moved her left forearm back, toward the rear, behind them, and she watched as the line lifted off the water and started back toward them. He felt her flinch. As the line repeatedly passed over their heads, high and behind, and she flinched, Scott explained "It won't hit us if we do it right, and even if it does, it won't stick you."

She felt her left arm stop and pause just for a second, abruptly, upright, and then Scott started her arm forward with his, as if they were one, and she could feel the rod tip flex ever so lightly, as the line appeared in the air now in front of them, pulled by a tight loop, almost in slow motion, as it rolled out smoothly until the tiny fly landed softly on the water, directly in front of them. It did not make any ripple. In that instant, as she was staring at the tiny floating fly, the water around the fly exploded and the fly disappeared. In the same moment, the loose line she was holding flew from her right hand, and the reel in her rod hand sang out. In a second, the line was again slack, the fly gone. Disappeared.

"My God!"

"Broke off. Nice fish, maybe fifteen, seventeen inches," Scott said flatly.

She looked at him over her shoulder, "What did *you* do? Did we lose it?"

"*We* did not lose it, you did. He broke you off. Look," Scott had retrieved the line, and he held up the severed tippet. The fly was gone.

"You owe me a buck seventy-five for that fly, a Parachute Adams, lady."

Jamie stared over the water where the fish had been. "That was easy, I mean my first cast. Let's do it again," a note of urgency in her voice. Scott tied on a new fly, and they moved to a different pool. While she was learning to cast, the pools were her best bet, he explained. He would teach her the riffles later.

For the next few hours as the light left the water and their eyes became accustomed to the settling darkness, Scott stood behind and held her, working her arm through the casting motion: forward and back, ten o'clock and two o'clock, he intoned. Raise, lift, stop at two o'clock; feel the pull on the rod tip—the rod loading, he called it; then, forward and stop at ten o'clock; like a gentle chopping motion. With each backcast, the fly line lifted gently off the surface, droplets of water trickled back toward them and fell into the river, each a tiny ripple, as the line passed repeatedly over them, a living thing, the line turned in the air over itself, led, pulled, urged by the loop in the line, the size and speed of which was directed by the height and angle of the slender rod tip, as they cast, over and over.

While he worked with her, he was conscious of her body against his— her hair on his face, the scent of her, the movement of her muscles as they rocked together in the rhythm of her casts, their two bodies joined by the delicate fly rod as if a part of it, an extension of themselves moving as one, back and forth, subtly yet powerfully. Again and again, they coaxed the magic fly line from one spot on the water to another, until at that last precise tense expectant moment, the line straightened ever so slightly and the tiny fly alighted on the water soundlessly, effortlessly, artfully, awaiting, tempting fate. Once when his right hand was working line off the reel, his hand came to rest against her breast. She looked up at him and down at his hand. He smiled. She liked the feel of his arms around her, holding her.

Together they stuck and hooked a few fish, but when he handed her the rod alone to play a fish, she lost it each time. As darkness descended, they worked their way back toward the cabin. Scott could see the warm light of windows through the trees, and he knew they would not have much more time tonight. Scott paused above a riffle that he had saved for last. He could still read the seam of the water on the edge of what he knew was a likely feeding lane. *They are here. Let's see if we can entice them out,* he thought.

"Let's try here, Jamie," he said softly, "And if this doesn't work, we will call it a day. O.K.?"

"Fine, I'm O.K.,"

"Not cold?"

"No."

Cautiously he moved her out into the water so that there would be room for her backcast. He did not want her to try a roll cast, too much to learn in one day. No fish were working that he could see, but he knew they were there. What was left of the sunlight was behind them; no shadows on the water. He positioned them above and across from what he knew was the seam, that moving line on the water separating the quieter water from the faster moving mass. His arms around her, they worked the line off the reel, let the fly drift, the pull of the water taking line off his hand. When he judged that he had enough line out, and the current had loaded the rod, together they raised the rod as he coached her, and they eased the line and leader off the water and cast it back overhead, and on the forward stroke he guided her arm slightly upstream, so the fly landed opposite them and above where he wanted it to be. He tossed a mend into the line, shooting the looped portion back upstream, and as it straightened in front of them he adjusted it a touch and the fly floated upright, drag free, past them headed for the slot he had imagined.

In the fading light he almost missed it, he said afterwards. But he saw the fish roll and come out of the water and slam the fly. Instinctively, he waited a second only and then he lifted the rod tip. He felt the line tighten and the rod bend, and the reel started its scream. His first thought was that this was one hell of a fish, get Jamie out of the way, and his second was that this was *her fish*—hers to land, theirs together. He stayed wrapped around her.

"Let it run, Jamie. Keep your hand away from that reel. Just let him take it," he said, his voice strained but cool.

"You take it," she offered.

"No way. This is your fish and you can do this. Keep that rod tip up."

The line ran off the reel, and he looked down. The orange tapered line was showing white beneath and they would soon be into the backing line at this rate. The singing noise of the fly reel had stopped.

"He is coming back!" Scott tried not to shout. "Rod tip up! Good! Pull the line in with your right hand! Down! That's it! Keep pulling!" he said. "Never mind the reel, just keep pulling that line in!" The retrieved line fell on the water in large loops and was washed away, but on the rod it was tight to the fish. "Good job!" And then the fish turned and was gone again, and the slack line she had recovered zinged back out through the guides and off the water.

"Don't move! Stay still! He's making a run." And as he said it, the fish broke water lifting straight up in the air, it turned, and for a second only, its body was parallel to the water, and then it dove.

"Wow!" he shouted now, "What a slab-sider! That's a nice fish, Jamie. Easy now."

Now, more line was coming off the water, and Scott realized that he had been keeping tension on the line with one hand. On the reel now and following Scott's instructions, Jamie slowly began to get line back, one foot at a time. The fish jumped three more times, and each time Jamie followed Scott's directions to keep the rod tip pointed at the fish, let it run, then put pressure on it, and the fight continued.

"I think you have him beat." He looked downstream and realized they had moved almost fifty yards from where they had first hooked the fish. Ahead, he could see a section of low bank where the grass ran into the water.

"Let's move down, but keep the rod tip up and pressure on him. Slack is our enemy, Jamie," he cautioned.

Behind her still, he reached down and tucked his hand inside her belt; he felt the warmth of her back against his wet hand. She did not flinch. Holding her, one hand on her belt, he gave her leverage against a trip or fall. They were able to keep pressure on the fish as they walked steadily to the landing place Scott selected. Now, they could see the fish.

"Swim him to the bank, use the rod," he instructed her. Jamie eased the fish, on top of the water now, toward the bank.

"I'm going in front of you" he said, "Whatever you do, keep the rod tip up and no slack."

All the line was recovered, and he followed the leader down with his hand, to the tippet knot and then down to the fly. Then he had the fish from behind, one hand tailing him, the other near the fly and he eased him toward the shore still in the shallow water.

"O.K., Jamie. You can set the rod down and come here. It's O.K., I have him," he said.

She moved forward and sank on her knees in the water. Her face was red, glowing. She was breathing audibly.

"You O.K.?" Scott asked gently rocking the fish back and forth in the water.

Silent, she nodded.

"Ok, see here is your fly, in the sinew of his lip. No blood. That is all that kept him on, that tiny fly. No barb on the hook. Neat, huh?" he looked at her. She said nothing and stared at her fish.

"Look at the colors! He is beautiful, Jamie. A big buck, maybe nineteen inches. See the green back and the spots," he pointed. "Gorgeous rainbow.

Look at that red lateral line and that fin, the small one in the back. That's how you tell he is a wild fish, a native."

He picked the fly easily out of the fish's mouth and then said, "O.K., now the hard part. I am going to lift him up, and you are going to hold him yourself, in your hands, and then you are going to kiss him. Got it?"

Jamie never uttered a word; she made no sound. Scott lifted the fish, and placed one of her hands under its belly, near the tail, her fingers straddling the rear fin, and her other hand behind the large jaws. And Jamie, as if she had done it all her life, lifted the fish on her own, took a long look at it, and then she kissed the fish on its nose and handed it back. Scott sat in the water and continued to work the fish back and forth. The fish moved slowly, regaining strength.

"Watch him," he said, "He will be just fine in a minute. See the gills working? By moving him gently back and forth we keep the water moving over his gills. Oh, he is ready to go," and the fish struggled against Scott's hand, and with one strong surge, he was free. "There he goes," Scott said. They watched as the fish, strong and vital, moved away and with one quick flick of its tail disappeared into the blackness of the current.

Scott looked up at Jamie. Without a word she sank down, and sat in the water. And the tears came. She leaned into him, and he held her as she cried, shaking. He waited for a few moments until she stopped. He took her face in his wet hands, and he brushed the hair out of her eyes.

"You O.K.?" he asked.

"He is, was, the most beautiful thing I have ever seen, Scott," she said looking in his eyes. "When he jumped, I wanted him so bad, and then to see him here, caught. That is the right word, *caught*. I felt so bad. That maybe I killed him, or that he would die. I felt like you were asking me to kiss him goodbye, like the mother I never knew. Is that crazy? Oh, God, Scott!" she sobbed.

He held her; neither of them spoke. Finally, he took her in his arms and kissed her long, deeply, and she responded with an ardor that seemed new, more intense. He tasted her tears, and they sat in the water of the beautiful stream, the night down, wrapped around them.

Jamie was overwhelmed with the moment, and then she realized that whatever fear she might have had with regard to Scott, whatever was holding her back, that was all gone now, released like her magnificent fish. She looked up at him.

"Scott?" They were both wet and now a little cold, and she put one damp hand on his face, and she wiped her tears away with the other hand. "Scott. I love you. There, that's it. I said it. I love you." He kissed her softly under each eye, then on the nose.

"Jamie, I have loved you since you walked into the bar after the award ceremony, and every day since. I was just so scared that somehow I would screw this up, or that I was not enough for you, or . . . You taste like trout! "

"Shut up," she said softly, kissing him on the lips. She started to stand, but Scott stood up first. She took his hand, and he helped her to her feet. "What do you mean 'the bar,' I thought it was when you saw me at the table?" she asked.

He had started toward the bank to recover the rods, and he looked back over his shoulder. She was standing still in the water. "Oh, yeah. Then too. Since then, too." he smiled.

She kicked, one foot in the stream, sending a wave of water up and into his face and hair. They laughed, and she took his hand and stepped up onto the bank.

They walked silently back to the cabin, and Scott quickly made the favorite drink he saved for fishing trips: a Bombay sapphire martini, up, twist of lemon, dash of bitters. Jamie watched him mix and shake the drink. While he was pouring it, she nodded, and he dressed the glass with the lemon twist and raised it to her. The icy sweat on the outside of the chilled glass gave the finished cocktail an irresistible look. He handed her the drink. She took a tentative sip, and he smiled and began to prepare one for himself. They sat silently on the deck as the moon rose. The night air hummed around them. They were both too tired to cook, so they had a second round and snacked on chevre and crackers until Jamie sighed.

"A bath, that's what I want. A soak."

"I thought maybe after all that, a shower," Scott teased, his lips close to her ear.

She straightened up, and stood. She ran the lemon peel over her lips and tasted it.

"A bath. A tub, Ames." She smiled and slowly stretched and arched her arms over her head, and satisfied with her choice, she flipped the lemon twist at Scott, and then she turned and walked inside.

After a while, Scott finished his drink and put the glasses away. He turned out the lights in the living room and walked into the bedroom. Jamie had left the lights off, and the room was backlit by moonlight through the tall windows, shadows painted the high ceiling. He recalled that he had slept on the couch the night before; neither of them had discussed it. He shrugged out of his shirt, shorts, and underwear, and took a towel from the nearby stand. He saw the light under the bathroom door, and he could hear her sounds just a few feet away. He opened the bedroom door and stepped over to the outside shower, naked in the reflected light, and he felt the water and moonlight wash over him, his back to the forest, as he faced the wall; the wall behind which he knew Jamie was bathing.

The rain showerhead poured over him plugging his ears, and he did not sense her, until he felt a hand on his back. And then her arms encircled him as she pulled him toward her, her breasts pressed against his back, her thighs against his legs. She raised one leg slightly, moving it up his as she leaned into him.

He turned, his skin sliding over hers, seamless, until he faced her. She was as wet as he, her body glowing, radiant in the moonlight; her hair shining. He looked down at her and then her mouth was on his, her tongue certain. He felt every inch of himself against every part of her, fit together as one, as the moonlight and the shower flowed over them.

She stepped back, and she looked down at him. She smiled, looked up into his eyes, and reached behind him to turn off the shower. Taking his hand she turned and led him off the stones, onto the deck, and into the bedroom. As they sank down onto the bed, Scott noticed that the covers had been turned back and his shorts and shoes, which he had left on the floor, were no longer there.

~

Scott lay on the bed, a sheet partly covered him. He looked at the light under the bathroom door and heard Jamie's soft sounds from within. The setting moon dappled the walls and the bed with a varied palette of light and shadow. The bathroom light went out, and Jamie stood at the foot of the bed, her wet hair silvery luminescent; a towel wrapped around. She smiled at Scott and settled down next to him. They studied each other, until she said:

"Scott?"

"Yes."

"Can I ask you something, personal?"

"Maybe," he sighed. She felt the warmth of his breath on her face.

"What took us so long? Why did we wait?" she hesitated and shifted so that she was now raised up, supported on one elbow, over him. With a fingertip she traced his jaw and mouth. For a moment he said nothing, looking at her. She felt a premonition, almost sorry for having asked. He sensed her hesitancy.

"Jamie, I knew this would be as perfect as it was. As it truly was, and . . ." he stopped,

"And what?"

"And I knew that for me there would be no going back from that moment on, and I wanted to be sure that I was ready, even, if . . . well, if you were not."

"What do you mean, if *I* was not, Scott? I do not understand?"

"Jamie, nothing like this has ever happened to me. Never. What I feel, or felt. What just happened."

"You mean seducing me after catching a big fish?" A smile at the corners of her mouth.

"No. I am serious, Jamie, I mean it." Scott eased out from under her, and he leaned back against the pillows, so that he could look directly into her eyes. He brushed back a wisp of her hair.

"I . . . I have trouble explaining my feelings, at least I used to. I was raised by an absentee mother, nannies, babysitters, after-school programs, single parent stuff. I always was on my guard not to get attached, I guess, because it was always changing, or I knew it would. And if I never got, I guess, involved, emotionally, then it would be easier."

"You mean it wouldn't hurt as much?"

"Yes, I suppose that is one way to put it. I have had my share of girlfriends, I even lived with someone for a year, but it never felt right, comfortable, and one day she just left and it was O.K.; actually she made it easy for me."

"How was that easy?" Jamie searched his eyes.

"You know, I didn't have to break things up, it was just over. If it ever *was* something. Can you understand that? Maybe it is nuts, or maybe I am," he paused, thinking as he shifted his weight and straightened. "You know, one time in a psych class I had to make a list of feelings, all kinds of feelings. I could only come up with about five or six. I had to look the rest up. I got 'happy, sad, angry,' those kinds, but 'shame, blame, relief, contentment, satisfaction, longing, desire, doubt,' I had to look those up, and I remember my surprise at reading the words, those feelings. I felt like I had missed something, or that maybe *I* was the reason, that there was something wrong or missing from *me*," he paused. "Is that crazy? Do you understand what I am trying to say?"

She leaned back, on one elbow, and then holding her towel close, she pivoted around so that she lay with her head on his chest. She felt his heart beating.

"I think we are a lot alike, Scott. I *have* thought a lot about it. About us," she said. "You know, I was raised by my father, a single parent. He never remarried after my mother died when I was born. I always felt sad for him, but I never had a mother. I had lost my mother. Never had a mother, for any of those things." She slowed. "He was—is—a great father, you could not ask for a better father, and I suppose that he gave me enough love for two parents." She stopped, her voice choked, and Scott watched her wipe a tear as she continued, her voice soft now, uncertain. "I always felt like I had killed . . ."

"Jamie! No! It's not your—" Scott interrupted.

"I know Scott, but it is how I *felt*. Feelings were what you were trying to explain, not facts, feelings," she said. "And wrong, stupid, whatever, that is what I felt then, and sometimes still feel. That if I had not been born, he would have had a wife to love and live with, even now. I cost him that. I cannot help it. That made me somehow lose trust in people, relationships, maybe not *lose* trust, but I was suspicious of it, because I did not want to cause anyone the hurt I felt I caused my dad, on one level. And on the other, I did not want to experience the loss myself, again. So," she continued, "I kept my distance. A safe distance. From girlfriends and boyfriends. Sort of like lending myself to others on an as-needed basis, but I did not give myself to anyone. I was unwilling to take the risk. Until now. Does that make sense?"

"Yes," he replied. "I never had a father, and I missed so much. I could see the other guys in sports, at school: 'My dad and I did this or that.' I was so jealous and resentful. But I was taught that he was gone and that was it. Couldn't get him back. That sort of thing. But that did not make it any easier."

"But you had information, pictures, didn't you?"

"No, nothing. I always wondered why we did not, but when I got older, although she never came out and said so, I knew my mother was never married to my dad, and that he had disappeared or had taken off, whatever. He had somehow died. No sense to worry or ask. He was not coming back. That was it. She never told me his name, and I was told to never ask. At some point it no longer made any difference who or what he was. He was not a part of my life, or even my past. I had 'surrogate' fathers, scoutmasters, teachers, coaches, great guys, but it was *so* not the same." He shifted, leaning forward, toward her. He ran his hand through her hair. He could smell the shampoo on her head and on his hand.

"So, we have the same thing going on, the same baggage, I guess you would call it," Scott said. "That has kept me focused on my work, away from a home I do not miss, that I do not care about, and a mother who is O.K. with it, so long as I send her a card now and then. That's it," he shrugged. "So, that is why I went home after our cruise and have gone out of my way to keep my distance. It has been killing me, believe me. But I was afraid of my feelings. But more than that, I was afraid that somehow I would hurt you, and damage ... well ... *us*. People do the most incredible things to those that they are supposed to love, or at least that they say that they love. I was not sure that I could trust my feelings for you. For me it had ... has to be permanent. Do you see what I mean?"

"Of course I do, Scott. Like you said, I let you off the hook, a hook you did not want to get off of. Oh, God, I can't believe I said 'hook'!" laughing. "But Scott, *I* am the one who went out to the shower." She paused and then said softly as she rose, now kneeling over him, her towel falling away, "I have been searching for you long before we met. I knew what I wanted, and when I met you, I knew it was—and Scott, *it is*—you that I want, now." She reached down and eased the sheet off of him. "And, Scott, I am certain of ... *this*." She settled gently on top of him as he slid down onto the bed to meet her.

~

Jamie turned off the light. She paused and looked down at the sleeping Scott. She adjusted her towel and slowly moved around the bed looking at him. *How?* She wondered. *How has this happened? The plane, beach house, his winning the grant, saving the pony, the bay cruise, all of it? How can this have happened to me? To him? To us? What does it mean? Is this real? This cannot be some kind of accident?* She wiped a single tear. *Is there more to this than I am seeing, feeling? But here we are,* and she felt for the first time . . . complete. *And yes,* she said to herself, *it is him. He is what I want, what I have been waiting for.* She let the towel fall to the floor, and she slid in beside him; fitting her body to his, she traced a small scar on his back. *Well, I do not care. If this is meant to be, if this is meant for me, then it will be, because it feels so safe and so right.* Whatever comes, she was no longer afraid.

CHAPTER 10

THE SIGN "VILLAGE OF EASTON" slid by, and Will Grant slowed and exited US 50. He glanced at a Post-it stuck on the dashboard and turned west on Maryland State Route 33. Ahead he saw "St. Michael's—26 miles," and he relaxed, comfortable now that the hard part, navigating from Washington, D.C., was behind him. The dashboard clock confirmed that he was early. He wound through the pleasant Maryland countryside, thinking back to the previous month when he and Kay had received the invitation:

Mr. Brad Williams
Requests the honor of your presence
at the marriage of his daughter,
Ms. Jamie Williams
to
Mr. Scott Ames,
Son of Ms. Ava Ames . . .

He decided that he should attend the wedding. As Kay had conflicting commitments to the charity that she headed, he went alone, in part welcoming the opportunity to experience what Kay said was the "Carmel of the Chesapeake," St Michael's, Maryland, and to renew his acquaintance with the father of the bride.

Over the years, when Williams had need of his legal services in California, Grant had represented his company, but always by mail or phone, usually by way of an employee or other attorney of Williams's growing company; never had there been a personal visit. In addition to the occasional business, not unlike soldiers who had served together, they had kept in touch after their shared experiences in that California court room long ago in what was, for Grant, one of his most interesting, certainly the most dramatic, of the cases he had ever handled. Throughout those years, both men had waited, hoping that someday that boy stolen from the courtroom, now a man, would reappear. But it had not happened, and Grant was now quite sure that Williams would never have the closure that he craved. They both knew that his son could be dead, And, for all practical purposes, he was dead, as far as Grant was concerned. But, for Williams, the father? Well, although he had a daughter now, Grant knew that Williams would never let go of the *son* who had gone missing. Grant was flattered to have been included in the joyous occasion that this wedding represented for his former client, and he was looking forward to meeting the daughter, Jamie, who had filled the void for the missing son.

The inn was set back from the frontage road and reached by a gravel drive, the informality of which belied the elegance within. Partly shielded by trees and a high hedge, guests were assured of their privacy on arrival and departure. The inn itself was three stories, white-sided, the top gabled floors only partly visible from the roadway. Grant pulled into a vacant space near a hedge, hoping for some shade. Exiting the car, he walked to the rear, where-upon he noticed a paved chopper landing pad. *Well, that tells you something about the clientele.* As he retrieved his garment and travel bags from the trunk, he realized he could have pulled into the drive-thru—*O.K., the porte cochère*—and allowed the attendant to park the car. But now it was too late. The bell-man was jogging toward him and his bags as he slammed the trunk shut.

"Welcome to the Inn on the Bay, I'm Jonathan," the bellman said warmly. "First time with us? Here, let me get those," the young man reached for the bags.

"Right," Grant replied, following his bags to the front of the inn.

"Great! Are you here for the Williams wedding?"

"Yes, I am."

"Great!" Jonathan said. "The wedding party and all the guests are in the veranda section of the inn. You will have a great room. Are you alone, or expecting someone?"

"Just me."

"Great," Jonathan held the door. They entered into the coolness of the reception area, more living room than an office, which had that studied elegant look that made Grant feel as if he had been admitted accidentally into someone's private home where he had better not put his feet on the coffee table or set his drink down without a coaster. That look-but-don't-touch feeling—scary comfortable. *Who decorates these places,* he wondered, *and how do they know to get it just right? I mean, how do you know if the guests are* Town and Country *or* Saveur? *He noticed both magazines on a table next to a love seat.* Chesapeake Bay Life*?*

"Good afternoon," the receptionist greeted him. "And welcome to our inn. You are Mr. Grant? Will Grant?" she inquired.

How do they do that? Sign language?

"Yes, I'm Grant, for the Williams wedding. I have a reservation."

"Of course, Mr. Grant. There is nothing for you to sign. Everything has been arranged by Mr. Williams. Jonathan will show you to your room. The wedding, as you know, is at 4:00 P.M. in the garden, on the bay. The garden is just there," she nodded, "through the reception area and out the French doors. You have about an hour to freshen up, if you wish. There is, I think, an envelope for you. Yes, here it is. And your key. Will one key suffice, Mr. Grant?"

"One is fine. Is there a bar?" Grant inquired.

"No, I am afraid we have closed it for the wedding, but there is a minibar in your room," she replied. Her tone included *If you can't wait.*

"Enjoy your stay with us, Mr. Grant, the wedding will be wonderful. Quite special, I think."

"Great," Grant replied. He accepted the key and the envelope, winking at Jonathan. "Let's go, Jonathan." They threaded their way among a small fortune in antiques, down a polished-plank hallway, and passed through a glassed-in breakfast or afternoon tea area, which opened onto a private garden. All incredibly tasteful, smelling of spices and a hint of lemon polish. The furniture gleamed, and he could imagine his reflection in the woodwork. On either side of the hall were beautiful sitting rooms, fresh fruit on the sideboards, flowers on the tables. The waters of the bay were visible through the rooms to his right.

"The inn is owned by Lord Nash and his daughter, Nancy," Jonathan offered. "Lord Nash built it for his daughter, a designer, so she could show off her products. The furniture is all original antiques." Jonathan turned sideways as he ascended the narrow staircase to the second floor. "Most from the colonial area. You will recognize the Nancy Nash trademark design in the window coverings, bedding, and towels, all—"

"—available in the gift shop." Grant completed the sentence for him.

"Great," Jonathan acknowledged, as they reached the top of the stairs. "Here we are, number 207." He opened the door and stepped aside. The room was beautiful, Grant thought; Kay should have come. "The climate control is here by the door. There are screens on the windows and on the door to your balcony. The bugs can be bad at night. Room safe is in the closet. Here is your minibar," gesturing.

"I can figure it out, thanks, Jonathan," Grant said, handing him a ten-dollar bill.

"Great!" Jonathan replied. "If you need anything, just dial eight for the concierge. That's me."

"Great," Grant replied. He closed the door.

~

Grant showered and changed into a white shirt, tie, and slacks; he hung his linen sport coat in the humid shower to coax out the wrinkles. He opted for a split of Pinot Grigio, admiring the wine selections available. Relaxing on the flowered love seat, he put his feet on the low table, swirled, sniffed, and sipped the chilled wine, and only then did he open the sealed envelope.

"Will, Thanks for coming. It will be a busy day for me and my family, so I wanted to take a moment to tell you how much I appreciate your taking the time and coming all this way to share this important day with us. It is not every day that a father marries off his only daughter, or welcomes into his family a "new" son. Over 20 years ago, you helped me through an incredibly difficult time. We did not stay in contact much, my fault, except for Christmas cards every couple of years, a phone call now and then, checking on one another after a couple of disasters—I called you after the '89 quake, you called me after Hurricane Hugo—and even though you helped me with some legal matters once in a while, which I appreciated, we never got to talk, just the two of us. I regret that, Will.

But, as this wedding became a reality, I thought of those people in my life who are important to me and with whom I wanted to share this day. They, of course, include you. It seems, at least I feel, I am starting a new chapter in my life, or maybe it is closure of another chapter. I think you know what I mean. Anyway, it is very important to me that you be here to be a part of our celebration, the beginning of a new life for Scott and Jamie. I hope that despite all the excitement and confusion that weddings include, that we will have some time, the two of us, to talk and that you will get a chance to meet and talk with Scott. He is a son-in-law to be proud of, and I am so proud of him and happy that he and Jamie have found each other.

Your friend, Brad.

Brad? Grant hesitated, and then he recalled that his friend had dropped "Rob," the name by which Grant had known him years ago (*something to do with the business or his partner having the same first name?*). He sipped his wine and then stood, checked his watch: time to go. He retrieved his jacket from the shower, and pleased with the results of his instant steam pressing, he headed downstairs. He could already hear the murmur of the guests on the veranda, through the open windows.

~

United Flight 807, Austin to D.C. was already late, very late; four hours in fact. Re-routed in flight for electrical storms over Tennessee, and then mechanical trouble that necessitated an unscheduled landing in Atlanta, and an "equipment change," airplane-ese for a plane that was broken and could not be fixed. That had been enough to convince the passenger in seat 4B that her long-standing fear of flying was justified. She could not remember the last time she had flown, and it had not been out of Texas. She glanced over at her dozing companion in seat 4A, and out the window. It was obvious that they had begun their descent into D.C.—she could feel the pressure change in her ears; she did not like the feeling. The annoying chime of the flight announcement system confirmed her conclusion.

"This is your captain, ladies and gentlemen. We have begun our descent into Dulles International Airport. We should be on the ground in fifteen minutes. Local time is 2:45 P.M., and the temperature is seventy-eight degrees.

On behalf of United Airlines, we would like to apologize for the difficulty which we have encountered in this flight."

Ava's assistant, Joyce, stirred in her seat, and then she sat upright.

"Our decisions to land and change aircraft," the captain continued, "of course were dictated by our concern for the safety of our passengers, and we hope that you are not terribly inconvenienced by the delay in your trip. We hope that you will include United in your future travel plans."

I won't forget United in my future plans, thought Ava. *I am never getting on another airplane, and I shouldn't have got on this one.*

"We are never going to make the wedding, Ava," Joyce said. "It's at least a two-hour drive from Dulles to St. Michael's, and with the traffic . . ."

"I know, Joyce, but I don't know what we can do about it. They were supposed to have a car meet us. I guess we'll be late. At least we can make the reception and dinner."

"Scott is going to be so disappointed if you miss the ceremony."

"And, I'm a mess, I can't walk down the aisle as mother of the groom looking like this, and God only knows where our luggage is, in Atlanta or on this plane!"

The plane banked and the seat belt sign came on. Ava could see the Potomac and parts of the capital below. A stewardess leaned over and handed her an envelope.

"Mrs. Ames?" she asked.

"Yes."

"This message is from the cockpit; we just received it," the attendant smiled and handed the envelope to Ava.

"You read, Joyce, it can't be anything but bad news, the way things have been going," Ava handed her the note. Joyce read:

Saturday 18 Aug 14:37 hrs
ZX0004897-001-04
To: Ava Ames
From: United Airlines, Red Carpet Services

Upon exiting the aircraft, you will be met by Mr. Odetto, United Customer Service Agent, who will escort you to Gate 909, nearby. Arrangements have been made to fly you and your party by helicopter to your destination. Your baggage has already been segregated and will be transferred to the helicopter. You should be able to arrive on time for the scheduled event.

Please accept our apologies for the stress associated with our delay, and Congratulations on the wedding of your son!

Mr. Meier

"Well, look at this," Joyce said, smiling and handing her the note, "Maybe things are looking up."

"A helicopter! That's all I need!" Ava groaned.

The airliner rolled left and leveled on final approach, and a slight jolt indicated that the gear was down and locked; the capital glided by below.

~

The inn, really three buildings built over time, was joined on the left by the dining room and on the right by a recent addition of guest rooms. The complex framed an expanse of brick patio and lawn that draped down to the bay. The patio was elevated above the lawn and ran the entire length of the buildings, broken up by brick planters and small trees planted in the largest pots that Grant had ever seen. The lawn was dotted occasionally with Adirondack chairs and small tables for drinks, books, and sketch pad, Grant surmised. The entire scene resembled some English lord's backyard, he thought. The late-afternoon sun glistened on the still waters of the bay, and the several, small boat piers and docks pointed invitingly to private estates across the water. The whole view was magnificent. There were no buildings on either side, and except for the few barely visible homes across the water, the entire area was at the same time completely open and yet totally private.

To the right of the lawn area, an aisle covered with a shiny white runner split the white fabric–covered guest chairs into the two traditional "friends of" sections. At the end of the aisle, almost to the water, stood a gazebo-like structure, laced with white roses, the floor of which was covered in rose petals. Pots and stands of flowers in large sculpted cement holders surrounded the gazebo and lined both sides of the seating sections.

The missing bar was in fact located on the brick veranda, and it was doing a brisk business with arriving guests who accepted champagne or mixed drinks as they mingled and slowly strolled to their seats. Grant estimated that there must be at least one hundred fifty people, and he decided not to do the math yet on the cost of the whole thing. He did not see anyone he recognized, but then he didn't know anybody except his host. He decided that the people he was looking at were some of the best-looking, well-dressed people he had ever seen gathered in one place.

Jonathan, in bow tie and black vest, had graduated to assistant bartender. He offered Grant a chilled glass of champagne. "Beautiful setup, isn't it?"

"Great, simply great," Grant panned, thinking they had that in common.

He looked around, studying the guests. His former client, as he remembered him, was nowhere in sight. Even though it had been over twenty years, a long time, he thought that he might recognize him from pictures sent with some of the Christmas cards. In any event, he would be coming down the aisle with the bride.

"Mr. Grant?"

He turned in response, "Yes."

"I thought so, I was looking out for you. Brad asked me to," she said extending her hand, attached to a well-tanned brown arm. "I'm Cecily, Brad's secretary, and I am pleased to meet you. We are so glad you could come. Was Mrs. Grant able to accompany you?"

"No," he said, realizing that he was still holding her hand.

"I see you have a drink. Is there anything I can get you?"

"No, thank you. I was just admiring the view and this incredible place."

"It is quite something, isn't it," she replied. "It is very old. The original buildings date from after the war of 1812. It is colonial style, and Lord Nash and his daughter have remodeled it and added a guest wing, but maintained the feel and look of the original home, don't you think?"

"I'm not old enough to remember the 'original look' or the feel, or who won that war," Grant smiled.

"I am sure that you are not," Cecily laughed. "Have you noticed the furnishings? The antiques are priceless. Lord Nash has spent years assembling this collection." she said.

"Do you know Jonathan?" Grant laughed. "Just kidding. Actually, I did notice the impressive sideboards and hutches in the rooms off the hallway. There are some beautiful pieces."

"Brad loves the inn, and when Jamie and Scott said they wanted to be married here, he was delighted. It is a special place. Do you know anyone here?" she asked.

"Just two, you and Brad," Grant said. "How long have you worked for Brad?" he asked.

"Almost five years now. I love my job. I was working for him when Scott was chosen for the annual grant. That's how he met Jamie. It is quite a story," she continued.

"I bet. I would love to hear it from the top; Brad gave me only an outline. I understand he and Scott really hit it off," he said.

"Yes, they did," she replied. "It is the old saying: lose a daughter, gain a son, and in this case it is so true. They have developed a remarkable friendship."

"I understand that," said Grant, recalling the note from Brad.

"Where is he, Scott, from originally? Do you know?"

"Scott grew up in Texas, Austin, where his mother lives. She is involved in the recording industry, quite successful I understand. In fact, we weren't sure if she was coming to the wedding until just recently. She is apparently totally involved in her work, a workaholic, Scott calls her, and she was, until a few weeks ago, so busy that she wasn't coming. Brad has never met her, since Scott and Jamie live in California. But, she is coming, I have been told; at least we are expecting her."

They had moved away from the bar area to make room for other arriving guests, and the ushers were beginning to seat guests. The front seats were rapidly filling, but Cecily did not seem concerned. They paused at the top of the brick steps, which led to the aisle and the gazebo. Guests filtered around them to their seats, some escorted by ushers, others on their own. The formality of the seating seemed voluntary, Grant observed, and he liked it.

"I hope I'm not keeping you from anything," Grant said, aware that he had taken up much of her time and that she might have more important things to do.

"Not at all," she said. "My work is finished. The inn has taken it over from here on. Unless there is some last-minute problem with regard to one of the guests, I am programmed to enjoy—in fact I have orders to relax and have a good time at the wedding," she smiled.

"So, Scott's mother is not here yet?" he inquired.

"No, and that was my most recent, and hopefully last, problem for today," she said. "She, her name is Ava, was flying in from Austin today, and she should have been here by now, but her plane was forced to land in Atlanta due to some in-flight mechanical problem, and she has only just landed at Dulles," she explained.

"Well, it took me almost two hours to make that drive; there is no way she is going to make it. Isn't this about ready to start?" he asked.

"Oh, she'll make it all right," Cecily continued. "We knew of the delay. I sent our pilot, our helicopter pilot, to pick up her and her assistant. They should be here any minute. They can land right in front of the Inn. She'll make it. We are not starting without her," she explained. "In fact, her timing is perfect." They both glanced skyward as the unmistakable sound of a helicopter carried over the buildings. As if on cue, the blue and gold jet chopper banked over the bay and dropped downwind of the inn so that the rotor wash would not disrupt the guests or the decorations. Grant heard the rotors wind down and the high-pitched whine dissipate as the chopper landed out of sight behind the inn.

"Excuse me," Mr. Grant, Cecily touched his arm, "But now I *do* have work to do, convincing the mother of the groom that she does not need a half hour or more to get ready. She has about five minutes!" She turned and walked back through the open dining room doors.

Grant opted to seat himself. He could never remember if it was the right or the left for the bride's friends. Reluctant to do anything "left," he walked down the outside of the right-hand section of chairs and picked a seat on the outside end, five rows back. To his left a couple in their fifties leaned over and introduced themselves. He promptly forgot their names, and he focused on the scene in front. He knew he would not get a chance to talk to Brad until after the ceremony, and he guessed that his friend was probably inside with the wedding party.

~

Ava knew that she was a mess and that there was no way she was walking down any aisle, or anywhere, dressed and looking as she did, wedding or not. She was still upset from the unscheduled stop in Atlanta, and she would have preferred to take the train back to Austin immediately. *And then, a helicopter, my God, what next?* she thought. Actually, the view of the capital was spectacular, and the pilot pointed out Chesapeake Bay and the town of St. Michael's. It was lovely, and the headphones, though destroying what was left of her hair, drowned out all the noise. She thought she might get used to it after all. The Maryland countryside was green and beautiful.

Williams's secretary greeted them when they entered the inn, and she escorted them to a private room. *"Her* room," she was told. No sooner had Ava stopped to catch her breath, when a serious-looking woman in a smock, carrying a suitcase, plopped her down in a chair and began to do her hair and makeup without so much as a word. This she could handle. Her luggage was unpacked as she watched in the mirror, and her clothes hung up in the closet.

"Which dress?," the secretary asked, and she indicated the one Cecily was holding. "It's in good shape, Mrs. Ames. No pressing needed," Cecily offered, and it did look fine to Ava.

She observed that now her hair was perfect, she had to admit, and her makeup was almost done. Ava looked up at the first strains of Pachelbel's Canon in D. *Must be at least two violins and even a cello,* she thought. *They are quite good.*

"Mrs. Ames, they are starting. Can I help you with your dress? Your hair and makeup look fine," Cecily said, leaning over her shoulder.

"Thank you. I can finish, I only need a minute," Ava said. "Joyce, get my satin shoes, will you? Thank you, Cecily, is it?" she asked. "Y'all have been so helpful," the soft drawl clothed her words. "Joyce and I can manage. Which way do we go?" she asked.

Cecily pointed to a door nearby. "Right through here. I will wait outside. The usher will seat you on the right side, front row. There is a short walk across the patio. It is brick, a couple of stairs, easy, and then the aisle. It is on grass, but there is a runner, fastened down on a hard surface. No problem with your shoes. Should be simple."

"That's fine. Joyce and I will be along in a minute. Thank y'all so much for all your help," Ava reached for her dress.

~

Grant studied the backs of the heads in front of him as the violins began to play. He turned toward the sound and found the trio seated on the patio to his right. *Canon in what, D?* he thought. At every wedding he could remember. Here in this setting, however, it fit perfectly the tranquility. The ushers appeared behind the trio on the patio, four young men in morning suits, tails, and spats, French ties. *First class,* thought Grant. The young men left the patio in a line and took up their positions in front of the right-hand section of chairs, short of the gazebo, facing the center aisle. Behind them a young man, six-feet or more, walked across the lawn, a broad smile on his face. As he passed the ushers, he shook hands with each, and he gave the last one a full hug: the best man, Grant guessed. The young man took his place at the head of the line, nearest the aisle, and turned to face the crowd. His white vest and white tie marked him as the groom. Brad was right, Grant thought: he is a handsome kid, and if he is as smart and nice as he looks, no wonder Brad felt the way he had described in his note to Grant.

The young man leaned toward the aisle. The guests followed the gaze of the groom, whose smile now broadened into a full grin. Down the aisle, on the arm of an usher, *that makes five,* Grant noted, came an attractive woman dressed in a floor-length flawless lace dress, close fitting but not tight. *Classy,* thought Grant, *something Kay might have worn.* Of course, remembering his conversation with Brad's secretary, she must be Ava Ames, Scott's mother. He certainly gets his looks from her, Grant thought.

She glanced neither left nor right. Granted noticed that her jaw seemed tense, her neck stiff, and her head held almost not quite straight, as if she was expecting something. A little like a deer in the headlights, he thought. But then he recalled that she probably knew almost no one here and that she had never met her son's father-in-law, Cecily had told him. And there was that mess with the flight and the helicopter ride. She looked fine after what she had been through, Grant conceded.

Scott joined his mother as she reached the end of the aisle. He took her arm and he kissed her on the cheek, then he led her to her seat. As she was seated, another woman, her assistant Grant presumed, came in from the side and took the seat next to her.

Then the music changed. Had it ever stopped? Grant knew the music but could not recall the title. Andrea Bocelli, maybe? He glanced down at the wedding program in his hand: "Con te partiro" ("Time to Say Goodbye"), of course. The guests seated next to him stood as Grant heard the murmur of the group swell. He stood and looked back over those behind him, and he caught a glimpse of the bride in her white dress, and of her father, as they stepped off the patio, preceded by several bridesmaids, five, Grant counted. They walked in that halting gait Grant always thought strange. The last bridesmaid took her place, all of them at an angle, under the gazebo, facing back down the main aisle.

The classic wedding march now sounded, and Grant could sense the excitement. Everyone was now standing. Grant glanced ahead. The groomsmen and the bridesmaids opposite them were all smiling, and he noticed the mother of the groom fidgeting with her hair as she stood, straightening her dress. She had remained seated during the early procession, which Grant thought odd, but then he had never been the mother of a groom. Grant turned to face the rear, and now he recognized, through the throng, Brad, taller it seemed than he remembered, as he stepped onto the white runner and started forward, his daughter's arm in his. As they approached, Grant thought he looked the same, still fit, his face a bit heavier, *but I would know him if he passed me on the street and said hello,* after a minute, he conceded.

Jamie was all in white, her long train attended by two young girls, her face covered in a white veil. They walked slowly, sort of like a perp walk, Grant thought inappropriately. He noticed Brad nodding at guests, and as they passed him, Grant could see the beautiful young bride smiling ahead at her groom. He turned and looked to the front as the two of them neared the gazebo. Scott was shifting his weight awaiting their arrival.

Ava was seated on the aisle in the first row in front of Grant, and she watched her son as the music began. She smiled at him, knowing from his look that he had seen his bride approaching. She turned and looked back down the aisle as father and daughter approached, slowly. She studied the bride, her dress and the train, and then looked at the father: Brad, she recalled. As they came nearer, she found herself focusing on him. Only yards away now, moving slowly in tempo to the music, she felt her mouth instantly dry, and she felt that the sound of her heart, or pulse, beating in her temples, resonated over the music. Joyce heard a swallowed, "Oh, no!" as Ava stepped around her, and started down the first row of seats away from the center aisle. Joyce started to say something as Ava lunged past the guests standing in her row, who were blocking her exit and didn't see her coming. Shoving, pushing, urgent, soundless, she was almost clear of the row when one of the guests stepped back to let her pass, and suddenly Ava tripped. She fell forward, headlong onto the lawn, with a sharp cry as she went down, and then her head hit a concrete aggregate base that was supporting one of the pillars of the gazebo under which the ceremony was to take place.

Grant saw her efforts, puzzled, and watched in amazement when she stumbled and then fell, almost in slow motion. From the sound of her head hitting the concrete, he knew she was hurt, probably seriously. The music abruptly stopped. Scott, who was standing almost directly in front of his mother, was the first to reach her, and he knelt by her side. Brad and Jamie froze at the end of the aisle. Grant forced his way through the rows of chairs in front of him and heard Scott call out: "Mother, my God!"

Grant found himself standing next to Ava's assistant, who was sobbing with tears pouring down her face. No one else had made a move. He leaned over Scott, and he could see blood running down the rough cement base and onto the grass. One hand on Scott's shoulder, he looked up at Brad who was now behind him: "Call 911, or whatever it is here!" Grant said, the authority of his tone left no doubt that it was serious. Brad turned and moved away, giving orders. He directed one of the bridesmaids to take Jamie inside. One of the groomsmen knelt beside Scott.

"Scott, let me have a look. I am an EMT remember?" he said.

Scott made room for him. "Mark, what happened? Is she all right? God, she is bleeding."

Mark moved her slightly, supporting her head, until he lowered it onto a jacket that someone had placed on the grass.

"She is breathing O.K.," he replied. "And head wounds bleed badly. I cannot tell. Mrs. Ames!?" he called into her ear.

Ava was still; no response. He felt for a pulse.

"Five minutes, they are on the way," a voice behind sounded. "The ambulance."

"Good," Mark replied. He had moved her head so that she could breathe, and he rolled her over partly onto one side, one arm under her. Searching for the wound site, he pushed her hair back behind one ear. He felt for the pulse on her neck as Brad, now returned, leaned in over Grant. There was a deep abrasion and what looked like a laceration in her scalp, and Mark took a towel handed to him by one of the hotel staff. As he started to put the towel against her head, Brad and Grant watched as the young man's finger traced a small S-shaped mark on her neck, behind her ear. It was not bleeding. Satisfied that the scalp wound was the source of the bleeding, he applied pressure to it with the towel, covering her neck and scalp area.

They heard the sirens, and in few moments the firemen took charge. The guests were asked to move away, and Grant and Brad moved back with them, watching from a distance. One of the firemen was using a portable radio, relaying information to a hospital. Williams stood silent. He had not said a word since they had moved out of firemen's way. Distant. *It is like he has "left the room,"* Grant thought; he could not imagine his friend's upset.

One of the firemen, accompanied by a uniformed sheriff, approached Brad and Grant with questions. The sheriff called Williams by his first name and seemed to be as concerned about him as he was for the injured woman, when it was clear to the deputy that this was an accident.

At one point, Brad started to walk back toward Ava; she was now on a gurney and hooked to an I.V., but then he abruptly returned to stand by Grant. Grant noticed that Brad never took his eyes off her, even though she was not visible through the shock blankets and bandages. The firemen quickly stabilized Ava, who was still unconscious, and began to move her through the parting throng toward their vehicle. Scott accompanied them, one hand on his mother. In a few moments Grant heard the wail of the sirens fade.

~

Grant and Brad followed Scott and Mark back to the inn. Mark had blood on his clothes. As they approached the door, Grant looked at the guests, who were standing by quietly.

He asked Brad, "What do you want to do about the wedding? Go on with it . . . check with Scott? Make some announcement . . . ?" The two men looked out at the group, all of whom were staring at them.

"No," Brad responded. "No, Will. There is not going to be a wedding . . . not today. You tell them that," and he turned away.

Grant looked at Cecily, standing next to him. She touched his arm: "I'll take care of it, I know most of these people."

Together they stepped off the patio and walked back toward the musicians. Grant took one of the microphones and handed it to Cecily who made apologies to the guests and a brief explanation. Many of them had not seen Ava fall, and they could only guess at what had happened. Cecily told them that the bar was open and they were free to stay and eat as long as they wished. Prompted by Grant, she declined to take questions. After, Grant stood with her while she accepted regrets and condolences for Brad and the couple. She promised that there would be a second wedding, that all would be reinvited. Within half an hour all the wedding guests had politely left. By then, it was dark. The two went inside. The small bar was open; Grant ordered a vodka for himself and a glass of Chardonnay for Cecily. He carried the drinks into one of the small meeting rooms where they settled down in easy chairs, facing each other.

"Well, now what, Cecily?" He took a long sip of his drink. The ice clinked as he lowered his glass.

She stared at him over her wine and replied, "I do not have a clue, frankly, Mr. Grant. I have been through some interesting . . . episodes with Brad, but nothing like this," she sighed, leaning back against the cushions. "Nothing like this."

"No one had ever met Scott's mother, is that correct? Before today?" he asked.

"Yes, that is right. She lives in Texas, and a meeting never happened. Scott finally told Brad not to worry. That he was sure she was coming to the wedding and, if she did not, well, that was her decision. They have an "interesting" relationship, Scott once told me. I surmised that it was what it was, and Scott and Jamie were so in love and excited that we left it up to them."

"What does Brad know about her? Anything?"

"Nothing as far as I know, except what I told you earlier, outside. Only what we have learned from Scott. She keeps to herself, it appears."

"Well, something happened out there to scare the *hell* out of her. Either something physical or something else. I saw her struggling to get out of the row of seats; she was determined to get away. My first thought was that she was going to be sick."

They looked at each other. Neither had an answer. *Not yet,* Grant mused.

~

It was after midnight when Williams parked in one of the spaces marked Emergency Room Only. There were no other cars. He cut his engine, got out of the car, and walked slowly up the ramp into a semidark entrance hall of the one-story hospital building. Scott and Jamie, who had followed the ambulance, had called him from the hospital when they were leaving: *Severe ankle sprain; require crutches for a few weeks at the outside; a mild-to-severe concussion; accompanied by a laceration to the head which required six stitches to close; beneath the hair, no scarring expected; nothing life threatening. They had not been able to talk to her.* That was the report. She had been given a mild sedative and had been transferred to a private room. Scott would bring Joyce back to the inn, and they would fill Brad in later. However, Williams had avoided them upon their return.

Williams pushed open the ER inner door and stepped inside. It was empty. A TV flickered; the sound off. A man in scrubs looked up. Williams, still in formal wear, but tie down and shirt open, asked for her room. The attendant nodded, and he easily found it, her name on the door. He paused. He had planned his questions if the opportunity arose to ask them, but now he was not so sure. *What the hell am I doing here?* he thought. He eased the door open. The room was that half-light that hospitals favored. He could see a woman in the bed. She was asleep; the sedative, he remembered. Her head was wrapped in a bandage that hid one side of her face and most of her hair. The sheet was up to her chin. He stopped at the end of the bed. She was breathing deeply. Monitors cast their eerie glow and shadows. An IV drip disappeared under one side of the covers. He strained, but he could not see enough to recognize her. He moved closer to the side of the bed. The line on one of the monitors jumped slightly. He stopped, staring at it. *Who are you?* he thought. *Why did you bolt out of the wedding? What are you afraid of? If that was it? Why do I think that there is more to this than . . .?*

She made a soft sound and shifted slightly in her bed. He took a step back and glanced at the monitor again. Nothing. He realized that there was no point in waking her. She was not going anywhere in the next day or so. Then he would have a chance to talk with her, to ask his questions. He ran his hand through his hair and bent closer, studying her face. Nothing. Suddenly exhausted, he turned and walked away, letting the door close silently behind him.

Behind him, unseen by him, the monitor skipped a beat, the pulse and blood pressure readings accelerated, and Ava's eyes, now open, followed him until the door closed.

In the hallway outside her room, he noticed a nurse's station. A young nurse sat in front of a computer, her back to the counter. She turned when he asked, "Miss?"

"Yes," she replied. And then, "Oh, aren't you Jamie Williams's father? There was a wedding today, wasn't there?" she asked.

"Yes, I am Brad Williams," his tired smile said the rest.

"I just came on shift," she said. "What happened? Someone was injured? Oh," she interrupted herself and standing offered him her hand. "I am Linda Caen, Mr. Williams. Jamie and I went to high school together. I was at your house for a party once, but it was long time ago," she smiled. "But I recognize you, and I saw your name referred to on the patient's, Ms. Ames's, chart."

"She was, *is,* the mother of the groom," he replied. "It is a long story," he paused, leaning down towards her. "Linda, I need some of the information from her chart, for insurance. She is from out of state, Texas, and I need to find out about payment by her insurance carrier for this . . . ." he gestured at the room. "Could you . . . could *I* . . . see her file and maybe get a copy of some of the biographical information, social security number, home address, that sort of thing?"

"Sure, Mr. Williams, I have the file right here. I was just starting to check her meds, the physician's orders. Why don't I just copy the 'Admit' part for you? It has everything you need. Just give me a minute." She picked up the file and walked to a nearby copy machine.

"That should be everything, Mr. Williams." She smiled and handed him several sheets of paper.

"Linda, thank you so much. This should help and if I need . . . ?"

"Just call me, if it is tonight. I am off at 7 A.M."

He shook her hand. "Thanks for everything."

She smiled, "You are welcome, Mr. Williams. Please remember me to Jamie. I hope it all works out for her and for you."

"I hope so. It will, I am sure." He turned back down the hall. Behind him he heard, "Mr. Williams, if you need to call back for another, or anything, just ask for me. Station Two," she said. He turned and gave her a half wave.

Outside in his car, he leaned back in the seat. He felt his fatigue—and what was it? Worry? Doubt?—wash over him. *It is nothing* he thought. *Maybe she had some sort of food poisoning, a bowel attack, the flight, being late for the ceremony, nerves; Scott said she never travels, hates flying . . . That must be it.* He buckled up and bent forward to start the engine, and he glanced over at the hospital records that he had set on the seat. He reached over and picked them up. He switched on the overhead lights and slowly read:

Name, WFA, date, address, arrived by ambulance. Name of the crew chief. Address.

    Next of kin—blank. No local phone. His eyes ran down the page. *1st responders start IV. Patient breathing without difficulty; non-responsive to voice or touch . . .* on it went. *Radioed condition to ER en route.*

He turned to the second sheet; it was the back of the first page.

Weight, height, age, description of injury . . .

He scanned the rest of the page, boxes checked and handwritten notes:

    Distinguishing marks or characteristics: Dark brown hair, appears dyed. Glasses, broken. Ring on right hand. Two finger nails broken. Small S-shaped scar behind left ear . . .

An instantaneous bone-deep chill washed over him. He felt the hair rise on the back of his neck, and he looked down at the raised hair on both of his arms. His stomach tightened. He was holding his breath. He read it again, aloud: *Small S-shaped scar behind left ear, not evidence of a present wound.* And he remembered. He felt his stomach turn, the taste of bile in his mouth; his chest tighten. He choked back a gag and stared at the wall of the hospital. The red ER sign warned: danger, trouble, help inside. He knew it *was* she. There was no way that this could be, but there she was. *"Someday when you least expect it . . ."* After a moment, he got out of his car. He paused and leaned back against the door, thinking, weighing the odds, the incredible unlikely possibilities. *Someday . . .* He shook his head and glanced at the darkened windows, one of them her room, and he imagined her lying there. Tamara! Mara! . . . Ava! *My God!* He straightened, and when he walked past his car, he slammed one hand violently down on the hood. Inside the entry he located the phone he had seen when he had entered a few moments earlier. He dialed the inn: "Will Grant, please?" He heard the phone ring, the connection made, "Will..."

~

Grant had returned to his room after bidding goodnight to Cecily. They had not seen Brad since he had left them outside earlier. The guests were gone. Grant learned that Jamie had changed out of her wedding dress and that she and Joyce, Ava's assistant, had driven to the hospital. Someone, Grant could not remember who, had heard that Ava had been admitted to the hospital, that her injuries were not life threatening. Shoes off, in T-shirt and shorts, Grant had just finished a call to his wife, in California, relating what little he knew, when his phone rang. He glanced at the clock. It was almost 1:00 A.M.

"Will? We need your room. I will be there in a few minutes. I'm on my way back from the hospital," he heard Williams say.

"Sure, but what—?"

Williams cut him off: "Dave Mosby is on his way there to your room. In case he gets there first, let him in. I'll explain when I get there." The line went dead.

~

It was late afternoon the following day. Clear, cloudless, warm, a trace of wind on the water of the bay. They were in Brad's office at the beach house: Grant, Brad, and attorney Dave Mosby. Mosby was in-house chief counsel for NEFCO and a trusted friend of Williams. Grant was still was having trouble processing what for Williams was fast becoming a certainty. It was just too unlikely. Too impossible even. But Grant had done what was asked of him and, as he was fond of saying, "We are all here to learn."

"O.K., Grant, what have you got?" Williams started.

"I got through to the clerk's office in California," he nodded at the other attorney. "The time difference helped. The file is closed. The paper file was destroyed long ago, but the court's orders are available on microfiche. That includes the order for custody and the order authorizing her arrest. I have a faxed copy. The certified one is being overnighted." He handed copies around. "It is the same order that you have, Brad. The reduced copy that you have been carrying around for years. Actually that sort of saved the day, because it had the case number on it, otherwise they might still be looking for the file."

"Good," Williams interjected, studying the order.

"The arrest warrant is another matter. This case predated the revision of the state's records. Now, they put all outstanding warrants online in a state database. These days they are picking up Californians returning from Mexico for outstanding traffic tickets. But back then it was all manual. They have not yet found the warrant," Grant explained and he continued, "But I spoke to a judge, whom I know. He remembers the case and is prepared to order a new warrant, now, perhaps as early as tomorrow. He wanted the certified order on his desk, and then he will do the paperwork. Bottom line, we should have it the day after tomorrow, Tuesday, here."

"I wish *we* could get things done that fast," Mosby said.

"There is more," Grant continued. "Because parental kidnapping is such a hot button issue these days, the sheriff and the local DA are willing to request formal extradition if, and this is the kicker, Brad, if we can prove that Ava *is* in fact Tamara Evans . . . Mara. *If* we can convince the local court. Remember, she has not been convicted of a crime, but she has violated a state court order, and there is an outstanding order for her arrest from California, which includes a warrant for her arrest. *That* is the key, the warrant. In that sense, she *is* a fugitive," he paused. "There may be federal issues, which we might get the feds involved in, maybe later, but that is all I could find out so far."

"Good work, Will. Thanks for that," Brad said. "Dave?" He turned to Mosby.

Mosby opened a file and passed around a memo of several pages. It was titled: "Ava Ames (?)" For the next half an hour Mosby reviewed what he had been able to learn regarding Scott's mother, a task given him the evening before at their meeting in Grant's room. Grant was amazed at the depth of information that the attorney had been able to gather so quickly. *Big corporations do have the advantages,* he thought.

Mosby had obtained her Texas driver's license; a printout of the State of Texas criminal index (nothing on file); her social security number matched the one supplied by Williams; her employment history; a copy of a real estate loan application when she purchased her home in

Austin; proof that she had never been married or divorced in Texas; and her health insurance information. He also had his own copy of her complete medical file from the local hospital, which included the admissions form that Williams had obtained. And, he had the Texas record of birth for Scott Ames. "It is all pretty routine, nothing exciting, except Scott's birth record," Mosby said.

"What about it?" Williams asked, looking at the document.

"Well, it's a duplicate, not an original. It is actually a substitute certificate, issued to replace a lost birth certificate."

"How does that happen?" Grant asked.

"In Texas," he explained, "if you are born at home, or the Hall of Records or the government building in some small town where the records are supposed to be kept burns down, or if they are lost somehow, or if there are no records in the first place, all you have to do is supply an affidavit of the circumstances of the birth, and the state or local clerk, either one, will issue a *substitute* birth certificate. That can be done anytime. And that is what this is," he held up the document. "See here, on Scott's birth certificate, where it says 'Name of Mother,' that is filled in: Ava Ames, but the space for the father, that is blank. We have not had time to cross reference the mother's name, her name, with any other possible records, but the absence of a hospital or attending physician suggests he was born at home, or somewhere other than a hospital."

"Look," Grant interrupted, "The date that this certificate was issued, at least on my copy, is illegible, it is blurred. Can you read it on your copy, Brad?"

Williams looked up at Grant, a thin smile forming, his eyes shining. "Mine is blurred also. But we *know* the date, don't we, Will? I am betting it is sometime *after* our hearing in California, after she left." He looked at the two men. "We need to keep her here, gentlemen, until we can get this settled. We cannot let her leave. Not after all this time. I know, I just know, that it is she. Now, how do we get this into some court to prove it gentlemen?"

"For God's sake, Brad," Grant was standing. "Do you realize what you are saying? What you are asking us to prove?" he paused. "Do you actually believe, think, that Ms. Ames is Scott's mother and that she ... that *you* are his father? Out of all the people in this country, that Jamie and Scott met ...! Jesus, Brad!" He ran his hand over his head. "None of this proves that, not even for openers. It is all circumstantial. And what if she denies it, which she surely will, unless she is a crazy. Then what?" They were silent staring at Williams.

"She will, and she is" he replied slowly. "And Will, you and I, counselor, are going to have that day in court that your judge promised us would happen, remember: 'someday, somewhere,' he said. Well, that day is now, and the place is here!" He stood and crossed the room. Facing them, "Your job now, gentlemen, is to find a way to keep her here, here in this county, in Maryland, and to get us into some courtroom, any courtroom. My sanity, my life depends on this and so do the lives of my daughter and ... my son."

"Brad, what are you going to tell Jamie and Scott?" Grant said, his voice almost a whisper.

"That's my job, Will. I will handle that tomorrow," he replied. "Now, here is what I want you to do, Grant." he said.

~

It was midmorning when Grant entered her hospital room. He was dressed in sport coat and slacks, his shirt open, no tie. He carried no pad or materials. He knocked softly, and hearing no objection, he eased the door open. She was in bed, facing the window.

"Mrs. Ames?" he asked softly. The door closed slowly behind. She turned toward him, her face expressionless.

"Mrs. Ames, I am a friend of Mr. Williams, an ... his ... attorney. I would like to ask you a few questions. It will take only a few moments." Grant walked past the end of the bed and stopped near the window, so that she could see him without straining. Her eyes followed his movements. Her head was still bandaged, and her left foot, wrapped in a bandage, extended out of the covers.

"How are you feeling?"

She nodded. "Better, but I would love to get out of here."

"What do the doctors say? When can you expect to leave?"

"Whom did you say you were?"

"My name is Will Grant. I am an attorney, and I was at the wedding. I saw you fall. I was worried that you might have been more seriously hurt. A concussion, I was told."

"Who told you that?"

"Mr. Williams, I think. Or maybe your son, Scott."

"What questions do you have, Mr. . . .?"

"Grant. Will Grant. Just a few if you do not mind, and if you find it too trying or tiring, I understand."

"All right, go ahead." She straightened up, leaning back on her pillows, her eyes now even with Grant's. He leaned against the windowsill and crossed his arms.

"Mrs. Ames, I have known Mr. Williams for many years. A long time ago I represented him in a case in California, Northern California. Have you ever been to California?"

"Never," she replied without hesitation.

"Oh, I thought perhaps we had met there, in California."

"We could not have, Mr. Grant. I have never been to California, north or south."

"Mrs. Ames, you are an experienced businesswoman, quite successful and respected in your field. Music, isn't it?" He paused for a reply; there was none. "So, let me be quite direct, and there is no easy way to do this, Mrs. Ames, or to say it. Are you the mother of Scott Ames?"

Her eyes narrowed just a trace, but he saw it. If her eyes were not cold before, they surely were now; her expression blank. *Does she recognize me?* he wondered.

"You know that I am his mother, Mr. Grant."

"Yes, I do, and I believe that. Where was Scott born, Mrs. Ames?"

She sighed, "In Texas, of course."

"In Texas. And who is his father, Mrs. Ames?"

"That is none of your, or for that matter anybody's, business, Mr. Grant."

Even now, he was not certain that it was she, he still could not be sure from the court hearings years ago. Her hair was short and dark, no longer blonde. She seemed heavier. Her face just looked different. He tried to conceal his doubt. But something about her tone and her control did not set right.

"Well, Mrs. Ames, I guess you could say *I* am making it *my* business." He waited for her retort. None came. She simply stared back at him. "Do you *know* who Scott's father is?"

She looked away from him for a moment, and then she turned back. "Yes, Mr. Grant, I do. Surprised?" she smiled. "I know who fathered Scott. Where and when it happened—all that. And it is none of *your* business, still."

"So, you know the name of Scott's father, but you are refusing to tell me who he is"

"It was a long time ago. Scott understands, and that is all that matters, Mr. Grant."

"Is Mr. Williams Scott's father?"

"You are serious, aren't you? 'Is Mr. Williams Scott's father?' you ask me. No, he is not. I have not yet met the man, unless you count his visit here last night."

"Would you be willing to take a polygraph, a lie detector test, on that?"

She did not answer. She sighed. She closed her eyes and wiped her forehead with a tissue. She opened her eyes and stared at him. He held her stare. He could not read anything into her expression. *She is either telling the truth, or is a very good liar,* he thought. Her eyes left his, and she looked out the window behind him.

"We are through, Mr. Grant, you and I, and I *am* tired," meeting his eyes.

Grant stood and moved closer to her. She gave no sign of anything. At the foot of her bed he stopped. She followed his movements. With one hand on the end of the metal bed, he leaned slightly towards her.

"*We* are not through, Mrs. Ames," he said. "I think you know that. *We* are just beginning. We believe that Mr. Williams is, in fact, Scott's father, and if we are correct, you know what that means, for Scott, Jamie, and yes, Mrs. Ames, for you." He paused. "I came here today to give you a chance to straighten this out, to acknowledge what you know and what we will be able to prove. *Prove.* That is the operative word, Mrs. Ames. I do not personally recognize you as the young woman who walked out of my courtroom years ago, but whether I do or not is not important. This is your chance to keep a lid of sorts on this, and what happens next is up to you."

"Get out, Mr. Grant. Get out of here!" her voice was hard and her face reddened. "How dare you come in here and accuse me of whatever it is you think I have done or I am! Get out!"

Grant did not move for a moment. Then he said, "I'll take that as a 'No,' Mrs. Ames. But we are not through yet." He reached into his back pocket and placed a folded, white, typed document on her lap. "That is a subpoena, Mrs. Ames, for you to appear in court, here in Maryland, two days from now. You have been served. And you will be there, not like the last time," he paused.

He could feel her hate. There was no disguising it now. He turned away and, as he reached for and pulled open the door, he felt something hit him in the back, and he knew when he looked down that it was the subpoena, balled up. He picked it up and lobbed it back at her. It landed between her feet on the bed. He stepped through the door, and as he did, he heard behind him:

"Do not tell me what to do, Mr. Grant! No one tells me what to do!"

He smiled to himself, remembering that he had heard those words long ago, as the door closed behind him.

The door closed, Grant gone, Ava reached for the phone on the bedside tray. In a minute, she said: "Joyce, get Steve Ryder on the phone now, and have him call me here. Never mind why, just get him!"

When Grant stepped off the curb into the parking lot, he felt for the inside pocket of his sport coat and with an index finger pushed the Stop button on his portable mini-recorder.

~

Williams hesitated outside of Scott's suite at the inn. He ran his hand through his hair, squared his shoulders, and took a deep breath. Then another. He knocked once and, without waiting for an answer, opened the door. Jamie was seated on a love seat looking out at the darkened bay; she turned as he entered.

"Daddy. I wondered where you were." She embraced him as Scott entered the room.

"Sit down, both of you, please."

They were startled by his tone. Williams took a chair from a nearby desk and positioned it in front of them. Scott sat next to Jamie. He held her hand.

"Mom is resting; she is a little better, stable," Scott began.

"I understand, Scott. I was at the hospital, after the two of you left," Williams answered.

"You went to the hospital, daddy? That was nice, but why?"

"I met your friend, Linda. She filled me in," he added. "It sounds like your mother should be fine, Scott, in a couple of days, except maybe for her ankle."

"Yes, that is what they told us," Scott replied.

"I need to talk to you, both of you," Williams leaned forward, his elbows on his knees.

Before he could begin, Scott said, "Brad, I am so sorry about the wedding, but I know something must have happened to my mother. We are not sure yet why she collapsed, but I want you to know that I can deal, well, cover the expenses with you. I feel responsible."

"That is not it, Scott, the wedding is off, anyway, for now, and I am not worried about the expense. My concern is for the two of you, and, frankly, one other thing."

"What do you mean, daddy?" Jamie asked. "We can always get married at a small ceremony later. What is important is Scott's mother. Whether, and how soon, she will be all right."

"Jamie, I do not think there is anything 'wrong' with her. I think she was trying to get out of there . . . in a hurry, and she fell. That is what happened."

"Wait a minute, Brad, but she must have been sick or something," Scott said. "Maybe she did not want to be embarrassed. Until we get a chance to talk to her, we won't know."

"Well, I am as anxious to talk to her as you. Believe me, Scott. But not about what happened today." He stood as Scott and Jamie frowned and looked at each other and then at him. Williams moved to the sidebar and opened a small bottle of sparkling water. He offered it to Scott and Jamie. They declined. He poured himself a glass, took a long sip, and set the glass down and returned to his chair.

"I need to tell both of you something, something that happened a long time ago, and I need you to listen and give me a chance to finish all of it." Puzzled, Jamie and Scott looked at each other and then at him. "All of it."

For the next hour, Williams explained in detail the birth of his son, the mother's flight to California, and his discovery and recovery of the boy—only to lose him during the custody proceedings—the years spent trying to track them down, with no success.

"That is why I moved here from Boston, Jamie. I needed to start all over after my grandmother died. I started the company, met your mother, you were born, Jamie, your mother died," his voice cracked. "But there has never been one day, not one single day of my entire life, that I did not think of or wonder about *my* son—where he was, what had happened to him, was he dead or alive. They were never found."

As he spoke Scott and Jamie listened transfixed, awed at both the story itself and marveling at his self-control as he delivered what was for him a wrenching and painful tale. When he paused, finished it seemed, no one spoke for a moment.

"You never found him, or her?" Jamie said softly. "You never told me, daddy."

"No, never," he replied. "And I did not tell you. I should have." He straightened in his chair. "Grant, Will Grant, was my attorney in California. He handled the custody trial, when all this happened."

"Oh, so that is the California problem you had. I thought it was something to do with the business," Jamie said.

"No, Jamie, it was about my son," he looked only at Scott.

"But daddy, what does this have to do with me, with us?"

Scott broke the silence. "It's me, isn't it?" Scott whispered. "You think it is *me?* My God!"

Williams said nothing, just stared at Scott. He knew he was right. The shock of what Scott had blurted out stunned Jamie, who recoiled from him as if she had been struck. Scott was on his feet. He took a few steps away and then turned, facing Williams.

"Are you out of your mind!? You think that you are my father!? Somehow, that *you* are my father?"

"Scott, I hope for all the world that I am not, believe me, but ..."

"Daddy! Scott! What does this mean? It was supposed to be our wedding day, Scott. What is going on?" Williams saw tears forming in Jamie's eyes.

Scott slammed his hand down on the arm of the couch and leaned in toward Jamie.

"Don't you get it, Jamie? Your father thinks that ... that I am his son. His long-lost son! Don't you get it? That makes you my sister." He glared at Williams, "Damn it, Brad why are you doing this to us? To your daughter?"

"Oh, my God! No!" Jamie burst into tears. Scott sat down, and he took Jamie into his arms, one hand stroking her head as she sobbed uncontrollably.

"Scott, listen. Grant went to the hospital to speak to your mother, to try to sort this out."

"Your lawyer went to what? To interview my mother!? While she was in the hospital? And you sent him there to question her? For Christ sakes, Brad, she has a concussion! She is hurt, or sick!" His face was red, his jaw clenched.

Williams felt physically ill. His throat seized, his mouth went dry; he was sure he could feel his heart pulsing. He looked at the two young people whom he loved, and he shuddered at the damage wrought many years ago. Afraid that his uncertainty showed, he continued deliberately:

"You have to trust me. You need to trust me with this, and believe that I am not crazy. But what is happening here is, well, it was meant to be, to happen someday, with your mother. And now we are about to find out the truth. This is no coincidence, Scott." Brad stood. He looked down at them. "A long time ago a judge told me justice is one of those truths, and that as unlikely as it may seem, it is inevitable that justice will not, cannot, be denied. For all these years I questioned that, I denied it, but I never forgot it. He was right, and I am not about to let it get away again. No more lies. Let me see it through. I know what I am doing,"

"What you are *doing,* Brad, is destroying the most important day—well, that's already done—of our lives. The rest of our lives. Get out! Now, Brad. Now!" Scott whispered fiercely.

Williams rose slowly and started to reach out to touch one or the other. Scott ignored his hand. "Get out! Please just leave us alone!"

Williams backed away, watching the eyes of the young man who was, a few hours earlier, to be the husband of his daughter—his son-in-law. He walked to the door, paused, and said:

"There is going to be a court hearing the day after tomorrow. Your mother will be there, Scott. She needs to—must—be there. And we will sort this out. I know that you think I have destroyed your lives. Jamie, since your mother died you have been the most important part of my life, you know that," he pleaded. She did not lift her head. "Scott, if you want this to end, *now, you* prove me wrong. Go talk to your mother. *You* ask her. *She* knows the truth. Up until now, today, *she* was the only one who knew that truth. But she knows. *You* ask her."

~

Early the next morning when Scott entered the hospital, Ava was not in her room.

He had comforted Jamie after Brad left; for a while she was speechless, and Scott just held her. Finally, Scott told her that they needed to talk. They were both astonished at Brad's "assertions," Scott called them, but Scott explained that he had always known that his mother's explanations, or lack of them, about the identity of his father and the circumstances of his birth were intentionally incomplete, and probably untrue. From early childhood, he accepted that he had no father; that he would never have one. A succession of surrogates, first the fathers of his friends who included him in their families and treated him like a son; then the counselors and scoutmasters who guided him; his teachers and coaches, they all provided a measured refuge from the heartache and separateness of a fatherless young boy. In his late teens, confident in himself and used to being on his own, with his mother bent on her career and content to let him wend his own way, his sense of longing for a father had waned.

He backtracked to the nurse's station and was directed to the dining room. His mother was in a wheelchair; her wrapped ankle elevated by a brace attached to her chair. The bandage on her head had been removed. She was facing the windows, away from him. He hesitated for a moment. He studied the back of her head, uncertain, and he wondered that if she had not come to the wedding, none of this would have happened. She saw his reflection in the windows. He stepped in front of her and pulled up a chair, sitting between her and the windows. The early-morning light warmed his back. There was a small bandage on her head. Her hair was brushed and down. She had managed to do her makeup.

"How are you, mother?" he asked.

A slight shrug of her shoulder, she leaned back, "I am all right, considering," she replied.

"Considering?"

"Considering that your future father-in-law and his lawyer have ruined your wedding. That they have, or are, accusing me of I don't know what. Have hauled me into a court in this godforsaken state, for God only knows what! How am I? Just great. And you?" she said.

For some reason, Scott oddly found himself disgusted with her self-pity.

"Well," he said, leaning back. "I do not have the slightest idea what is going on. Really, I do not. I was hoping that you could tell me."

"*You* don't!? Well, wake up, Scott, because someone has gone to an awful lot of trouble to sabotage your wedding. *Someone* has apparently decided that you should not marry his daughter, and don't ask me why. I have never met the man!"

Scott found he was holding his breath; he exhaled slowly, his thoughts tripping over his rising anger.

"What happened to you yesterday? Why did you so suddenly have to leave? Where were you going, do you know? What did the doctor say?"

"Slow down, Scott. Slow down," she shifted in her wheelchair. "I don't know what happened to me. The music started and I was watching you, and the next thing I know I am in this hospital, hooked up to tubes and things. God, it was, is, awful."

"You don't know anything?"

"No. And no doctor has said anything to me except that I have a concussion and a sprained ankle, which hurts badly, Scott. Even now," she winced noticeably.

"Mom, you must have been sick or something. I saw you trying to get out to the side before you fell. Why?"

She shrugged and nodded here head, "I don't remember any of it. I was dead tired. The flight was the worst. I swear I will take a train back to Austin," she shook her head slowly, leaned back, her eyes closed. "Maybe I had some kind of spell, or one of those panic attacks. I do not know."

Scott studied her for a moment. She said nothing more, and he realized she was waiting for him. Her eyes were still closed.

He leaned forward. "Who is my father? What is his name? I need to know. I never cared before. Oh, I cared, wondered, but I gave it up. You made it off-limits." He waited. She had not moved, and she said nothing. "I want, I *need*, to know. A name, just give me a name."

She opened her eyes; she seemed to be looking at the ceiling.

"I know what they are up to, Scott. Why they are doing this. They cannot get to you, so they are using me. I have my own life, you know. You have yours. For some reason they have decided that you are not, I do not know, *good enough*, or whatever. Some reason why you should not marry that girl."

"That girl? That girl would have been my wife if you had not been here. We love each other! That girl?"

"Well," she leaned forward slightly. "You are lucky, Scott, that I was here, because they wanted you out and they would have done it sooner or later. His lawyer, coming in here, asking me questions, here, in my hospital bed!" She sagged against the chair.

Scott stood and walked to her. He leaned forward and put a hand on each arm of her wheelchair, his face inches from hers.

"I always took care of myself, so that I would never be in your way. I even went away to school and you hardly ever—make that *never*—called. You probably would have skipped the holidays, if I had not come home to see my friends. I have a career fifteen hundred miles away from you, and you couldn't care less. Well, that is who and what we are, mother. You and I. I can, and I have, lived with that. And finally I have found real happiness. I do not know if you ever have. And I do not know what this is about or where it will end, but I love this woman. She is not a 'girl.'" He paused collecting his breath. "So, here is the question, *the* big question. Only one. Yes or no? Is Brad Williams my father? That's all, that's it. Yes or no?"

She had kept her eyes fixed on his since he had bent over her. Now, that gaze, those eyes turned dark, wary.

"This is so preposterous. No, he is not your father, Scott. He is not. I have never seen him before."

Scott straightened, took a step back. He glanced over at the windows, the trees and grounds now in full sunlight. He shrugged a kink out of his back and looked down at her.

"They are going to ask you that in court the day after tomorrow, do you know that?"

She nodded.

"Brad Williams is a good guy, mom. He is a good man. There is a reason why he is doing this, and it can only be one. Only one reason," he paused. "He would never intentionally hurt Jamie, nor me, either. I think, I *know,* he loves us. Both of us. I know that. So, part of me hopes that you are telling the truth, mother. I get Jamie, and Brad as the father I might have had. But if you are not, I lose Jamie, the woman I love, but I get my real father. Quite a mess, isn't it? Like one of those awful Greek tragedies."

She said nothing; her eyes tracked his, defiant.

"But if what *they* tell me is true, if you are lying, *you* are the big loser. Perjury in Maryland, and a fugitive from California. Jail, prison, either way."

"I do not think so, Scott. Not quite," she was looking at the window reflection, at the image of a man approaching them from behind. Scott looked up over her as she smiled.

"Steven, this is my son, Scott. Scott, Steve Ryder. My attorney from Austin,"

The attorney, dressed in a suit and tie, carrying a briefcase, extended his hand, "Scott, ah've heard a lot about you. Ava is quite proud of you, suhn" he said. "Pleased to meet you."

Scott shook his hand.

"Got here as soon as I could, Ava. Took a red-eye. Is there someplace, private, where we kin talk?"

"Yes, Steven, we can get a room. Scott was just leaving."

CHAPTER 11

THE TALBOT COUNTY COURTHOUSE, established in 1711, was a marvelously preserved two-story brick building of federal design. Set among stately Maryland oak trees, it dominated the town square. It was a few minutes before 9:00 A.M. when Grant mounted the six steps to the entry, pausing to admire the ornate cupola towering over the entrance. *This is how courthouses are supposed to look. Why the French call them "palais justice,"* he thought, *a building worthy of the serious business to be conducted within.* When Grant paused to hold the door for Mosby, who was a member of the Maryland Bar (also the D.C. and New York Bars), he saw Scott and Jamie cross the street headed toward them.

The courtroom of the Hon. Payton Sheridan, Circuit Judge for Talbot County, was made entirely of hand-crafted wood, reflective of another century and a skill now almost impossible to find. The single, long counsel table spanning the front of the elevated bench was a masterpiece of workmanship. The curves and bevels of the ornate witness stand gleamed with polish and care. The only concessions to a modern age were two microphones and speakers. Everything looked, Grant mused, as if some fiery Maryland patriot attorney might rise at any moment to address a matter of colonial import against the Crown. *If this were not so damn serious, it might be fun to try a case here,* Grant thought as the attorneys passed through the gate and selected their seats at the table; the usual plaintiff and defendant markers were absent.

"We need to leave room here, on the left, for the county prosecutor," Mosby said, moving to his right. "One chair, and Mr. Ryder can sit here, at the end," indicating the far right of the table. "With one seat for Mrs. Ames. That should do it." He counted the available chairs. As he finished, a young, well-dressed attorney approached and shook hands with Mosby. They conferred briefly, and the attorney, nodding to the others, left the courtroom.

Over the previous two days, Mosby, as Williams's local attorney, and Grant had worked out the arguments that they would make this morning. The court had reviewed their legal briefs and granted them an immediate hearing, with the express understanding that the proceedings would not take longer than one day. Each of the attorneys had agreed to waive the notice period, usually several weeks, which would otherwise have been required. The court had also sent word that it was accommodating them because of the unusual nature of the issues and recognizing that the attorneys and clients were from three different states.

Attorney Mosby, Williams's in-house counsel, had taken the lead and filed a petition in court to determine whether the marriage license issued to Scott and Jamie by the Easton County Clerk was void because of the emergence of the facts that they were, as it now appeared, related. Grant had provided background information on the California proceedings. The parties named and involved in this petition, in addition to Scott and Jamie, included Scott's mother and Jamie's father, both of whom had been subpoenaed to testify.

In order to save time, Steve Ryder, the attorney for Scott's mother, who had flown in from Austin, had agreed that the petition could be deemed denied without his having to file lengthy, time-consuming opposing papers, so sure was he that there was no merit to these proceedings and so anxious was his client, and he, to return to Texas. Ryder was confident that the matter could be simply and quickly resolved in Ava's favor.

The petition which Mosby and Grant had filed alleged, on "information and belief" (legalese for "maybe"), that a dispute existed over Scott's parentage and that this issue was of grave import because of Scott and Jamie's intention to marry. Maryland statutes and the laws of most states prohibited a brother and a sister from marrying. In order to guarantee that Ava would attend the hearing, Grant had supplied the local sheriff with a copy of the California contempt order with its accompanying old, but still very valid, arrest warrant, establishing that she was believed to be a fugitive.

Ava, through her attorney continued to deny that she was the person named in the California papers, and she had reluctantly agreed not to leave

Maryland until conclusion of the proceedings, otherwise the sheriff had made it clear that he would take her into custody or require that a substantial bond be posted to guarantee her appearance in the Maryland court. So long as she denied that the arrest warrant was not applicable to her, the local authorities could not charge her with any crime until they had more evidence.

Scott and Jamie had just taken their seats in the front row when Ava and her attorney, Steve Ryder, stepped through the gate and took the two remaining seats at the counsel table. The court clerk nodded at the shorthand court reporter, who returned his nod, indicating that she was ready to begin. Nothing could start without a verbatim record of the proceedings. The clerk rang a small hand bell, and a door opened behind the bench, at which point the uniformed, armed bailiff standing to the far left against the wall intoned:

"All rise. This Honorable Circuit Court of Talbot County is hereby in session, the Honorable Payton Sheridan, Judge, presiding. Be seated."

By the time he finished his announcement the judge had taken his seat at the bench. He nodded at the bailiff, who sat back on a high stool against the wall, eyeing the parties with a protective mien. Grant had seen clerks, bailiffs, and judges enact this little bit of theater in countless courtrooms, and the familiarity was comforting. *You should be able to walk into any courtroom in the land and be confident that justice will at least be attempted, if not assured; that at least you have the opportunity to be heard,* he thought. *That is what our constitution is all about. And here we go.*

"In Re the Matter of Williams/Ames and the County of Talbot, State of Maryland," the clerk read from of copy of what Grant recognized as their petition. "Appearances, gentlemen?" he asked.

Mosby stood, "May it please the court, David Mosby for Ms. Jamie Williams." Jamie had reluctantly agreed that she had to be the primary named party, since it was *her* marriage license with Scott that was at stake. Scott was so totally confused, concerned, and angered that he was not asked to take an active role. He did realize that he might have to testify, and that he would be bound by the outcome of these proceedings in any event.

"Mr. Mosby. Good morning to you, sir. We have met before, but not in this circuit, I believe," Judge Sheridan smiled down at the attorney.

"That is correct, Your Honor. It was a few years ago," Mosby responded. The judge nodded to him. Mosby continued, "Your Honor, I have the pleasure of introducing a distinguished member of the California Bar," he put his hand on Grant's shoulder, the signal for him to stand. "As discussed at our meeting yesterday, we ask that the court permit Mr. Will Grant to participate in this proceeding on behalf of Mr. Williams. Mr. Grant has provided the clerk with proof of his good standing with the California Bar, and my office will serve as his sponsor and co-counsel."

"Very well, Mr. Mosby. Mr. Grant will be recognized. That will be the order," and he nodded at his clerk. The court addressed Grant as he took his seat: "Mr. Grant, I think that you will find our rules of evidence quite similar to those of your state, and Mr. Mosby can guide you as we go."

"Thank you, Your Honor." Grant replied. "I was thinking as I entered this magnificent courthouse, that it is one of the wonders of our constitution that a citizen and his attorney can walk into any courtroom in this country and be assured of virtually identical protections of their rights, whether in the far west where I practice, or in this, the first state, wasn't it, to join our union?"

"Close, Mr. Grant. Delaware was first, but we were the seventh," the jurist smiled. Looking at the end of the table, the court asked, "And you, sir?"

Ryder pushed back his chair and stood. "May it please the court," his drawl set him apart from the others. "I am Steven Ryder of the Austin, Texas, Bar, Your Honor, and I am pleased to represent an interested party, Ms. Ava Ames, Your Honor." Ryder paused and smiled at the judge.

Judge Sheridan looked to Mosby, his brows raised, questioning as he asked, "Maryland, California, *and* Texas, Mr. Mosby?"

Mosby stood, "Yes, Your Honor. Mr. Ryder is a member of the Texas Bar and a partner of one of Austin's oldest and finest firms. His firm, actually Mr. Ryder himself, is Ms. Ames's personal and business attorney in the State of Texas; he has represented her for many years, Your Honor. We have agreed, subject to your approval," he paused, "that Mr. Ryder might appear 'specially' to represent his client in these proceedings, so that all persons are before this court and would have the benefit of counsel."

"Subject to my approval. Thank you for *that*, gentlemen," the judge said. "Let us begin and see where this takes us, and we can address that request at that time." Turning to Ryder, the judge added, "You, and your client, since you are already seated at the counsel table may remain there for now." Picking up his file, the judge looked up at the attorney. "Mr. Mosby, you may proceed."

"Thank you, Your Honor. First of all, we had expected that the County Prosecutor's Office would participate in the matter, since they have an interest if the marriage license in question is determined to be void. Deputy Prosecutor Kenneth Bennett was here a moment ago, and he is in agreement that we may proceed without his presence, so long as Your Honor has no objections. He has read our papers and is content to let the matter be determined by us, on the condition that we of course advise him of the outcome, which I agreed to do."

"That is acceptable to the court," the judge replied. "Next?"

Mosby continued, "Your Honor, we intend to offer certain records, we hope without objection, in the interests of time. I would, therefore, make the following offer of proof," he paused. The court studied the attorney's faces in front of him. No objection was forthcoming. The judge nodded at the attorney. Mosby continued. "We have had these pre-marked by your clerk. The first is Exhibit A, a copy of the birth certificate of Jason Williams, Massachusetts State Records. This record lists Jason parents as follows:

"Father: Robert B. Williams. The "B' is for Bradford, Your Honor, and Mr. Williams is present, and he will both corroborate his birth and clarify the name." Mosby handed the document to the clerk who passed it over his head to the judge. Mosby handed copies to each of the attorneys.

"Mother," he continued, "Tamara Evans." He glanced at Ms. Ames, who was staring straight ahead. "B. Exhibit B, Your Honor, is a certified copy of an order re custody of the same Jason Williams, issued by the California court, and Exhibit C is a certified copy of a companion order of the same court in the same proceedings, holding the named Tamara Evans in contempt for absenting herself from those custody proceedings, while they were in progress, and taking the minor child, Jason, with her from the courthouse," he paused, " to which is attached a certified copy of a warrant issued by the sheriff of that county for her arrest." He placed the documents into the waiting hand of the clerk. "While these documents are over twenty years old, twenty-six to be precise, it remains our position that they are still enforceable, and Mr. Williams will corroborate them and the proceedings from which they derive, Your Honor."

Ryder stood, a hand up, to catch the court's attention. "Your Honor, some of these documents are not certified, at least the ones I have been given are not, and I fail to see how they relate to my client, or to these proceedings," he objected.

"Mr. Mosby?" the court asked.

"Your Honor. The California documents are copies which Mr. Williams has carried with him since the disappearance of his son, years ago, for just a moment such as this. They are certified, that is to say the copies are made from certified copies, and the markings can be clearly seen. The Massachusetts birth certificate of Jason Evans we obtained through a reliable, licensed, records retrieval service in Boston. We have ordered a certified copy and will replace this copy with the certified one when we get it. We have no reason to question this copy, however, and it appears correct as to form. As for the relevance—"

"Mr. Ryder," the court interjected, turning to Ava's attorney, "I have no problem receiving these records at this time unless it appears later that they are incorrect, which I think unlikely. And, do I understand that the witnesses will testify in any event on these matters?" the court looked at Mosby and the other attorneys.

"Yes, Your Honor, exactly," Mosby quickly added.

Ava's attorney remained standing and in a drawl more pronounced than before, stated, "But Your Hon-ahh . . ."

The court gestured to Williams's attorney and asked: "What about the relevancy, Mr. Mosby?"

Mosby replied: "One of the issues, *the issue,* if you please, is the parentage of Scott Williams, and we intend to show, Judge," he paused for a brief moment, "we, intend—"

"His intentions are not evidence, Your Honor, at least not in Texas," Ryder interjected, his voice raising.

"Mr. Ryder, his *intention* I take as an offer of proof, not evidence," the judge glanced at Mosby, who nodded. "And they allow offers of proof, even in Texas, sir," he said. "So," he continued, "if that is your objection," he looked at the man still standing, "it is overruled. You may continue, Mr.

Mosby," the judge said, directing his attention back to the other attorney. Ryder sat down.

"We intend to show that Mr. Robert Brad Williams," gesturing to the man seated next to him, "and Ms. Ava Ames, otherwise known as Tamara Evans, are in fact the parents of Scott Ames, whose real, birth name, if you will, is Jason Evans," and he turned and pointed to the young man seated in the first row. Scott looked at Jamie, who stared at the floor. "And Your Honor, we intend to show . . ."

Ryder made a sound, but before he could form a word a glance from the judge silenced him.

"We intend to show that it was Ms. Ava Ames, Your Honor, who kidnapped—"

"Objection! Objection! Obj—!"

"Mr. Ryder, please hold your objections until counsel has completed his statement," the court cut him off. Ryder rocked in his chair, tilting it precariously back.

I hope he falls on his ass, Grant thought.

Mosby continued, "Ms. Ames is the same person as the Tamara Evans named in the contempt order and in the arrest warrant, and it was Ms. Ames who kidnapped her son, those many years ago," Mosby concluded.

The court now addressed the fuming attorney, "Mr. Ryder, in order that we might move along, hold your objections. I have them in mind, I assure you, and I will rule on them when we get through these preliminaries. This is only an offer of proof, Mr. Mosby, correct?"

"Yes, sir," he answered.

"Fine, proceed," the judge said.

In quick order, Mosby produced the State of Texas birth record of Scott Ames issued by the Clerk of Travis County, where Austin is situated. Grant pointed out to Williams that Scott's certificate was issued *after* the date of Jason's kidnapping. Williams frowned as copies were passed down the table to Ryder. Grant did not look at Ava. The records also included a certification from the Secretary of State of Texas that there was no record in Texas of any birth of one Tamara Evans *or* of Ava Ames prior to the date of Scott's birth as shown on his birth certificate. On Scott's Texas record, the space labeled "Father" was blank.

"That's it, Your Honor, for now. We would offer these in evidence as official government records, if you will," Mosby said.

Ryder was already on his feet. The judge spoke first. "I will receive these marked for identification, not yet in evidence, Mr. Ryder," he addressed the Texas lawyer. "The certification formalities are less of a problem for me, but I understand the relevance objection," this to Mosby. "Once you link them up, or tie them in, we can then deal with whether they ought to be admitted, and for what purpose or to what extent." To Ryder, "That is my ruling, Mr. Ryder, and the record can reflect your ongoing objection. Proceed, Mr. Mosby."

"Thank you, Your Honor. We will call Mr. Williams, and the examination will be conducted by Mr. Grant." The judge nodded his assent.

~

Williams was sworn and settled into the witness chair. He stated his name and gave his local address. Grant rose, asking, "Your Honor, may I stand while I question the witness?"

"Certainly, Mr. Grant. Make yourself comfortable," the jurist smiled.

"Thank you, Your Honor. Mr. Williams, you gave your name as Brad Williams just now. What is your full name?" Grant asked.

"Robert Bradford Williams."

"Yet, you go by your middle name?"

"Yes, I do. I used Rob, the abbreviated form of Robert, when I was growing up, in fact until I came to Maryland. As an adult, I was always known as Rob."

"You changed it then. Why?"

"When I first went to work for the original company, it was very small. The owner's name was Robert, and he had always gone by 'Rob.' So, we agreed, almost from the time that I started, that I would use my middle name; it was my idea actually. And so the other employees, well, the customers and accounts—we only had five or six employees—they came to know me as Brad, and I just kept it." Williams straightened the crease on his pants leg.

"And you have kept that name, as your preference, or what you were called by, to this day?"

"Yes, that is correct."

"The employees and those with whom you have dealt as your company grew, they know you as 'Brad'?"

"Yes. In fact, I doubt that anyone knows that Robert is my correct, my legal, first name."

"So, now I want to take you, us, back to the birth of your son and the events that subsequently transpired in California. During that time, what name were you known by?"

"Only Rob. Rob Williams. I never used my middle name. In fact, I hardly ever signed anything with the 'B.'"

"No one did, or would, have called you Brad, or referred to you by that name?"

"No one."

Grant reached for and picked up a copy of a birth certificate that had been marked previously during attorney Mosby's remarks to the court.

"May I approach the witness, Your Honor?" he paused at the end of the counsel table.

"Yes, of course, Mr. Grant. I run a relaxed courtroom," the jurist smiled at Grant, "and you need not ask for permission. I appreciate your courtesy in that regard, but I do not perceive that either the witness or this court is endangered by your approaching the witness," his smile showed at his eyes. Grant nodded and handed Williams the document.

"Mr. Williams, can you identify this document?"

"Yes. This is the birth certificate of my son, Jason R., the 'R' is for Robert, Williams. I have had this for years; I kept it."

"And Jason was born when?"

"February 23, 1970." Williams stared at Scott, who met his gaze.

"And on this birth certificate, the parent's named are . . ."

"Mother, Tamara Evans. Father, Robert Williams. I left the 'B' off even then," he looked at Grant.

"Who provided the information for this document?"

"Objection, hearsay, Your Honor. And leading," Ryder announced.

"Overruled," Judge Sheridan replied immediately. "It seems preliminary to me anyway. Continue Mr. Grant."

Grant nodded at Williams to answer. "I did," he said.

"Did you ever marry the mother of your son?"

"No, I did not."

"After the birth of your son, did you maintain a close relationship with his mother and with the boy?"

"Yes, I did. Very close. Probably weekly. Every week."

Grant went on to draw out the story of Williams's involvement with the mother and his son, tracing quickly the events that transpired and his growing concern over the boy's welfare.

"Directing your attention to the summer of 1972, specifically June, what occurred at that time."

"Jason was a little over two; two and a half almost. They disappeared."

"Excuse me? What do you mean 'disappeared'?"

"She left, taking Jason with her. I thought she knew that I was not happy with her lifestyle. Maybe she knew I had consulted an attorney about custody. I do not know. But she left."

"And when did you see your son next, Mr. Williams?"

"Thirteen months later, when we got him out of the house where they were living in California. Over a year. And not a word the entire time."

"Move to strike the last as nonresponsive, Your Honor, and ask that the witness confine his answers to the questions," Ryder interjected.

Judge Sheridan's frown was palpable. "It may stay in, Mr. Ryder. I take 'see' to include 'hear from or about' in the context in which it was asked and given. However," he swiveled to face Williams, "Mr. Williams, please try to avoid what we call a 'narrative,' even though it does help us move along," glancing at Ryder. "Specific testimony is preferred." He nodded at Grant to resume.

Grant had been standing behind his chair. Now he moved to his left, and Williams turned his head slightly to follow him.

"Tell us what happened next, after you got Jason in your custody," Grant asked.

Led by Grant, Williams explained the court proceedings, the progress of the trial, the evidence of the squalor and inappropriate conditions in which the young boy was living, and finally, emotionally, his disappearance from the courtroom, and ultimately the loss and later finding of her car. The courtroom was deadly silent; the judge sat erect in his chair, his eyes fixed on Williams and occasionally scanning the face of Ms. Ames, who remained still and expressionless. Ryder was furiously taking notes.

"What was the date again of his disappearance from the courthouse?" Grant asked.

"September 15, 1973; it was a Thursday."

"And you have not seen your son since that time?"

"No, sir. God knows I looked. But no, not since then." Williams looked down at Scott, seated next to Jamie. Scott's hands were apart, his fists clenching and unclenching. Jamie had one arm looped through his. They both had their eyes cast down.

"Neither one? Not his mother, Tamara Evans, nor your son, Scott Williams, or Evans, perhaps? They were never found?"

"No," his voice even.

"And you have carried a copy of the court order, the one awarding you custody, and a copy of the arrest warrant with you every day since?" Grant asked.

"Yes, I had them reduced and laminated. I have one in my wallet and another copy in my car." He looked over at Ava. "I look—looked—at them every day for the past . . . for all these years."

Grant moved back to his chair. He set down his notes and reached for a set of papers. Resting the documents on the back of his chair, he continued:

"Mr. Williams. Since that day when she left the courthouse in California, have you ever seen Tamara Evans?"

Ryder roared, "Foundation. Lack of foundation, Your Honor!" He was on his feet. The volume of his objection echoed in the room. The judge's face reddened slightly. He leaned forward.

"Mr. Ryder. I am only scant feet away from you, sir, and I can assure you that your normal, modulated voice can be heard up here!"

"Your Honor. I, we, have suffered through this drama, wondering when, if ever, it would appear that it had some relevance. Suffered without objection, for the most part, in the interest of what I suppose you might call full disclosure, to move this matter along. I submit, Your Honor, respectfully, that this entire line of questioning and the answers elicited, well, we have a word for them in Texas, that may—would—not be appropriate here."

"I can imagine, Mr. Ryder. Perhaps, in fact I cannot. If that is an objection, sir, it is not one recognized by me and it is overruled." Turning to Grant, "Mr.

Grant, I presume that you are going to connect these dots. Sooner rather than later?"

"In fact *now*, Your Honor."

Grant nodded at Williams. "Do you have the question in mind, Mr. Williams? Wait, let us have the reporter read it back?" Grant nodded at the reporter who reached down and sorted through layers of stenographic notes, lifted a loop of transcript and read:

"Question. 'Mr. Williams. Since that day when she left the courthouse in California, have you ever seen Tamara Evans?'" Grant looked to Williams, his eyebrows raised.

"Yes, sir, I have." Williams replied.

"When and where?"

"Last week at my daughter's wedding." Someone behind Grant gasped. Grant looked at his witness. "I saw her, I am fairly certain. She is seated right there, at the end of the table."

Ryder exploded out of his chair, which tumbled over backwards.

"Your Hon-nah. We 'ave taken about as much of this as anyone cud tolerate!"

"Sir, I advised you that if you had an objection, to put it in the form of a legal objection. Otherwise, sir, it is an outburst, and *I* do not tolerate outbursts in my courtroom."

Grant thought that the instant pallor of the jurist's face, his jaw set tight, was in marked contrast to Ryder's redness, whose collar was about to snap.

Ryder turned and grabbed at the chair, only moving it farther away. The bailiff had moved, as if on autopilot, behind Grant, and he picked up the chair and arranged it for Ryder to sit in. He did not move away until the attorney had taken his seat and shifted the chair forward. The bailiff moved past Grant and winked at him.

"Mr. Grant, you have more?" the court asked.

"Yes, Your Honor, we do," Grant replied. He turned back to his witness. "You have indicated that the woman seated to my right, the record should reflect, at the end of the counsel table, identified in these proceedings as Ava Ames, the mother of Scott Ames . . . that you believe her to be Tamara Evans, the mother of your missing son, Jason Evans?"

Ryder cleared his throat, something like a gargle. Grant paused. The court looked over at Ryder.

"Objection, Your Honor, if you please." His voice was firm and controlled. "On the grounds of lack of foundation, calls for opinion. Opinion *and* conclusions, in fact. Including to the extent that expertise may be required, a lack of qualification as to this witness. And," he paused as if waiting for the court, "it calls for the ultimate issue of fact here before this court, perhaps."

The court looked down at Ryder, expectant. The attorney realizing that the court was waiting on him added: "That is all judge. Those are my objections, sir."

Grant started to respond, but the judge shook his head. Grant waited.

"On foundation, he has given us the time—last week; the place—the wedding. Overruled. On opinion, there are two objections, one that it calls for opinion and, if so, that it may involve expertise. He was asked to make an identification, Mr. Ryder. That is not an opinion. Even if it was phrased or understood as 'Do you have an opinion whether she was so and so,' which it was not. The witness can make an identification or give his opinion on that subject. One can opine whether a car was, or is, his. Whether that is his horse. Certainly, this witness can testify whether he recognized the mother of his child, that he believed she was that person. It does not call for expertise for one to recognize his former spouse or lover. To the extent that the question assumes parentage, while that is the issue for this court to decide, again I believe it is essentially identification related." He paused looking at the attorney. Ryder stared back but said nothing.

"Overruled." He nodded at Grant to continue.

Grant nodded to the reporter. She was ready for him and immediately began to read: "Question: You have indicated that the woman seated to my right, the record should reflect, at the end of the counsel table, identified in these proceedings as Ava Ames, the mother of Scott Ames … that you believe her to be Tamara Evans, the mother of your missing son, Jason Evans?"

"Yes, I do," Williams replied.

"Mr. Williams, please tell this court the basis of that identification."

Williams recounted the late arrival of Ava at the wedding, that he had not met her before the ceremony, and the circumstances of her fall. He continued, "She went down just to the side of us, in the first row. I did not know who she was, only that there was a woman on the ground, bleeding. I heard Scott cry out, 'Mom' and that was the first I knew that she was his mother. She was right there on the ground in front of me. It was awful. Jamie was panicked, crying. We did not know what had happened."

"Then what happened," Grant interposed, maintaining the flow of his testimony.

"You were kneeling near her and you asked me to call 911, so I left for a moment to be sure that someone had made the call, and then I went back. She was down on the ground. One of Scott's friends was an EMT, emergency medical tech, attending to her, and he turned her over to check her head, to see where the blood was coming from. That's when I saw it."

"When you saw what?"

Out of the corner of his eye, Grant saw that Ryder had stopped taking notes and that Ava was erect in her chair, staring at Williams, impassive as stone.

"The scar, on her neck, under the hair, behind her ear. I was not sure at first. But Mark, Scott's friend, was looking for wounds, to see where she was bleeding from, and he traced his finger over this little mark. It was not bleeding, and he then covered the larger wound with a towel." He paused.

"And?" Grant coaxed. Ryder was silent.

"Well, I did not think anything about it at that time. It was later. They had her on a stretcher, one of those collapsible ones, and they were getting ready to take her to the hospital. It was grating on me, like a bell rung, but I could not get it. While she was laying there, before they took her away, I even started to take a closer look at her, but I did not know why. It was just something." He paused.

"Did you mention that to anyone, that you had a question about this mark or scar? What was it, a mark or a scar?"

"No, I didn't say anything. I stood there with you, and it was all so surreal, the wedding interrupted. We had no idea what had happened. Just that she fell and hit her head, we guessed."

"So, what happened next?"

"Later, after we had decided to call off the wedding, Jamie had gone to change to go the hospital with Scott. At some point, I think it was Cecily, my assistant, who confirmed it was Scott's mother who had been hurt. But we still did not know what had happened to her, or why or how she got hurt. We were concentrating on getting her medical attention." Williams reached for the water pitcher and poured himself a glass. He took a long drink, and when Grant nodded at him to proceed without waiting for another question, he continued.

"Tamara Evans had a small S-shaped scar behind her right ear, under her hair, which then, twenty-plus years ago, she wore long. I saw it the first night we met." He paused and met her gaze. Her eyes were cold, dark, unmoving. "And I saw it many times after that. And then it hit me. That mark on Ms. Ames's neck. I could not believe what I was thinking, but I could not get it out of mind, and I had not even thought of the consequences. So, later I went to the hospital." He stopped and shifted his weight. He crossed and uncrossed his legs.

"You went to the hospital where?" Grant asked.

"The Easton Clinic. There is only the one. Where they had taken her. I thought maybe we could talk. I walked right into her room; no one was there. I had this idea I could, well, look at her neck." He halted, thoughtfully. "But when I got inside I knew that was stupid. She was asleep or maybe unconscious, I did not know which. And her head and neck were covered with bandages. I just looked at her, and I was not sure. It seemed all so impossible. So I left."

"Did you speak with her?"

"No, I just left, and then in the hallway I thought about the records, the medical records. I went to the nurse's station. The duty nurse turned out to be an old friend of my daughter who agreed to give me the admission report. I just asked, and she made me a copy."

"Your Honor. Objection, if you please. If he plans to tell us what was in some report, that is A) hearsay, B) an invasion of my client's right of privacy. That should do it. I object."

The judge looked down at Grant, who had several sheets of paper in his hand.

"Do you propose to use or offer the medical records which you, or rather your client, received from the night nurse? That might be a problem."

"No, Your Honor, not *per se*. I have here the copies which the nurse gave him . . ."

Ryder was on his feet. "He snuck into my client's room, in the dead of night, alone. She is in a coma, or concussed, same thing; and then he cons some inexperienced nurse friend of his daughter out of my client's medical file. Judge, please. This is highly objectionable. Actionable in fact."

Judge Sheridan turned to Grant. His expression presented the question for Grant.

"Judge, these are the copies he got from the nurse that night," Grant replied as he held up several sheets, and then he held up a stack of papers, clipped together with a printed cover sheet on top, as they were handed to him by Mosby. "These we subpoenaed from the hospital, and . . ." anticipating the direction from the court, "the record should reflect that I am handing a copy to counsel. The only reason we raise the facts surrounding the receipt of the records that night, Your Honor, is to lay the foundation for other evidence that we will get to later today. These sheets given to Mr. Williams are contained in the subpoenaed records, verbatim."

"All right, for that limited purpose, I allow it, subject to Mr. Ryder's motion to strike if it goes beyond that. This is not, thankfully, a jury trial, and I can sort it out later," the jurist ruled, looking at Ryder.

Grant had both sets of records marked, and handed the small set to Williams.

"Mr. Williams, are these records the ones given you by the night nurse?"

"Yes."

"What did you do with them?"

"I took them with me, and I got into my car to drive back to the inn. I was sure that I had made a terrible mistake, that there was no way that this could be Tamara. I threw the records on the seat. I began to start the car, and I stopped. I picked them up and then I read—"

"Judge," Ryder urged.

"I'll allow it, for now."

Grant nodded for Williams to proceed.

"I looked them over and on the back of the first page there was a section 'Characteristics slash Distinguishing Marks,' etc. And written there by . . . I do not know who . . ."

Ryder's groan was cut short by a look from the judge.

". . . it said," Williams looked at the form and read: "'S-shaped scar behind right ear; not wound.' And there it was. I knew. I just knew."

"As you sit here now, today in this courtroom, can you identify the woman seated at the end of this table as the mother of your child, Jason Evans or Ames."

"Yes, I believe so," as he looked at Scott.

"And you realize the consequences of that identification, what it means to your family?"

"Move to strike, Your Honor. Irrelevant."

"Sustained," the court answered. "That will go out, madam reporter."

"Nothing further, Your Honor," Grant said.

"We will take our morning recess. Ten minutes." The judge rose and disappeared as he stepped off the back of his bench.

~

By the time of the bailiff's "All rise," the attorneys and parties had returned to their places in the courtroom. Williams was back on the witness stand. "Be seated," the bailiff intoned, and the judge directed his attention to Ryder.

"Mr. Ryder, your cross, if you will."

Ryder stood. "Thank you, Your Honor. Just a few questions."

He moved down the table and stood directly behind Grant. *Right,* thought Grant.

"Mr. Williams, are you, sir, as you sit here today, at this moment, able to identify this woman, this Tamara Evans, in this courtroom?" he asked.

"I said, 'I believe so,' Mr. Ryder. She is your client, seated over there," he pointed to Ava.

"You believe so? Is that your testimony?"

"Yes, sir."

"Well, Mr. Williams do y'all believe that tomorrow the weather will be pleasant, like, say, today?"

"I do think so, yes."

"You *think* so. So now you *think* so. You expect so, you suppose so. Would those be fair statements, sir?"

"Yes."

"Do you *know,* sir, what the weather will be like tomorrow?"

"If it is like today, I know it will be fine. Yes."

"Yes. And the difference is the 'if,' is that it?"

Williams did not answer. Ryder, his voice lower now, exact, slow, continued. "Do you *believe* in God? In heaven? Do you *believe* in the tooth fairy?"

Grant was on his feet at the first word. "Objection, please, Your Honor. He is badgering the witness. It is argumentative, and he has not allowed the witness to answer the pending question."

"Argumentative, Mr. Grant?" the Court replied. "This is cross-examination after all. Overruled. But," looking at Ryder, still standing behind Grant, "allow the witness to answer before your next question. And, sir, please step back from behind Mr. Grant, so that he, all of us, may observe your examination."

Ryder smiled at the court as he moved back toward his seat. Williams immediately responded without waiting for another question: "Yes," he said, "the difference might be the 'if,' in that question."

"The 'if' was in your answer, sir." Ryder stopped moving and faced Williams.

This bastard is good, Will thought, *really good*. He hoped that Williams remained cool and patient, and that he could weather the assault when it came, but Grant knew that he had underestimated Ryder's passion. He did not think that the Texan would be this interested. But he clearly was. He felt Williams's tension and his studied glances. *Patience*, he whispered under his breath to himself.

"Well, Mr. Williams, I suggest to you that we are not interested in your *beliefs*, but rather what you *know*. There is a difference; do you agree?" He leaned forward, resting his arms on the back of his chair, looking at Williams.

Williams, shifting his weight, said nothing.

"Well, let's see if we can move to the realm of certainty. This is a court after all, and we are in search of the truth."

Judge Sheridan interrupted, "Your next question, Mr. Ryder, is?"

Ryder returned the court's look and then focused back on Williams.

"So, let's define our terms, Mr. Williams." Ryder stood back. He placed one hand on his chair. "When I say that I *recognize* this chair," tapping the chair back, "Ah mean that I know that this is a chair and that it is my chair. I don't *believe* it is my chair, don't maybe *think* it is my chair. I *know* it is my chair. Fair enough?"

Williams nodded.

"Y'all have to say somethin' on the record, Mr. Williams, for the reporter to get it. I am sure your attorney told you that."

"Fair enough," Williams answered, his distaste evident. Grant had warned Williams, told him to be patient, to stifle the anger he would feel, to wait their turn. It would come.

"So, sir, now that we have defined our terms, when you saw my client on the ground, bleeding profusely, unconscious, right there just inches in front of you, did you *recognize* her, sir, as the mother of your long-lost child?"

"No."

"You did not know at that moment that it was she?"

"No."

"And when, while she was being attended to medically, unconscious still, and you saw her hair pushed back as they searched for her wounds, you saw some mark on her neck?" he paused.

"Yes, I did. It was a scar."

"A scar. Did you know at that time that it was a scar?"

"Well, no."

"You did not know that it was a scar until later when you read the medical record you conned out of the gullible night nurse."

"Objection, Your . . ." Grant needed to buy time for Williams, who looked uncomfortable.

The court cut off Grant's objection: "Overruled. I remind you that this is cross-examination of what appears to be a central, perhaps, crucial witness, Mr. Grant." The judge's stern tone conveyed his growing displeasure with Grant's repeated objections.

"Yes, Your Honor, but—"

"But nothing! Overruled. Continue, Mr. Ryder."

Ryder's smug glance at Grant said it all. Ryder continued.

Grant caught Williams's eye. He appeared to have relaxed.

"You did not know it was a scar when you saw her on the ground?"

"Correct."

"And when you saw this mark, as she lay on the ground, did it occur to you that this was the mother of your lost child?"

Williams sighed noticeably. The judge studied him.

"No," he answered.

"All right, now while you watched them attend to her, put her on the gurney, take her away, did it occur to you then, that this was the mother of your lost child?"

"No."

"And while y'all were waiting for the ambulance, or they were treating her, at some point the local sheriff arrived and took a statement from you?" Ryder leaned over and picked up a sheet of paper. Grant could not tell what it was, but he bet it was the police report. *How did he get that so fast?* he wondered. "Is that correct?"

"Yes."

"Did you tell the sheriff or anyone then. I mean this was your chance to have her arrested, to use the warrant you had with you. You had it with you in your tux, that warrant, at the wedding? Correct? That this was the woman who had stolen your child. She was a wanted woman, a fugitive?"

Grant stifled his obvious "compound" objection, hoping Williams would sort it out.

"No, I did not tell the officer or anyone. And, yes, I had the warrant in my wallet. In my tuxedo." Williams replied deliberately. "And, yes, she was a fugitive," he finished, looking at Grant.

"I see. And at the hospital later, as you spied upon this unconscious woman, in her hospital bed, did it occur to you that this was the mother of your lost child?"

"No."

"Do I understand, sir, that it was your intention while in that hospital room, to dislodge and look beneath her bandages to see her neck, to confirm this fantasy that—"

"Objection! Beyond the scope of direct; argumentative and speculative." Grant's voice echoed throughout the room.

"Sustained!" Grant was sure the volume of the judge's ruling matched his.

Ryder paced back and forth near his chair, pausing behind Ava, and asked, "So, you got the medical records and sat outside in your car in the dark of night and came to the conclusion, formed the *belief,* that because of this mark on my client's neck, which you barely saw and then read about, that she must be your long-lost fugitive. That's it?"

Williams sagged noticeably in his chair and looked at Grant. They waited. His "yes" was barely audible. They all saw the judge look over to the clock.

Timing is everything in a jury trial, Grant thought. Thank God this a bench hearing, without a jury.

"Let's see, suh, if ah have this ko-rect," Ryder straightened, no notes in his hand.

"When you saw her on the ground bleeding, saw the mark on her neck, watched her being treated, when you were questioned by the police, when you invad—visited—her hospital room, you did not recognize her as the woman who stole your child, twenty-plus years ago?"

His "no" came quickly, too quickly for Grant.

"And finally, I promise Your Honor," Ryder said, looking at the court. "As you sit here today you do not recognize her as that woman?"

"No."

"And you do not, today, now, here, *know* if it is she, do you?"

"No, I do not know, but I believe—"

Ryder's "Move to strike!" perfectly timed, cut off Williams's answer.

"That will go out, after the word 'know,' madam reporter," the judge stated. "Anything else, Mr. Ryder?"

Ryder held his hands palms up and shrugged.

"We are in recess." The gavel banged, and the judge was gone.

~

Fifteen minutes later, back in session, the court looked at Grant.

"Redirect, Mr. Grant."

"None, Your Honor," Grant replied.

"You may step down, Mr. Williams."

As Williams stepped down and moved to the empty chair next to Grant, the judge said, "Call your next witness, Mr. Grant."

Grant seated, looked over at Ava at the far end of the table and, watching for her reaction announced, "We call Ava Ames, Your Honor." Not a flinch. *She expected it. Sure,* he thought. *Ryder knew I would take her out of order, and she is ready. Well, this will be very interesting.* And then Ryder was standing.

"Your Hon-uh," he drawled. "Ah have a motion to make at this point."

"Yes, Mr. Ryder?" the court responded.

"Judge, this here hearing is supposed to be about revoking, or consider- ing to revoke, a marriage license issued to these two young people, one of whom is my client's son." He paused and looked over at the couple and then back at the court. "Now it seems to me, to us, me and Ms. Ames, that the basis of this is that they, Mr. Williams and Mr. Grant, think that Mr. Williams is the father of my client's son. Have I got that right? Yes, I believe I do. I *know* I do. Got to be careful of my own stuff," he grinned at the judge, who nodded but did not smile back. "So here is mah problem. They have accused my client of being some sort of fugitive from California. Now that might make this a *criminal* proceeding, might'n it? So I think I may have to assert her fifth amendment privilege not to testify, unless . . . ?" He looked over at Grant who was standing, his hands behind his back, turned halfway toward the other attorney.

"Mr. Grant?" the judge asked as he leaned forward, one arm resting on his bench.

"This a civil proceeding, regarding a license matter. No part of it is crim- inal, Your Honor. So, unless she were to commit a crime in this courtroom today, such as perjury, and I know that Mr. Ryder is too good an attorney to let that happen . . . " Grant smiled at Ryder, who tossed his head slightly, " . . . there can be no criminal implications to come out of this case. She is not at risk."

"But Mr. Grant, if she is who you think, *believe*, she is, and I do not know and I have no opinion on the matter, isn't she incriminating herself by testi- fying perhaps that she is not?" the judge asked.

"Not at all, Your Honor," Grant responded before Ryder could react. "If she denies what we believe to be the case, that is not a crime, beyond per- jury, and you have to decide the license issue. If, however, she admits it, and we have considered the implications, the license is invalid and the warrant is outstanding in all events and that would be up to this state to deal with extradition." Grant paused, letting it sink in, and then he continued, sur- prised that Ryder had not objected. "If she refuses to testify, that creates a certain inference that we are correct, which you can consider in this case, but I do not think that she can take the fifth in this, a *civil* case, not likely to have criminal consequences, notwithstanding the outstanding warrant." Grant turned toward Ryder, whose arms were crossed, one finger stroking his chin. *Now what, you son-of-a bitch?* Grant thought. *Gotcha! Maybe . . .*

"Mr. Ryder?"

"One moment please, Your Honor," Ryder said, as he took his seat and huddled with Ava.

Grant could not see her face, blocked by Ryder, nor could he hear them. After a moment, Ryder straightened as Ava stood and, smoothing her skirt, with her cane, walked slowly past Grant to the witness stand. She settled into the chair and placed her cane against the side of the witness box.

"Mr. Ryder?" the court asked.

"Your Honor?" he asked, waiting.

The judge frowned his impatience with the Texas attorney. "What is your position with regard to her testifying, sir?"

"She is prepared to, wants to, testify, Your Honor. She understands the issues."

"And?" the court responded, leaning forward toward Ryder.

"And nothing, meaning no disrespect, Your Honor," he said.

The judge regarded the attorney for a moment, then he sat back rocking in his chair.

"Swear the witness, madam, clerk," he announced, fixing Ryder in his stare.

"I do," was her answer, the first words Ava had spoken. "Ava Ames, Austin, Texas," she continued, the hint of an accent in her long A's.

"Ms. Ames, you understand the discussion we had, the attorneys, over whether you should testify here today and whether there might be consequences, even criminal, consequences?" the judge asked.

She faced the judge, turning slightly, "I have committed no crime, Your Honor, and I can think of no reason why I should not testify here."

"Your attorney has discussed this with you? Just a moment ago?"

"Yes. He told me—"

"Stop! Ms. Ames," the judge interrupted her, one hand up. "You are not to tell us anything that he told you! There is a sacred privilege that prohibits you from being asked to reveal any communication between you and your attorney."

"I know that, but he told me I may not have to testify, and I told him that this whole unpleasant matter needed to be over and done with, and that I had nothing to hide. So here I am." She straightened her shoulders and turned to face Grant.

"Your Honor," Grant was standing close to the witness box, the counsel table behind him; he leaned against it. "It would seem in all events that with counsel present, if the privilege not to testify were to apply to these proceedings, assuming it did, which I do not admit it does, even so, she has voluntarily waived it. That is a question, Your Honor."

The judge looked at Ryder. "Mr. Ryder?"

"Agreed," Ryder answered without hesitation.

"You understand that you are under oath here today, Ms. Ames?" the jurist asked.

"Certainly," she responded.

"Very well. Mr. Grant you may proceed."

Grant stood with his arms behind his back and regarded her: soft brown hair, makeup enhancing her well-formed face, stylishly dressed. He tried to recall how she had looked twenty years ago. He could not reconcile this confident, mature woman with the out-of-control young woman in his courtroom in California. But there was something about her, the tilt of her head, the sureness in her eyes. He agreed with Williams, without the scar he would never have recognized her. But with that tip-off, maybe, just maybe. And as Grant looked at her, met her gaze, he knew that she knew, and it was, well, *game on!*

"Your name is Ava Ames, is that correct?"

"Yes." No lack of confidence in her tone or answer.

"Have you ever been known by the name of Tamara Evans?"

"Never."

"What is the name of the father of your son, Scott Ames?"

"Mr. Grant, I do not know."

"Excuse me. You do not the name of the father of your son?"

"No."

"How can that be, Ms. Ames?"

"He never told me his name." Nothing more. Grant was amazed at her obvious candor and control. He tried to remember, to reimagine, this woman on the witness stand in California, and he felt doubt coming in his backdoor. Missing was the hesitancy, the total lack of confidence, even the victim attitude of that hearing. This was a different woman, accomplished, certain, in control, unembarrassed by the most personal questions, and not even angry. Grant continued.

"Why?"

"You would have to ask him."

"Didn't you ask?" There it was a slight, barely perceptible wince. A flash and it was gone.

She smiled, just at the corners of her mouth. Grant doubted that the others saw it.

"There was not much time, Mr. Grant."

He leaned toward her. "Because . . . ?"

The smile again, "Because what, Mr. Grant?"

"Were you ever married to the father of Scott Ames, Ms. Ames?"

"No."

"Were you ever married to anyone?"

There was the smile. "Have I ever been married? Is that your question, Mr. Grant?"

Who is examining whom? he pondered. *She is correcting my syntax. Damn!*

"Have you ever been married?" he asked.

"No."

"Have you ever met Mr. Rob, or Brad, Williams, the gentleman seated, here," indicating.

"No. And we have yet to be introduced," she nodded to Williams.

"Do you have here, with you, your birth certificate, or a copy of it?" Mosby had not been successful, so far, in his attempts to get the birth certificate of Tamara Evans from the State of Massachusetts. So Grant took a shot.

"No."

Grant picked up Scott's birth certificate, which Mosby had obtained from the Travis County records in Austin. He handed it to her. She studied it for a moment; Grant waited.

"I have handed you a copy of a birth certificate previously marked by the clerk. Do you recognize this document?"

"Yes."

"Yes? What is it?" Grant asked. *Nothing is easy with her*, he thought.

She studied it and then looked at Grant. "This?" she said.

He wanted to scream. "That, in your hand. Your right hand, Ms. Ames." He thought the judge flinched at his sarcasm.

"This is Scott's birth certificate, issued by Travis County, Texas, on September 10, 1975." She looked up.

"It reports his date of birth as . . . what?" he asked.

"Isn't it on your copy, which you have in your hand, your left hand?" she replied.

"Yes, it is Ms. Ames. But I want you to tell us, and the court, what the date is."

"You know what the date is, all of you have this," she said.

"Please answer the question, Ms. Ames," the judge interjected.

She smiled back at him, "Of course, Your Honor. March 23, 1970, Galveston, Texas. Actually it was in Fullton, just outside of Galveston, that is where I lived with my parents. He was born at home. With a midwife. Is that sufficient, Your Honor? Oh, the space for the name of the father? It is blank." She looked down at Grant.

"Was there ever a birth certificate issued for this birth at or about the time your son was born?"

"No."

"Why not?"

"He was born at home and I did not need one, until later."

"Later?" Grant asked. When was that?"

She smiled at him. "Why, when Scott started school. You cannot enroll in school in Austin without a birth certificate. I applied for one in Austin on September 10, 1975. The date is right here. They issue them the same day. He was to start kindergarten the following week."

"Do, or did, they require anything from Galveston, or do they just take your word for it as the mother?"

"I supplied the information, and it is under penalty of perjury, Mr. Grant, as you can see."

"So, as I understand it, no birth certificate was ever issued in, or by, the county where he was born? Is that correct?"

"Mr. Grant, I could not testify to your understanding, but aside from that, you are correct."

"Thank you. And this certificate was the only, the first one, ever issued as to Scott's birth?"

"Yes, as to both."

"And he was five years old at the time?"

"Five years, seven months."

"Where do your parents live?"

"Objection, Your Honor." Ryder was on his feet, his chair pushed back. "I have allowed counsel considerable latitude because my client wanted to cooperate, but now he has, as we say in Texas, 'gone fishin.' That's it. This is not a deposition. Enough, Your Honor, please."

"Mr. Grant? Mr. Ryder has a point and an objection," the court's frown was evident. "I wonder if there is end to this."

"I will withdraw it, Your Honor." Grant replied, and in the same breath—*what the hell, let's roll the grenade,* he thought—he asked without hesitation,

"Have you ever been to California, Ms. Ames?"

Just as quickly, she replied, "Never."

"Are you Tamara Evans?"

"No."

"Is Robert Bradford Williams the father of Scott Ames, your son?"

Ryder was on his feet. "Asked and answered. Objection, Your Honor!"

"Not exactly. I will allow it. Overruled." To the witness, "You are to answer the question, Ms. Ames. Do you want it read back?" the judge asked.

"No."

"'No' what?" Grant asked.

"'No,' I do not want it read back, and 'no,' Robert Bradford Williams is not the father of Scott Ames, my son."

She glanced at the judge and then trained her eyes first on Grant and then at Scott. She looked again at Grant. Grant thought he caught that trace of a smile, cold, in the eyes maybe and gone.

"No further questions, Your Honor."

The judge looked at Ryder, "Mr. Ryder? Questions or reserve?"

"Reserve, Your Honor." Ryder replied.

Right! Grant thought. *You are never putting her back on this stand. No way!*

"It is 11:45 A.M., gentlemen. We are in recess until 1:00 P.M.," the judge stood and pushed his chair back under his desk. "I remind you that we have until 5:00 P.M. today, gentlemen, and that is it."

Timing is everything, Grant smiled to himself, satisfied that he had finished with Ava and that the noon recess had intervened before he was to call his other witnesses. If he had to put them on before the break, the recess would have given Ryder an hour to prepare his cross-examination. Now, the other attorney would have to scramble, and if Grant caught him by surprise, well . . . Timing was everything.

"Please take your belongings ladies and gentlemen, This courtroom is locked during the noon hour," the bailiff announced, holding the gate in the railing open for them. Ava and Ryder were out and gone, Grant noticed as he picked up his papers. *She does pretty well on that cane.* Deep inside he knew that he had not accomplished much. As he started down the aisle toward the door, for the first time he noticed a man seated in the last row of the courtroom. As he passed, the man stood and stepped into the aisle behind Grant, and he heard Williams say, "Paul, thanks for coming. Join us outside for lunch. Did you hear any . . ." and Grant stepped outside into the brilliant fall day.

Mosby's secretary, anticipating their noon break, had arranged for sandwiches and drinks, which were already set on a picnic table under one of the giant oaks to the side of courthouse building. Grant, with Williams and the attorney, Mosby, sat on the benches, some of their papers piled in front of them. Williams introduced Paul Sloan to them, and he sat across from Grant.

"Paul, did you get it finished, all of it?" Williams asked, leaning forward, his voice low.

At that, Mosby tilted his head at Williams as he saw Scott and Jamie take a table behind, a few yards away. Ava and her attorney were nowhere to be seen.

Paul nodded. "In here, my report. Just like you said it would come out. It was something getting it done, but it is," the man replied. Williams reached across the table and shook his hand.

"Well, Grant," his remark directed to Mosby, "what do you think?"

"We are O.K. for now, Brad. It was tough on you. I am sorry."

"Never mind me. How did the kids take it?" indicating, with his head, Jamie and Scott at the other table.

"From what I could see, not good," Mosby said. "I sat sideways part of the time, so I could only see them a little bit. Scott is just angry, I guess at all of us. And Jamie, she would not look at me when walked out here."

"Do you think we should say anything to them? Could I say something?" Williams asked.

"No way," Mosby and Grant answered in unison. "Let this play out, just like we planned," Grant added.

"Yeah, remember she *is* his mother, whatever has happened," Mosby cautioned.

Williams's shoulders sagged, and he put down the sandwich he had been nibbling with little interest. "God, how I hate this and what it is doing to them," he sighed.

"By this time tomorrow, sooner, maybe today, it will be over, one way or the other," Grant offered. "O.K., here is the deal when we go back in . . ."

~

Gray hair worn long over his collar, his bushy sideburns concealed the earpieces of his horn rims. The wrinkles on his neck and slacks complemented each other. His sport coat might have been slept in.

"Sloan, Paul Sloan, S-l-o-a-n," he answered, and he was sworn by the clerk.

Grant leaned back, wishing for a leather swivel chair, his back stiff, a tablet on his lap.

"Mr. Sloan. Good afternoon, sir," he began.

Sloan nodded.

"We have met, spoken, prior to this moment, have we not?" Grant inquired.

Satisfied with his morning score, Ryder had not inquired whom Grant intended to call in the afternoon, and he did not ask now the purpose of this testimony. If he had, Grant would not have told him. No rule required him to divulge his plans in advance, though he would have been hard pressed to ignore such a question had it come from the court.

"Yes, we spoke on the phone, last night, and we met today, outside, for the first time, within the past hour," Sloan replied.

"And that is the extent of our relationship?"

"Correct."

Setting his tablet on the table in front of him, Grant leaned forward on his elbows, feeling the relief in his low back. "We discussed your testimony here today?"

"Yes," the man responded. "You had asked me to run several tests to determine parentage in this case . . ."

There was a noticeable scraping sound as Ryder pushed his chair back, but he remained seated, Grant saw out of the corner of his eye. He did not want to look at Ryder, not yet. *Got your ears up now, I bet*, Grant thought.

". . . you had provided us, me, actually, with specimen materials from several individuals . . . I see, two people," consulting a file in his lap. "Yes, two individuals."

"And were you able to, and did you, run those tests, sir?" Grant continued.

"Yes, I did, at my lab. It was extremely difficult, given the time constraints, but we did it, I am happy to say. It was a first for us, the speed with which this was done."

Now Grant stole a look at Ryder. The attorney was bent over, writing furiously.

"All right. Now Mr. . . . Excuse me. It is *doctor*, is it not? *Dr.* Sloan?"

"I have Ph.D.s in chemistry and biological science. Yes, it is 'doctor.'"

"Then with regard to your qualifications, Doctor, have you brought your CV, your curriculum vitae or resume with you?"

"Yes, I have." He handed a multipage document to the court. The judge reached over and took the paperwork, and handed it to his clerk. Grant now stood and walked to the witness stand. The clerk handed him the doctor's resume.

"I have made copies of this, Your Honor," Mosby said as passed two sets over to Ryder and to his client.

"Perhaps, in the interest of time I might offer a brief summary of the witness's education and experience in lieu of a complete inquiry, and maybe then Mr. Ryder might be in a position to stipulate to his qualification as an expert witness in his chosen field?" Grant offered, looking over at Ryder, who made no response.

"Let's try that," the court said.

For the next several minutes, Grant related Sloan's educational and professional experience. The doctor was one of the owners, a major shareholder in his lab, the G-Mark Corporation, which was licensed by, and under ongoing contract with, the FBI, the CIA, the Treasury Department, and a host of other federal as well as state agencies to conduct DNA testing, and it had been doing so for years. Dr. Sloan had personally been qualified and accepted as an expert witness in twenty-two different states and over a dozen federal districts.

"With that background, did you, as you stated, conduct genetic testing at my request on two individuals in this case?"

"Yes, I did. Most certainly."

Glancing at them, Grant saw Scott and Jamie straighten in their seats, staring at the witness; Scott skeptical, Jamie frightened.

"At this point we intend to delve into the doctor's testing and the results if Your Honor is satisfied as to his expertise." Grant halted.

"Mr. Ryder?" the court said. Ryder remained bent over his pad and simply raised one hand in apparent resignation.

"Hearing no objection," the jurist said, "you may proceed, Mr. Grant."

"Thank you, Judge. Dr. Sloan please describe for us what you did, if you will?"

Grant knew that the question called for an objectionable narrative from his witness, but he gambled that Ryder would not risk the wrath of the judge on dragging out what was sure to come anyway. He guessed correctly.

"Yes, well, at my direction, you, Mr. Grant, obtained and marked as I instructed, and forwarded to me by overnight air, a toothbrush from one white adult male, a sample which was marked 'Scott Ames.' Also, a hairbrush reported to have been used to brush the hair of a white adult female, marked one 'Ava Ames.' I received both items in sealed plastic envelopes, tagged and labeled as I have just stated. I have the items and the envelopes here with me. The envelopes and tags are dated and signed. The signature in each case appears above a typed name. On the Scott Ames sample is written 'B. Williams,' which indicates to me that Mr. Williams had obtained that sample. On the hairbrush, 'W. Grant,' which indicates . . ."

"Stipulate to the chain of custody, Your Honor," Ryder offered without looking up.

The court smiled, pleased that Ryder had read his mind, that he welcomed the opportunity to skip the preliminaries and move matters along.

"Continue, Doctor, if you will," Grant directed.

Sloan continued, "I also was provided with a buccal swab from Mr. Brad Williams. I had instructed you, Mr. Grant, to obtain a sample by swabbing the inside of Mr. Williams's cheek, inside his mouth. That is what was sent to me per the tag on the sample." Grant had moved to stand by the end of the table, so that he could address the doctor and at the same time watch Ryder's reaction. Ryder had not looked up since the doctor had begun his testimony. Now Grant saw Ryder wipe his forehead with the back of one hand and then run his hand through his hair. *He's got it dialed in now*, Grant thought.

"And then, Doctor, what did you do with these samples, please tell us?"

"Of course, my pleasure." Sloan crossed his legs, and he turned to speak directly to Judge Sheridan. *I love it when they do that*, Grant thought. *With really good expert witnesses, you can pull the string like a wind-up doll and go out for coffee!* Sloan was that good.

"My objective, Your Honor, was to conduct a test using the latest, most reliable, and incidentally, quickest, methodology, the polymerase chain reaction, or PCR, technology, which has supplanted it, is so much easier and more reliable than the traditional earlier RFLP, the restriction fragment length polymorphism method, particularly with regard to parental testing, and PCR is really the standard for such organizations as the FBI, in any event . . . " *Here is where I go out for coffee*, Grant mused.

Over the next few minutes, Sloan walked an attentive judge through the testing process, until finally the court held up one hand to him, and said:

"Doctor, you have been qualified as an expert witness, absent a request by Mr. Ryder to voir dire, or challenge you as such, perhaps at this point we can get to your opinion and findings?"

The court glanced briefly at Ryder, who was locked into conversation with Ava, both their heads bent low. The judge did not wait for an answer from Ryder. He nodded at Grant,

"Based on your tests and utilizing your experience, do you have an opinion as to the parentage of the subject Scott Ames?"

"Yes, most assuredly I do."

"And what is the assurance or range of error in the application of your tests to your conclusion of parentage? That is to say how accurate is it, I guess, is a better way to state, or ask, Doctor?" Grant asked.

"The tests performed by me on the samples given, all of which were excellent samples by the way, they were not degraded in the slightest, have a degree of accuracy in each instance of 99.999 percent. That is to say, it is correct in 99,999.99 times out of 100,000 in determining whom the parents are. It is as exact as science can be, or get, Mr. Grant."

"And what then is your opinion? Who are the parents of Scott Ames?"

"In my, opinion the mother of the subject Scott Williams is the subject Ava Ames."

"And the father?" Grant asked, his voice almost, he thought, a whisper.

"The father of the subject Scott Ames is . . ."

Even though he was looking right at him, Grant never saw him pick the gavel up, but the crack of the judge's gavel resonated like a rifle shot throughout, and it sucked the air out of the courtroom. Grant had never seen anything like it in more than thirty years trying cases. Sloan jumped visibly in his seat, recoiling away from the judge as if he had been struck. Ryder's mouth was wide open, and for a second Grant wondered if the judge had shot him, so disorienting was the interruption. Before he could arrange a thought, he heard the judge command:

"Recess! We are in recess! Now! Bailiff, everyone is to remain in this room, you understand? No one is to leave!" The bailiff was off his stool at the bang of the gavel, and he was already halfway to the courtroom door, a key in his hand.

"Yes, Your Honor. This courtroom is secure," the bailiff announced!

Standing, Judge Sheridan continued, "I will see counsel in my chambers, now!" He disappeared in a swirl of his robes.

~

The judge was standing as the three attorneys, escorted by the bailiff, filed into his chambers. He motioned for Grant, who led the way, and Ryder, who followed, to take the two leather chairs fronting his elegant cherry desk, a table actually. The top of the desk was absolutely bare. The clerk pulled a third chair forward, and Mosby positioned it to the left of Grant. The three sat, as if on cue. The judge nodded to his bailiff, whom they heard close the door behind him. Judge Sheridan's office was as period-oriented as his courtroom. A shaded Tiffany lamp cast a soft light on the desktop. High windows provided an afternoon glow over the interior. The sidebar behind the desk included a computer, phone, and small printer. Oddly missing, Grant observed, were those ever-present, weary, never-read leather law books, the ones that left oil smudges on your hands and desk. Judge Sheridan had opened his robe. He was standing, looking down at the three of them.

He pointed over their heads, "Samuel Chase, gentlemen." They turned to look at the portrait of the handsome man behind them. Regal nose, prominent lips, high forehead, shoulder-length hair. *He could be a rock star,* Grant mused, *if the picture was not clearly so very old.* "Samuel Chase, gentlemen," the judge repeated. They turned back to face the jurist. "A Maryland native, signer of the Declaration of Independence, member of the Continental Congress, successful attorney, Chief Justice of the Supreme Court of Maryland, and for sixteen years until his death, a Justice of the United States Supreme Court."

Grant had never heard of him.

"I keep his portrait here in case I weary of this task of judging, to remind me that there are men like Justice Chase . . ."

His respect and admiration are palpable, Grant thought.

". . . who gave so much, who worked so hard for this thing we call 'justice.'" He paused. "There is lot to be learned from our patriots, gentlemen."

Grant felt himself nodding in agreement; he stole a glance at Ryder, who seemed bored.

"So, we have something of a . . . well, a mess, is what it is, gentlemen. While that does not sound very judicial, it is accurate, I *believe.*" He smiled at Ryder.

They heard one knock, and the door opened behind them. The judge's clerk approached the jurist and handed him a slip of paper and immediately withdrew, closing the door. Judge Sheridan glanced at the note, tore it in half and the pieces disappeared under his desk.

"My clerk advises me that the reporter, as excellent as she is at getting everything down, that she did not hear and, therefore, did not record, the answer to the last question you put to the witness, Mr. Grant," he said, and with that he sat down. "I did not hear it, and I presume that neither of you did either." He scanned their faces. "Therefore, at this point in our case the question of who is the father of 'the subject, Scott Ames' remains unanswered, thanks to my declaration of this recess, and the record reflects that to be the case," he looked at each of them in turn. "I suggest that we review this situation before, as someone once so aptly said, 'the toothpaste gets out of the tube.'"

Grant looked at Ryder, whose jaw was set, cheek muscles bulging. The judge concentrated on Ryder.

"At this moment, Mr. Ryder, assuming something I *believe* to be true, but do not yet *know*," Ryder flinched, "your client is one sentence, maybe as little as two words, away from outright, I would submit, intentional, perjury. Several counts of perjury in fact, obviously planned, premeditated, and for you, Mr. Ryder, I am going to further assume, totally unexpected; committed in open court, while under oath, on the record. This is not some ill-conceived, lame, lie-to-an-investigator, what we usually see and ignore as not worth prosecuting. This is well, perjury *per se*, gentlemen, as inglorious as it gets!"

"Judge," Ryder interrupted. The jurist held up one hand to stop him.

"Not yet. Let me finish, please, Mr. Ryder," he said. "I suggest that before we return to my courtroom and reconvene this hearing, which we will do and which we will complete today, that we, all of us, discuss a 'resolution' of this matter. And that you assume, for this purpose, Mr. Ryder—and you can tell your client this—that it appears to me, as the judge who is to decide this case, that she is exactly whom Mr. Grant says she is," he paused.

Grant was certain he was studying the portrait of Chase behind. *Justice Chase never had a case like this,* Grant thought.

The jurist continued, his arms now on the desk in front of him. "I have no particular desire to incarcerate in Maryland this woman from Texas for her California missteps. That should be done, if at all, in California. But I cannot, I will not, allow her to come into this state, into *my* courtroom, and boldly violate her given oath to tell the truth. No, gentlemen, that will not happen. Now, starting with you, Mr. Grant, do you have any idea, if you could script the outcome of this case, how this might be handled?" he asked. "It seems to me, at this point, that your client—and God help his daughter; what heartbreak—has the greatest, what, *interest* in that outcome?"

Grant took a manila folder handed him by Mosby, and he opened it. He presented a single typed sheet of paper to the judge, and Mosby handed a copy to a startled Ryder.

"Yes, Your Honor, we do have a suggestion for you. And for Ms. Evans." The use of her name, Evans, did not surprise anyone. "We took the liberty of working up a stipulation which is agreeable to us, Your Honor, just in case the, ah, opportunity presented itself. I think, hope, that you might find it acceptable. Obviously we might *tweak* it a bit after Mr. Ryder has had an opportunity to digest it."

Ryder said, "Judge, if I might, without breaching any privilege, I assure you that I had no idea of the DNA evidence. If I had, I never would have . . ."

"I accept that, Mr. Ryder. I really do. Let us leave it at that. Perhaps we will not have to revisit that issue if we can resolve this," the judge said. "Now, let us review Mr. Grant's proposed stipulation and see if it accomplishes justice, gentlemen." He took a pen from his shirt pocket and, leaning back, began to read.

~

Thirty minutes later, Grant stood, the marked and corrected stipulation in his hand. Ryder stood and stretched and said, "I will need a few . . . more than a few minutes to go over this with my client, Your Honor. I mean it . . ."

"Take all the time you need, Mr. Ryder, but we will do this today."

"Thank you, Judge," the attorney replied. "I believe that she will sign this. It is quite fair, considering. I will certainly recommend it."

"Mr. Ryder, I too *believe* it is fair, and I *know* that you will recommend it," the judge said as he stood and extended his hand to Ryder, a slight smile showed on the judge's face as Ryder shook the jurist's hand.

Mosby had left the judge's chambers to discuss the matter with Williams, and as Grant was about to leave, he paused when behind him the judge asked, "Mr. Grant, a moment please."

Grant stopped and turned. He took a few steps closer to the judge, who was still standing.

"Off the record, Mr. Grant? You had that stipulation, quite detailed, I note, all worked out? You expected that this would happen?" he asked.

"Well, we *hoped* so, Your Honor. Off the record?" The judge nodded his assent. "We only got the final DNA at noon today, but we had a preliminary read out last night. So, yes, we had a good idea where we would end up, and we wanted to be in a position to suggest a disposition to you. I mean this is, well, complicated to say the least. In case we got a chance to wrap this up without, I guess, *hurting,* you could say, anyone any worse than has already happened over the years."

"But, my God, Grant, that young couple, what they are going through."

"Well, Judge," Grant smiled, "that little bit more of testimony that we agreed on, without objection from Mr. Ryder, that may . . ."

"Your Honor," the clerk had leaned in the open door, "Mr. Ryder says he is 'good to go,' whatever that means, sir."

~

"Your Honor," Ryder was on his feet. "We have reviewed the proposed stipulation, and while we have some reservations, we are prepared to put it on the record," he stated as he looked to Ava for confirmation. She nodded slightly, but she did not look up as she studied her hands in her lap.

The court acknowledged Ryder's statement and looked to Grant, who now stood and moved behind his chair, sliding it forward. He rested his tablet on the back of the chair, a pen in one hand. It had been almost twenty minutes since the attorneys had left the court's chamber to discuss the matter with their clients. Grant and Mosby had gone outside to their picnic table and sat with Williams. It had taken only a few moments to review the matter with him, since they had agreed, should the chance arise, on what was acceptable to them, and there was very little difference in what they had worked out with the court and Ryder.

Ryder had remained in the court building, in a side room reserved for juries. On more than one occasion a vague, undecipherable shout had been heard from their windows, which opened to the area where Grant and his party were sitting. Grant was sure that he had heard Ryder state at least once "I am not losing my ticket over this," and he could only imagine what was else was being said. They had agreed in advance not to discuss the agreement with Scott and Jamie. They were not sure how Scott would react to what might easily be viewed as an attack on his mother, whatever their relationship. She had already accused Williams of sabotaging the wedding and destroying Scott's life. They had agreed that they should let the case run its course, as planned, rather than risk interference, whatever, from Scott. Once it was done, it would be over.

"Mr. Grant?" the judge intoned.

"May it please the court, Your Honor, I am prepared to offer a stipulation, of some length, which we have initially discussed in chambers and which is acceptable to our client, Mr. Williams, only at this point. We are aware of the consequences of this agreement as to Scott Ames and Jamie Williams, but will reserve comment until, as agreed, we complete the stipulation and the further testimony, Your Honor," Grant stated.

"Very well, proceed," the judge leaned back, his eyes on Ava.

"Your Honor, on behalf of Brad Williams, also known for these purposes as Robert, or Rob, Bradford Williams, we offer to stipulate as follows," he looked down at his pad,

"One: Ava Ames is to admit, on the record, by stating specifically as such, that she is Tamara Evans . . .

"Two: That her son is Scott Ames, who is also known as, and in fact is, Jason Evans Williams . . ."

Jamie's cry, "No-o-o-o!" stilled the courtroom, and Grant paused. He did not look back at her. He noticed that Williams, seated to his right, stiffened his neck and shoulders, but he did not turn around. Grant continued to read from the stipulation.

"Three: That the father of said Scott Ames is Robert Bradford Williams . . ."

"What are you doing to us? Goddamn it, why are doing this?" Scott shouted. "Why!?" Grant felt his mouth dry. He felt sick. He could not look back or down at Williams. The judge saved him.

"Mr. Ames, I realize this is incredibly painful for you, and I am deeply sorry, but please keep your composure, or I will have to ask you to leave. And I believe, sir, that you need to hear this out," the judge's voice was soothing of deep concern. Grant noticed that the bailiff was standing next to his stool, but he had not moved forward. Grant resumed when the judge looked back at him.

"Four: That on September 15, 1973," Grant felt his voice constrict, and he paused, "on September 15, 1973, you fled . . ."

"'Left,' Your Honor," Ryder interrupted, "My notes show we agreed on 'left,' not 'fled.'"

Grant nodded his agreement and made the change on his pad, and continued, "left the jurisdiction of the Marin Superior Court while the proceedings there were in process, and thereafter intentionally secreted yourself and your son, Jason Evans Williams, also known as Scott Ames, from his father, Robert Bradford Williams, throughout the minority of said child."

Grant had pressed for a statement that she had hidden him to this date, but conceded the point that, after he achieved majority, Scott was free to go anywhere and technically no longer was "secreted" by her. It made no difference.

"Five: That within sixty days, said Ava Ames will turn herself in to authorities in Marin County, California, to answer to the pending contempt citation and warrant of arrest, and that whatever sanctions and/or sentence that court should impose, which may include incarceration, that Mr. Williams will advise that court of her cooperation here, in these proceedings; and that it is his position that justice would be served by a sentence of no more than thirty days, which may be served in a minimum security facility, halfway house, or similar facility; and . . .

Six: That said Ava Ames shall be required to perform community service at her place of residence, that is in Texas, upon her return, preferably working with troubled youth for a period of time to be determined by the California court; and . . .

Seven: That in order to assure compliance with this order, including her appearance in California, that she shall forthwith, before leaving this courthouse, execute and deliver to her attorney, Steven Ryder . . . "

Grant paused, "We should have an appropriate form, Your Honor, very soon. Mr. Ryder has requested that a deed be faxed here to your clerk, who was kind enough to give us the number . . . Oh, you have it already? Great," Grant said, acknowledging the indication by the clerk who was sitting in front of him that she had received the form. He continued,

"Shall execute and deliver, in a form to be attached to this stipulation . . ." Grant looked at Ryder who nodded his agreement to this change . . . "said deed shall convey her residential property and acreage to Mr. Ryder's firm as trustee. When the California proceedings and the Texas community service are completed, then the deed shall be cancelled and returned to her. In the event of noncompliance with this stipulation in any respect, Mr. Ryder's firm is directed to, and shall immediately, sell the entirety of said property, the proceeds of which shall be distributed to charitable organizations in the Austin area to be selected by Mr. Ryder and Mr. Williams," he paused and he looked down at his pad.

"Finally, eight: We reserve the right to recall here today Mr. Williams and one other witness to testify on matters which it is agreed are not to be deemed admitted as to Ms. Ames, and she and her attorney agree to waive any right to examine those witnesses."

Ryder looked up and added, "Subject to, and so long as, that neither that testimony, nor any evidence is to be admitted, nor shall it constitute evidence, *against* Ms. Ames, for any purpose."

"I have that, Judge," Grant responded. Grant ran down his notes and then looked up. "I think that does it. The understanding is that if this is agreed to by Ms. Ames, on the record, that the testimony presently pending shall be concluded, that no further questions nor answers will be elicited from Dr. Sloan as to Ms. Ames. That should do it?"

The court reviewed the copy given to it and then caught the attention of the court reporter. The reporter nodded that she had taken it all down.

"All right," Judge Sheridan said, "Mr. Ryder will you and your client please stand?"

They stood.

The court continued, "Ms. Ames you are still under oath, do you understand that?"

She nodded.

"You must state so for the record, verbally, Ms. Ames."

"Yes," she replied, barely audible. The court glanced at the reporter, who nodded that she had recorded her response. If she had not, the reporter would have asked for a clear statement.

"Now, you have had an opportunity to discuss this matter with your attorney and you understand the details and, more importantly, the consequences of this agreement, and it is acceptable to you?"

Her "yes" was so faint that the reporter looked up at judge, questioning.

"Was that a 'yes,' Ms. Ames? The reporter could not hear you, nor could I?" he asked.

"Yes!" her voice loud, clear.

"Now," he continued, "I am going to ask you a series of questions, and I need you to answer each and every one of them as agreed. Do you understand?"

She nodded, looking down.

"Ms. Ames?"

"Yes." She glared at Ryder, straightened her shoulders, and waited, her head up.

"Are you Tamara Evans?"

"Yes," clear without hesitation.

"And, is your son . . ."

Ava interrupted in a strong measured tone, "Scott Ames is Jason Evans Williams, whose father is Robert Bradford Williams. And on September . . . whatever date, I took him out of that courthouse, and we have been hiding out in Austin, Texas, ever since. Is that what you want? Is that good enough!?" this last shouted, almost. She had turned so that she faced Williams, seated to her left. He returned her stare, emotionless, waiting. It was quiet.

"Ah, Mr. Grant?"

"Almost, Your honor." Grant looked at this woman who had destroyed his custody case and who had caused Williams and now her son such incredible pain, and he wanted to scream at her. But looking at her, he added: ". . . from the Marin Superior Court, in California, while the proceedings there were in process . . . on September fifteenth," stressing the *fifteenth*, "1973 . . . ?"

When she did not respond and they continued to stare at each other, the court interjected, "Ms. Ames? The Marin Superior Court, in California . . . in progress . . . September 15, 1973?"

"Marin, September 15, 1973," she replied, stonily. She sat down.

"Mr. Ryder, is the stipulation as read into the record acceptable to you, and do you have your client's authority to agree to it?" the court asked Ryder, who had remained standing.

Without looking at her, Ryder replied, "Yes, Your Honor, so stipulated."

"That will be the order," the court responded. "Now, gentlemen, rather than take a recess, in order that we might complete the remaining matters, Mr. Grant, you have a witness?"

"Yes, sir. We recall Dr. Sloan, Your Honor." Grant looked to the back of the courtroom.

Jamie had collapsed into Scott's arms; Scott was staring at the floor. "Doctor . . ."

Sloan, seated three rows back, stood up and walked slowly to the witness stand.

~

Grant began, "Doctor, you are still under oath"

"Yes, I understand," he replied.

"Doctor, although we did not go into it when you testified earlier today, you have known Brad Williams for many years, is that correct?" Grant asked.

"Yes, that is true. At least twenty, maybe more," he replied.

Grant moved closer to his witness. As he did, he caught Scott's angry, hateful glance. He was sure those eyes remained focused on the back of his neck as he turned toward the witness.

"Tell us how and when you first met Mr. Williams, if you please."

"I cannot give you the date, but we were building a new laboratory. Our company, G-Mark Corporation, had expanded as we got more and more into genetic fingerprinting for our clients, most of them governmental agencies. We hired his, Mr. Williams's, company to design and construct several clean rooms for us. He came highly recommended."

Grant interrupted him, "And he did several other projects for you over the years, is that correct?"

"Yes, he did."

"And during one of those projects, did you have occasion to do some DNA testing for him, personally? And could, or would, you explain that Doctor?"

"Yes, of course. During one of our many meetings in my office, Brad had seen a piece, a chart on my wall, it looks to the casual observer like a work of art. It was actually a graph I had made of my family, their DNA, color-coded to show the common factors," he paused.

"Go on, please Doctor," Grant prodded.

"Well, he admired it and asked if I could do one for him. I had never done any others, I had only done mine, but I told him 'sure' I could do it. I knew his wife had, sadly, passed away in childbirth. He wanted to surprise his daughter. I recall she was about ten years old, or so, at that time. I said I was pleased to do it for him."

"And . . ."

"And I told him to get me material: hair, a toothbrush. I took a swab from him myself the same day. We laughed over it at the time. The same swab that I testified to earlier. We kept those results. He brought me a bunch of her hair, in a baggie as I instructed him, to get it from her hairbrush." The doctor kept pausing, waiting for the next question; he was accustomed to avoiding the "narrative" objection. Grant nodded that he should continue.

"I ran the tests to get the data necessary to create the graph. Then we would color, dress it up like mine. When we finished, I called him and I suggested that we meet for lunch." Sloan shifted in his chair, as if he was trying to distance himself from what he was about to say.

"It was very difficult. We had become good friends, I liked him, still do."

Grant heard and felt the shifting of bodies behind him; the tempo of the tension had risen. His eyes were drawn to Williams's hands on the counsel table, tight fisted, knuckles strained white. Ava stared transfixed at the witness. Ryder was erect, his body away from the chair back.

"What was so difficult, doctor? Was there a problem with the sample or with the result? The test did not come out?"

"No, Mr. Grant," Sloan looked only at Grant. "I had to tell him, to be the one to tell him, that he was not his daughter's biological father." Grant heard a stifled sob, but he dared not turn around to look at Jamie.

"Of all tests I have done, you know, we seldom know or meet the people whose material we test. That is it, just their material. This was different. This was personal. It was awful, but it *was* the science. I can still see the look on his face." he looked down at his friend and was shocked to see him composed, relaxed.

"So then, Doctor," Grant turned sideways, so that he was facing Scott, whose arm was around a bewildered Jamie. *Grant hoped that Scott now understood what was coming.* "What does this mean as to the parentage of Jamie

Williams?" He kept his eyes trained on Scott, his back to the witness. *Now he's got it.* Jamie raised her head, eyes wide.

"The conclusion, my opinion, is that Brad William is not, cannot be, it is biologically impossible, 99.9% impossible . . . He is not the biological father of Jamie Williams."

"And, Doctor, do you have an opinion on whether, therefore, Scott Ames and Jamie Williams are brother and sister, siblings?"

"They clearly are not. Absolutely are not."

"Thank you, Doctor, no further questions."

"Mr. Ryder?" the court asked.

"We waived, Your Honor, but 'no,' none anyway," the attorney said.

~

The court signed an order presented by Mosby, confirming that the marriage license as previously issued was valid. The attorneys signed the formal stipulation that had been read into the record. Mosby's secretary arrived to notarize the deed to Ava's residence, which was then entrusted to Ryder. As the two attorneys walked out of the courthouse, Grant handed Ryder a small cassette.

"What is this?" Ryder asked as they descended the steps.

Grant placed a hand on the attorney's shoulder and said, "Just a little something. In case we needed it. We didn't." He shook the attorney's hand. They both smiled, and Ryder, looking at the cassette recording, a frown on his face, turned and walked toward his car.

Scott, Jamie, and Williams had gathered under the trees.

"Daddy, this has been awful for you, I just cannot believe that you never told me any of this." Jamie held his hand. "Why?"

"Honey, it is almost as if I had two lives. The first with Scott; he even had a different name. And the second with your mother and with you. Too short, way too short with your mother," he said, holding her. "After your mother died, you were all I had, and I was not about to lose you. Not the way I lost Scott."

Jamie stepped back and pulled Scott toward them, the three held each other. Jamie looked up at him.

"Jamie, about your mother, I . . ." Williams started.

Jamie stopped him, her hand on his arm, "Dad, not now. Someday, maybe. But not now. Here, today, this is what is important."

Williams kissed the top of her head, and he looked up. Ava was getting into a car across the lawn. She paused, one foot in the car, and glanced over at them. Their eyes met, and she disappeared into the car, which pulled away.

"You are right, Jamie, and you too, Scott, someday. Maybe someday, son."

AFTERWORD

SCOTT AND JAMIE WERE MARRIED at sunset on the deck of Brad's beach house. Brad was the best man; Cecily, the maid of honor. Afterwards, Vera served the four of them dinner as the sky darkened and the afterglow was chased by a thousand stars, a prelude to the full moon that soon rose over the bay. Later, the couple walked on the beach, their footsteps glistening in the moonlit wet sand of a falling tide. Scott stopped, and he took Jamie into his arms and kissed her for a long, long time. Then he stepped back and looked at her, her hair radiant in the dim light. She read his mind and as one they shed their shorts and tops, and hand in hand they followed the moonlight into the dark water. Scott dropped her hand, and he turned and walked back to where their clothes lay. He picked them up and moved them higher, to dry sand. He looked for and quickly found a piece of driftwood and a few stones. He made a small cairn, marking the spot of their clothing and where they had entered the water. Then he turned and walked slowly back into the water. Out of the darkness ahead, Jamie's soft laughter wafted over the gentle swells of the moonlit bay.

~

Kay heard it first and answered the phone on the third ring. The clock radio read 11:23 P.M. "It is for you," she said, handing the phone to Grant, who took it and rolled over onto his back.

"Will? It's Brad." Grant recognized the voice.

"Is everything O.K., Brad?" he asked.

"Fine, Will. I just wanted you to hear it from me, personally. They got married, here, tonight, Will. Jamie and Scott. On the deck. We are at the shore, remember? Judge Sheridan did it, Will. They are married." Grant could feel the joy in his friend's voice.

"That's great, Brad. Please give them my best."

"I will do that, Will. I just wanted, again, to thank you for everything. All those years, Will, and now it is over. Who would have thought . . ." His voice broke, and he paused for a moment. Grant was about to respond when he heard Williams say softly: "He's home, Will. My son, he's home."

Grant felt his throat constrict, his eyes well up.

"Good night, Will," he heard, and the line went dead.

Kay raised up on one elbow, looking over at him. "It was Rob—Brad—Williams, wasn't it? Is everything all right?"

Grant let the phone fall to the floor beside the bed, and reaching over, he folded Kay into his arms. "Perfect," he said. "Everything is perfect."

EPILOGUE

AVA SURRENDERED AS AGREED. The Hon. Homer J. Halsey (Ret.) came out of his retirement for one day, to sit *pro tem*, in order to deal with his contempt citation, which he had issued over twenty years earlier. The judge had asked to speak with Ava Ames, a.k.a. Tamara Evans, off the record. Grant sat in the back of the courtroom. No one ever knew what they talked about. Afterwards, the judge read the Maryland stipulation verbatim into the record, and he confirmed from Ms. Evans her understanding of his authority regarding the imposition of sentence. He then ordered that she serve thirty (30) days in the Marin County Jail, forthwith, and the bailiff immediately took her into custody, cuffed her, and escorted her into the nearby holding cell and out of sight.

With credit for good behavior, she was released three weeks later. Outside the jail, she was met by a car, and by 8:00 A.M. the next morning she was back at work at her desk in Austin, Texas. Her fellow workers thought it odd that after all this time, she, who would never take a vacation, finally had, and yet she had no pictures to show them.

She began her community service within a week of her return and completed it within eighteen months.

~

Almost two years to the day of the Maryland hearing, Ava answered her phone at work. She had not heard from Scott in a long time; only one brief conversation since that day in Maryland. He now explained that he had just been visited by two agents of the FBI, a man and a woman. They wanted to know why his DNA, recently entered into the national database, had been linked to an unsolved murder in some Central Valley gas station years ago.

POSTSCRIPT

PARENTAL CHILD ABDUCTION REMAINS A CONSTANT PROBLEM. In the year that inspired this work of fiction, the laws regarding parental abduction were few and difficult to enforce. In answer to a growing problem, new laws were enacted to provide for national recognition of custody proceedings in a successful effort to avoid inconsistent orders, eliminate *forum* or court shopping, and to create uniformity in custody laws throughout the United States. Federal statutes were enacted that made parental abduction a serious crime. Most states have criminalized acts of parental abduction.

One of the first comprehensive studies done on the subject determined that 203,900 family abductions occurred in 1999 alone.[1] Most abducted children were returned or located. Some, however, were never found. The AMBER Alert System became federal law in 2003 and enhances the chances of recovery of an abducted child. Most states now have well-established policies and procedures for dealing with reports, investigations, and timely pursuit in such cases, and while some progress has been made on prevention and recovery, the "2013 rates of abducted and missing children did not differ statistically from the corresponding 1999 rates."[2]

The author never learned whether "Jason" was ever found by his father, with whom the author lost contact. Perhaps the release of this book will provide the answer to whether Jason is still gone missing.

---

[1] *National Incidence Studies of Missing, Abducted, Runaway and Thrownaway Children. (NISMART).* The study was updated by NISMART's 2 and 3, the last in 2013. For more, see the Report of the Dept. of Justice, Office of Justice Programs, Juvenile Justice Bulletins (OJJDP); and reports of the The Child Fund of America Program, website; *et al.*

[2] Childfindofamerica.org/resources/facts-stats